A Bowyer Book
Published in the United Kingdom
by Bowyer Publishing in 2018
Copyright © Paquita Lamacraft
All rights reserved

ISBN 978-1-9996273-2-4
Book Design by Tiger Ink, Hampshire, England
Author's Web Address: www.paquitalamacraft.com
Bowyer Publishing
A Division of Archer Business Group
PO Box 666, Eastleigh
Hampshire, England SO50 0PA

THE CUBAN APPROACH:

The art of letting go.

How to read the winds of change
and adjust your sails to ride them.

Paquita Lamacraft

DEDICATION

This book is dedicated
to all who are in danger of losing hope.

Travel with me in my journey of self-discovery
during a month with no plan in Cuba.

Smile at the stories within.

Ponder the thoughts.

Then apply *The Cuban Approach*
and hold fast to your dreams.

ABOUT THE BOOK

The Cuban Approach has nothing to do with a standoff between nations. Instead, this is an adventure into self-healing.

It gives insight into how, when we give ourselves time away from our daily distractions, our subconscious extracts things stored in that chest of drawers called 'can't deal with it right now' to be freshly reviewed. Then, they can be stored in less jagged spaces in our memory.

As the author carries us with her on a trip from family to family in country areas of Cuba, the stories within give vivid description to the side of Cuba most tourists don't see.

The trip is interlaced with fascinating tales of an interesting life – one that obviously hasn't been easy.

It is a story of resilience.
It changes perspective.
It renews hope.

Its story lets us reconsider the challenges of our own lives and gives courage to go forward.

Once we do, perhaps so we too can take 'The Cuban Approach' to heal our souls.

THE CUBAN APPROACH

CONTENTS

All human beings should try to learn before they die,

what they are running from,

and to,
and why.

James Thurber[1]

---

[1] *James Thurber was a much loved writer and humourist who had the art of caricaturing the foibles of us all. His plays 'The Male Animal' and 'The Secret Life of Walter Mitty' have been adapted to award winning films, and his cartoons and short stories make rich contributions to American literature.*

PREFACE

Dreaming Aloud:
Making the dream a reality

Dancing always takes you places beyond the dance floor, and so it was for me. It was in the early 2000s that I first fell in love with Argentinean Tango, which quickly became a passion. That passion led me to another, dancing salsa, and enjoying the culture and environment that went with it.

Having danced in different countries since, I now realize how fortunate I was with my teachers. In Melbourne, Australia, they were Christian Drogo and Kristina Diaz, and in London, Cesar Velasquez.

My good fortune was that all three are not just beautiful people (in looks and in personality) and remarkable dancers, but they gave me the dance in context of passion that is particularly Latino.

Later, I was to find that as a single woman I could safely go alone to any truly Latin Bar and be treated with old-world Latino courtesy. Without an escort I could safely enjoy memorable evenings of dance.

I make the differentiation between a truly Latino-inspired and operated establishment, and those run by non-Latinos where they teach steps but not what the dance is all about.

I also exclude those who run bars that just label themselves for marketing purposes but have none of that defining quirkiness that makes a Latino bar hum.

In 2001, while studying with Christina and Christian, I joined the annual student trip to take classes in Argentina and Cuba – the one for tango and the other for salsa. It turned out that sadly, due to my work commitments, I was unable to go to Argentina. Instead I joined the group en route to Havana at the airport of San José, Costa Rica.

I had stayed overnight in San José in a charming traditional hotel. It had a gracious courtyard and welcoming hosts. They kindly suggested that before walking into town I might be wise to remove the small gold chain and locket around my neck, and my diamond ring.

Having previously read of tourist muggings in the city I had been a little nervous about walking there alone, but was assured I would be fine as long as I removed these things of value. So it proved.

In my exploration, I sat in a park at the edge of town and watched the schoolchildren rehearsing for the big Independence Day celebratory march the following morning, wandered about taking photographs, got a feel for where to stand to watch the big parade the next morning, and ate in small local restaurants.

At exactly 6pm on the 14th September, radio and TV stations in Costa Rica broadcast the National Anthem. It seems as if the whole country sings along to start the celebration of independence from Spain that had been proclaimed for the whole of Central America in 1821.

The parade the following day is enormous. It takes hours to pass. I felt for the young marchers, for it was indeed a very long route.

Both the rehearsal and the march were performances worth the invested time. I came away delighted to have experienced the community of social interaction that makes such events successful:

- the mothers who made the costumes,
- the teachers who trained special skills,
- the companies who donated instruments and other materials and provided sound systems.

After all the celebrations during which I felt truly an outsider, I walked back to my colonial style hotel with its wide verandas and friendly gecko who shared my room. It is at times like this that the lone traveller feels the immensity of loneliness.

Alone, I have visited some of the most romantic places in different parts of the world. In each place this ache has been there.

The absence of those loved with whom to share the adventure is one of the things we miss most from the separation from those we hold dear. However, the option is either to go and make the best of it, or hide away with your wounds of aloneness.

I choose to go.

The memories I have made in doing so have coloured the long days and nights thereafter with the particular magic each experience offered me. They have left me a treasury of memories.

At the airport the next day I joined my friends who were exhausted from a week of tango indulgence in its heartland.

We arrived in Havana late at night and endured over two and half hours of waiting to be processed by immigration at José Marti Airport.

The humidity was stifling, with almost no air circulation. Russian-styled immigration stations slowly released people onto Cuban soil.

The rest of my group had pushed ahead energetically but then had to wait for me and the other side of the barrier was just as hot and steamy. I was one of the last to have the pleasure of being processed and by then I was wondering why I had bothered.

Eventually, we arrived at our hotel in the UNESCO World Heritage City of Old Havana. As we checked in, our Spanish-speaking teacher Christian started an animated conversation with a local and turned to me to ask if I wanted to go to sleep, or go out.

I replied that I had not come to Havana to sleep – and so it was that with some fellow dance students we rode in an old classic taxi into Central Havana. At that time it was illegal for tourists to do so and naturally that added to the delight of the whole experience.

We were headed to a bar near the Havana *Libre*, the former Havana Hilton Hotel. It was in a basement and almost empty when we arrived just before midnight. I visited the toilet but then didn't emerge for some twenty minutes. When I did, the place was packed and the music was on loud, louder, loudest volume – typically Cuban.

My friends shouted at me: "Where have you been?"In reply I just grinned and said, "Look at me".

With that, I held my arms out and slowly turned around in a full circle. "You could just stand me in the corner and I could be a glitter ball".

The reason I had been gone so long was because I had been generously glittered by the locals.

In front of the mirrors and wash basins, local girls had been primping and adjusting their dresses. Some were putting on their party makeup from shared resources – of which glitter made a fair part.

I had playfully engaged with one whose top had nothing but just laces across the back. She and her friends quickly grabbed me and told me that I needed glitter. They duly applied it amidst lots of laughter.

This is the sort of interchange that shows you don't have to speak the language to connect with people. A smile and playfulness are universal languages.

Back at our table, one of my new friends arrived beside me, telling me that her 'brother' wanted to dance with me ... and could I introduce her to my dancing teacher so she could dance with him?

I think that was about quarter past midnight.

We left just before six in the morning and I had danced almost non-stop the whole time.

This was Cuban salsa at its best. Dancing with one person, I turned to find another person had taken his place. Another turn and someone else popped up between us and took his place. Hand contact included a sort of sliding departure so your partner's hand slid down your arm in a shiver of seductive movement.

The whole thing was one immense and passionate dance event.

About four in the morning I danced close by my dance teacher and said, "Christian. Christian". He looked at me questioningly as I asked: "Do you know what happy is?" He raised an eyebrow.

I went on in reply: "THIS". I pointed to myself and my wide smile:

"THIS is happy!"

One of our group was very buxom and blonde and there wasn't much of her dress between a very short skirt and low cut neckline. As we waited for a taxi afterwards, she was extremely indignant. Referring to the hand slide I have just described, she said: "They were touching me".

I laughed and said: "I thought that was one of the best parts". Another student agreed.

By the time we got back to the hotel where we had arrived weary from long travels and had just found enough time to drop our bags in our rooms before going out again, there were just two and a half hours in which to sleep before our first dance lesson. It was a case of 'sleep fast'.

When the alarm went off we were all probably still running on adrenalin from the previous night, but we headed off to our class.

That morning during a break in our first dance lesson at the Academy of Dance, I looked at my fellow students and said: "...and we thought we could dance!"

What we were learning took us to another level.

This was my introduction
         to a country and its people.

It was then that I realised that if I was to understand how to dance Cuban salsa properly, I must learn not just the steps and the moves, but also to understand the source of the sheer exuberance that dance releases when danced with passion.

It seemed apparent that to make the most of this learning I would need to learn more about the place, the people, and perhaps, the politics. Thus began my journey to the soul of Cuba.

Over six more trips I made friends with some of the locals and became a godmother to a little Cuban girl, stayed in apartments where I could cook for, and entertain up to fourteen of my new local friends in spontaneous fiestas – and learn Spanish from them, for they spoke almost no English. I didn't actually learn Spanish. They say children don't learn languages - they acquire them. Just as if I were a child, I acquired Spanish.

Fast forward nine years.

Life events had overtaken me and my plans with some rude awakenings and there was no chance for such indulgence as a trip to Cuba.

My ability to speak Spanish evaporated in the heat of other priorities and through lack of use.

On my last trip, a Cuban friend had given me a small laminated picture of a saint and told me that it would bring me back. It has lived in my old battered wallet ever since. In the intervening years, every now and then the saint fell out to remind me of that promise.

Given my love of Cuba, when I started my website *www.discover-interesting-places.com* it was natural that the website included a large section on Cuba.

As I built each page of the new site, the saint was on a mission to fall out of my wallet as often as possible – but without getting lost in doing so.

It was against this backdrop that I wrote on the website that Cuba was calling me back. At the same time, privately I had mentioned to friends that I had all of December as leave. They suggested a return to Cuba, but I had replied that the trip was beyond my financial reach. Then came a call that made everything possible: my friends Jane and Greg Zeuschner donated the flight points for the fare.

It was a gift of dreams.

It seemed that I had spoken my dreams into reality.

So it was that in December 2011 I flew back to Cuba – this time to explore more of the island.

The person returning after this trip was one quite changed from the experiences of the month with no plan.

As my flight left Havana on my return, I thought of the Cuban saying that if the year ends well, it is a positive omen for the oncoming year.

Certainly the year had ended well for me:

- I was a happier and more relaxed person than on my arrival in Cuba.
- I had laughed heartily and well every day, been cared for by my friends – and cared greatly in return.
- I had seen the Cuban Cuba and not just that of the tourist routes.
- I had thought a lot, taken many photos, made heart connections, and reconnected with my soul.

Over the years I have tried to not look too far into the future. Experience has taught me that no matter what futures I have planned – and I have planned quite a few – these have never emerged in any form that matched the dream. It seemed that the Universe had other plans for me, and these were what directed my fate.

As a result of this, my coping strategy is to affirm to myself that it is best to try to have no plan. Instead, I just trust my guardian angel who has brought me intact through life's twists of fate.

Now, as the New Year approached, I was returning from a month with no plan in Cuba that had been a way to end the past and begin again.

Perhaps we try too hard to control our fate.

*With a focus on control we forget to read the tides
and so lose the chance to raise our sails
to catch the best winds to ride them.*

These were my thoughts as the year started – and so began this book. Its stories distil what Cuba teaches me. It teaches me that:

*The important things in life are not things.
Life goes better
when I take 'The Cuban Approach'.*

The Cuban Approach employs fifteen principles to give new perspectives on life and yourself.

- Speak your dreams into existence.
- Plan ahead but carry your lifeboat with you.
- You can be lost without feeling lost.
- Trust your judgment – and then trust others.
- Be kind.
- Challenge your mindsets.
- Some of the best memories have no photograph.
- Rough terrain is best crossed in good company.
- The way things are is the way things are.
- A smile is a universal bridge.
- Time doing nothing is well invested
- Perspective is not just for artists to learn.
- The quickest way through is often around.
- If you give of yourself you give twice.
- Sometimes you are somewhere not for your benefit – but for the benefit of others.

Employing these principles gives enough space to let new options reveal themselves.

I hope my month with no plan has meaning for you too, and that when life redirects your course, you will be ready to apply '*The Cuban Approach*'.

CHAPTER ONE

Reserve A Parking Place

Have enough of a plan to let the plan evolve

My plan was to have no plan. Having spent enough time in Havana on previous trips, I knew from experience that this was usually the best plan to have, and so it proved.

However, I am a responsible person and I was travelling alone, so when I arrived I had enough of a plan to last me four days out of my month. This short parking space would enable me to acclimatise. I could then make sure whatever form my No Plan took, it wouldn't leave me at risk.

I thought four days was enough time to let the No Plan start to take shape.

Cuba was ingrained in my heart because I had previously had the rare privilege of learning it through Cuban eyes, and not through those of an isolated tourist. The key had been the people.

But how to find the people who had so coloured my soul with the love of Cuba on my early trips?

Nine years' absence is a long time.

Even in Cuba, where moving house is fraught with the complications of an elevated version of 'Let's Make a Deal', people do move. At the time, in order to move you had to swap a house or residence because there quite simply aren't enough to go around.

It makes for complicated negotiating. This you can witness in the parks of Havana.

Beneath the cooling foliage of aged trees people who want to move sit beneath or beside small placards advertising their residence and their desired swap.

Of course, as with any country, although perhaps here at more frequency, such deals often resulted not from this sort of patient advertising but from 'The Village Telegraph' described by my mother as: 'Thou hast a friend and thy friend hast a friend'.

Perhaps that is how my friend from the past had disappeared.

The quotation my mother used was actually directed at the folly of telling someone something 'In Confidence'. She knew that they in turn would tell others 'In Confidence'.

Friends who are the exceptions to this rule and hold the trust of confidence sacred are real treasures.

Three and a half hours of travelling with my new friends around every square block of the old residence of my former key contact proved fruitless.

We met lots of people – none of whom could help. It was tiring work and we needed refreshment and to sit and let the reality of things drift slowly over us.

Not that much had changed in Havana over the period, and it all seemed clear and familiar.

As we sat and watched the world go by, chatting about all sorts of things not related to my month of no plan, the table next to us became the scene for an interesting exchange between two tourists. A loud argument in English ended, and one of the two men struck up a conversation with one of my new friends who had intervened to try to inject some humour into the increasingly heated discussion.

I became very quiet, not wanting to engage. One of my failings is being able to listen to someone sound off at the poor character of the locals of the country which I am visiting or where I am living and not say anything to correct it.

So far I had managed to keep quiet, but then this chap then got very vocal claiming that people who spoke to you were all just trying to take your money.

He added that he had told his companion – who turned out to be his brother – that he shouldn't trust them as everyone was just on the make: they were light-handed and he would find his wallet stolen.

The brother had the temerity to make a judgment for himself and it was to the contrary. This was the cause of the loud exchange of opinions. The older brother went on and on about untrustworthiness of the locals and how he had told his brother that he 'had been warned'.

This was a bridge too far.

I got up, moved around the table, and sat down next to this self-righteous fellow.

With a big smile I pointed out that it had been impossible not to hear their conversation and asked him why he believed all people offering him directions to the evening's events were trying to steal from him.

His answers didn't sit well with my experience and I said so. I then asked why he thought that he had the right to insist that his brother follow his judgment and not make his own.

He replied that his mother trusted him as the older brother to make sure his sibling came to no harm.

Both men were obviously over forty years old, so we then had an extremely interesting discussion about the fact that it was time for both of them to think for themselves as adults and not be constantly under mother's watchfulness.

I pointed out that they were now some thousands of miles from their home in Canada; and that what was normal in their corner of Canada might not apply in another corner of Canada, let alone in another culture so geographically distant from theirs.

In the course of what turned into a very wide-ranging discussion, I suggested that instead of the many visits to what he called 'his shrink' that he described as guiding his life, he should consider speaking with his friends.

I said that it was my experience that friends give you an uncluttered mirror in which to review your own actions as well as see those of others from a perspective different from your own.

A friend's view of your actions doesn't compromise the friendship but it is the duty of a friend to pull you up when you are out of order, because you know they love you anyway.

I went on to say that friends keep you honest. They also remind you who you are when you have temporarily lost your way.

He replied quickly: "Not my friends".

I got up to leave and in parting suggested that he should re-evaluate the quality of his friendships. He reached out and shook my hand emotionally, telling me he had been paying for therapy for years and what we had discussed made more sense than anything he had heard through all those sessions.

My Cuban friends were much amused and tagged me with a nickname 'Counsellor'. They laughingly told me that I didn't have to defend Cubans.

I replied that I did, because my experience was to the contrary but also because it is so rude to carry on like this when you are guest in a country. You wouldn't go to dinner at someone's house and start insulting them. What's the difference?

As I had pointed out to the man in question:

> *If you find people untrustworthy all the time*
> *you had better look in the mirror*
> *instead of through the window.*

It might have been this exchange that prompted one of my new friends to make the offer that was to define my No Plan trip.

He was the partner of the lass to whom I had brought gifts from her friends in Germany and was the person who had first engaged the complaining tourist in conversation. Fascinated by my intervention and the exchange that followed, he had watched quizzically but silently.

Now he spoke. Apparently in the past this chap had guided tourists on personalised trips inland. He now made me the offer that was to give structure to my month in Cuba. He could do the same for me. We could travel from relative to relative and see the Cuba not advertised in the tourist brochures, as well as that which is.

It is a favourite saying of mine in some circumstances that 'It would be rude to say no'. This was just such a case.

I accepted on the spot, but went on to explain that first I needed to rent an apartment in Havana as my base. When we returned it would be close to Christmas and I was sure that the limited number of suitable apartments would all be taken by then.

I didn't want a room in someone's home, although my friends showed me one that would otherwise have been top choice. It had a stunning rooftop terrace with views over the *Malecón*.

My choices are limited by my lifestyle preferences:

I write. That means I don't want to be disturbing others while my muse takes me far into the early hours.

I also cook. I want my own kitchen. This also helps with the budget – which for me is always slim. When I cook for my Cuban friends this can be a lengthy affair due to the limitations of a Cuban kitchen and its equipment and utensils.

Sharing someone else's house had an additional limiting factor. In the past, some of my best memories are from impromptu parties at my apartment and the left-over guests who stayed – including their children.

So what I needed was an apartment to myself.

I had a plan about how to find an apartment, but it didn't work out quite according to my expectations.

I couldn't find one that was suitable.

I asked my new Cuban friend for help. She asked about amongst her contacts and soon there were two apartments to be seen.

We hailed a pedalo and she negotiated a fare for one tenth of the price I had paid for the same route the day before, and off we went to view them.

On my previous trip I hadn't negotiated a price first, nor did I know roughly what that should be.

Local knowledge is a great asset.

The first apartment was at the back of an apartment block that could have doubled as a cell block in a B Grade movie. There was a long, narrow corridor with dim wall lights to led to an apartment at the back. No natural light was able to squeeze through until some drifted in through a very small window inside the apartment.

We politely declined.

The next was a little further along the road, but we crossed to find an airy and well-appointed place. It had its own balcony overlooking the road, just up from an intersection that divided two central Havana neighbourhoods.

It was high season and apartments were in much demand. While we were inspecting this one, two more calls came through to the owner seeking rental of the same apartment. Nevertheless, she was not to be diverted by other potential tenants and our deal was done on no more than a handshake.

My offer of a deposit was declined with a smile. My word was good enough.

It was not that she knew my new Cuban friend and was basing her trust on that. She just trusted me at face value. After some small talk we departed.

I was set. The price even included washing and ironing from a delightful neighbour.

My No Plan was working well.

Having accomplished our goal, the afternoon stretched into evening. We drove to one of the good music bars to dance – as one does.

While it was being checked out to see if was worth going that night I fell asleep in the car.

This pre-check was something I understood to be normal after experiencing the same on previous Cuban trips where this sometimes happened two or three times before the right music, or mix of staff was considered suitable and it was agreed to be the place to go.

Before leaving Germany I had been working long hours and also trying to cram in work on my website before leaving fast internet connections. I hadn't yet caught up on the lost sleep.

My friends say I can sleep on a washing line. It's a gift to be able to fall asleep in unlikely places. So, while the bar was being reviewed for suitability, I leaned across the now vacated driver's bucket seat and in a flash was sound asleep.

After some time I was roused with the news that the best band was not there that night but would be tomorrow.

I knew from going to several really fine bars in Havana on past trips in the company of Nemo, that often such a reconnaissance mission may have other purposes.

Some bars and restaurants give a local commission for bringing in a tourist. I had discovered this on an early trip when Nemo stopped me just as we got half a block from a particularly lovely rooftop bar we had just left. He instructed me to 'Wait here' and set off at a trot back to the bar.

Returning, he was chuckling in delight.

I looked puzzled and he opened his closed palm to reveal two dollars. As he opened the purse that held the trip kitty, my money, he looked incredibly pleased with himself as he stuffed the two dollars in and said, '*Comisión Paquita*'.

This was very honourable. I would never have known and he could have pocketed the extra money. Instead, he respected the trust I had placed in him.

I don't know whether the reason for us not going to that particular bar on this night had any more basis than that announced, but since I was being given the option to come back tomorrow night, it probably was.

It was hard for me to evaluate.

From my side this was a half-awake conversation and I slowly awoke to its expansion to the earlier offer of our planned travel inland.

There, in the warmth of a Havana night, we discussed where to go and for how long and at what cost, and agreed we would leave tomorrow.

We also agreed that the little red car in which we were travelling was not up to the effort. We had already suffered two flat tyres and had to replace the front one whose metal belting had come completely free from the rubber in which it was embedded.

The window winders were kept in a jumble in a pocket by the front seat and were passed back to anyone needing to open a back window.

The clutch was almost non-existent, but it seemed that, if you pursed your lips exactly in the right way, the gears could be changed with minimal pressure – as long as you were swift in doing so. There was also an ever-present smell of gasoline.

On the basis of this summary of the failings of our little red car, it was agreed that I would rent a vehicle.

So the no plan began with the need to first find a rental car in Havana in high season.

I found a car – but at a high cost. Cost proved to be not the only problem. When I investigated further, the car turned out to be no more than a theoretical construct. There may have once been a car at that price but as the conversation proceeded toward details of the basics of where and what, it proved from side conversations taking place at the other end of the phone during the call, that in fact there was now no such car to be had after all, at least not at this moment in time.

My Cuban friends had no plan about how to find a car. They just asked about and were passed from this person to that.

We stopped and had some beers.

The names of Cuban beers always seem well-suited to the island and its history: 'Bucanero' for all the pirates that used to work the straits of Florida; and 'Cristal', perhaps for the clarity that drinking several cans of beer can bring to the development of a plan.

In the course of our travels from one contact to the next there were a few cars supposedly available. These also turned out to be more concept than reality. However, eventually a real car at the right price was found from a friendly official rental place in the Plaza Hotel.

By then it was late afternoon and we hadn't eaten, so we settled down for a meal. A few Bucaneros and Cristals later, we agreed that it was quite late to start and we would set off tomorrow.

In Latino time, 'Tomorrow' is often code for 'The Day After Tomorrow'. Knowing this, I was quite relaxed about our schedule. In the warmth of the previous night we had agreed we would leave 'tomorrow'. It therefore appeared to me that we were keeping to the agreed timetable.

From previous experience of being in Havana I knew the need for acclimatisation.

By acclimatisation I don't mean the marked contrast between the sultry weather of Havana in December and the German winter I had left behind me. Instead, I mean the completely different world into which I had placed myself.

This is a world where for many there is no promise in tomorrow and so living the fullest in each day is a way of life.

It is a world where no single person seems to understand the complexity of all aspects of a system designed in the late fifties and overlaid with new and emerging political realities, each seeming to have competing agendas.

It is a world where infrastructure outside the tourism boundaries is quite literally crumbling through inattention. Verandas and internal walls collapse with some regularity.

This is the result of pressures of housing that causes more and more people to be crammed into once single family dwellings that are now honeycombed with improvised layers as families expand.

This is a world where so many of the basics we take for granted – like being able to put toilet paper down the toilet – require different protocols.

With a fragile sewer system and no repairs on the supporting infrastructure, the Havana of my visits was slumping into decay a little more noticeably with each visit.

Of course this is not the case in the well-appointed tourist hotels where you are isolated in a make-believe world. These are places sanitised from the daily experience of the hardships of life around you. They are hotels of best world-class quality and are exquisitely decorated. I had one for my parking place.

From experience I knew that we visitors need time to readjust our expectations and judgments – even when staying in such a well-appointed hotel. Therefore, I had reserved this parking place so I could do so.

I hadn't specified details of what my No Plan should entail and just had a vague concept of what I wanted to do.

Since I had no plan, if my early ideas didn't work out I could dream up some new ones and see how they went.

I wouldn't have lost anything in the process, as I had no plan to start with.

Such was my thinking when I first arrived:

- Have four days in a hotel
- Rent an apartment and a car, and
- Do some trips outside Havana.

That was it.

My new Cuban friends met me while I was in my parking space. As it turned out, they were the key to me seeing Cuba through the lens of a Cuban perspective.

Had I been rushing about making a plan, I would have missed them.

I would have missed them because a plan indicates that there is something next to do.

A long wait with no advice about why, or when the waiting will end definitely gets in the way of a plan that expects something to be done next.

I would have missed them because they had things happening in their lives and no means to communicate with me to let me know that the appointed meeting time needed to be stretched – even beyond Cuban standards.

As it turned out, I spent a fair amount of time sitting waiting, and while waiting, watching the world go by.

If I had a plan, I might have just left a message that I was busy doing the next thing.

When I say waiting, I mean for periods of hours.

On one memorable occasion my waiting stretched to two and half hours. I was then greeted by a smiling and satisfied friend who announced happily that everything was in order.

I laughed in a sort of resigned fashion and we set off. On the way to our destination the story of the delay slowly unfolded.

In the middle of the night he had driven to collect a friend who was dealing with the results of an accident caused by a man stepping out in the dark in front of his slow-moving car.

His car was slow-moving because the headlights were magneto-driven and prone to dim when their stored battery strength waned.

I had a car like it once. We used to say: 'Lights by Lucas, the Prince of Darkness'.

The accident in this case had resulted in the windscreen of his friend's car having a head imprint in it. I was later to see this for myself when we surveyed the damage before setting out for a replacement, but that was some days later.

My friend described the rest of the intervening period since we had last parted.

He had juggled various minor family crises, made sure his partner and daughter had alternative arrangements for transportation to and from her dance classes on the days ahead, driven a friend to another town and sorted out the proposed absence from work while he was to undertake his Tour Director duties.

All these duties had meant going here and there to speak with various people. There were several other errands he had completed for the wider family because he was the one who had a car, but now he was here with everything settled.

This summary was delivered in a matter of fact manner and ended with a satisfied smile.

If you were Cuban you would find delays quite normal, but I was to discover that my Tour Director stretched even those boundaries.

For those of us who are not brought up in Cuba, but in places where it seems the clock dominates our expectation of life's rhythms, it is not at all normal.

Resignation in such situations was something I had gradually learned during my earlier trips.

Similar experiences through past Cuban holidays had taught me the merit of having patience. I had found that usually things ended up taking unexpected directions that made for a better time than I had anticipated – and these never would have happened if I had shown my frustration at the reconstruction of the concept of time.

Another part of the No Plan was that on this occasion, as so many others, once so collected after the long wait I didn't know where we were going – or why – but it turned into a great evening.

We first stopped to collect the rest of the family and were a bit late arriving at our destination due to the progress of a saintly icon that was making its Christmas travels around the island.

I hadn't realised she *was* the destination.

This much-revered patron saint of Cuba is the *Virgen de la Caridad de Cobre*. She is surrounded by 400 years of belief, mythology, and colourful stories.

Official records show she was carved in Toledo. Legend has it that she was created to give sailors someone to whom to pray and from whom to seek protection from the pirates and buccaneers of Cuba's early Spanish history.

This is probably accurate.

On what ship the Virgin was originally installed is unclear, but we do know several versions of the story of why she was elevated to reverential status.

According to some reports she was found by the 'Three Johns' (one of whom I discovered in an old document to be actually named Rodrigo – but one would hate to spoil a good story by pointing out this detail).

The three Johns found the Virgin when, as children of about ten years old they were out at sea in a small boat. She appeared floating atop the waves holding the baby Jesus and standing on a plinth that proclaimed her to be the Virgin of Charity. Despite floating on the waves, she was dry.

Another version has the Virgin being found by fishermen. She appeared to them during a storm – also quite dry despite the lashing waves – and her appearance was credited with saving them from certain destruction.

Whatever the source of her recovery, she was an uneasy spirit.

Many of the Virgin's early resting places didn't suit her. She kept disappearing from where she had been installed and appearing in other places, despite both locations being behind locked doors.

After several places didn't make her happy, the Virgin was eventually relocated to a mountain retreat in the *Sierra Maestra* Mountains. It seems that this was a spot that she chose herself.

The *Sierra Maestra* is the highest mountain range in Cuba and is mostly in Santiago de Cuba province. During the many battles of Cuban history the Sierra Maestra Mountains have been the refuge of many a guerrilla fighter. In the early 1950s after the failed attack on the Marcado Barracks that provoked the future revolution, Fidel Castro also found refuge there.

What attraction the mountains held for the Virgin is not known.

Perhaps she had exhausted the pleasures of sea voyages and thought the rebels of history needed her more than the sailors.

How this became her final residence is said to be because of her frequent appearances to a little girl called *Apolonia* who went to the mountainside to pick flowers.

Apolonia's claim to being in the company of the Virgin of Charity wasn't at first believed, but the Virgin appears to have been nothing if not insistent: she kept being seen there.

Eventually, the locals acceded to the presumed request of the Virgin to move to the *Sierra Maestras*.

Consequently, a chapel was built on the mountain of her choice.

Since then, the Virgin of Charity seems happily at rest and receives her pilgrims 'at home'.

It was there, high in the Sierra Maestras that Ernest Hemingway deposited his Nobel Prize medal in her care. She even drew the Pope to visit her here on her mountain.

These days the Virgin no longer departs on solo travels. Now her trips appear to be the wish of the people rather than her own, and certainly she never travels alone anymore.

Since communism and the church have become easier companions in the social life of Cuba, the Virgin has taken to travelling widely, but always under escort. Now, her travels follow preannounced itineraries that share her graces with the wider communities of the island of which she is patron saint.

Now, with no more mysterious disappearances and reappearances beyond locked doors, when the Virgin travels it is to an approving and rapturous public.

Part of the magic of the unexpected of my No Plan was that on this night we were all part of that audience.

On the night when I was privileged to see the Virgin, the narrow streets where once I had photographed a donkey-powered street tram were a shoulder-to-shoulder mass of adoring people.

At first I had no idea where we were, or why.

My Spanish was in rehabilitation mode after years of disuse. Finally, I grasped the situation but by then it was impossible to get close to the church where the Virgin had briefly stopped.

As we were being moved along on the swell of humanity, I was surprised to realise that this was the very church where my Cuban goddaughter had been christened so many years ago. The picture of her in my arms that day has stayed by my bed ever since – but I have lost track of the whole family. I wondered if they were perhaps there in the crowd.

Ever resourceful, my friends pulled me with them away from the eager throng and through the packed street towards a house nearby.

There was a hasty discussion with a tall man who was watching the whole scene from his doorway with the bemused gaze of someone who had seen it all before and wasn't getting too excited.

My friends pushed me ahead of them urgently and told me to hurry upstairs.

We duly tramped through the adjacent house and climbed onto the rooftop. This gave us a bird's eye view just as the Virgin, still smiling enigmatically within her glass case, left the church en route to her next destination.

Once again it had been proven that by letting go of my expectations they had been exceeded.

What did the Cuban Approach accomplish?

My parking space gave me a few days with some predictability and a slow reintroduction to a culture whose priorities were different from mine.

From there, the plan started to evolve. Had I tried to control it, my invitations would have departed and I really would have had a No Plan – as in nothing happening.

From my parking place I could regain my Cuban perspective at a slower rate than if I had been thrown into urgent need to:

- Get a place to stay in Havana.
- Decide where to go outside the capital.
- Rent a car, and generally to,
- Have a plan.

Step 1 of the Cuban Approach: *Reserve a parking place:* Sometimes we need to take a slight pause before we pull back out onto life's highways.

Reserve a parking place: Have enough of a plan to let a plan evolve.

Reading the winds: When there is no wind, use some of the tools of the sailor.

Wait for the wind.
Sailors know that on a warm day there is no need to rush breakfast because usually the wind picks up in the middle of the day.

In life, let the day inform your level of activity as it unfolds with all its options.

Use the tide. Let it define your direction.

If you do so it is useful to bear in mind the old proverb of the Breton sailors:

Trust in God but row away from the rocks.

In life, swimming against the tide is known to be self defeating - but we so often do so because we respond with emotion and discard rational thought.

Instead, we can go with the tide and let it carry us to safe lagoons along the way where we can regroup and emerge to strike out to the shores of our choosing.

Look for 'cats' paws' on the water.

These are the small patches of ripples that reveal a puff of wind travelling on its own across the water.

In life, these are the tiny things we never notice when we are busy because we have a plan.

They are the things that often show us the direction of travel of a situation that, if well-read, positions us to take an easier route towards our goal.

Use good navigational techniques.

Plot a course but know that if your calculations are a degree off you may end up increasingly diverted from your objective, while still making great time in your travel.

This is something we are all prone to do. We measure activity, not result.

In navigation you use latitude and longitude, both measured by degrees.

Thanks to 'The White Hat Crew'[2] here are some examples of what it can mean if you are *just one degree off* in your route.

They use aviation and not marine examples, but I think these work to show the results of deviation caused a seemingly small error:

- After travelling from San Francisco to Los Angeles (a trip of about 614km or 382 miles) you'd be off by 9.6km or 6 miles
- If you took the scenic route to San Francisco around the globe departing from Washington, DC, you'd end up in Boston – over 700 km or 435 miles off course
- Travelling an even more scenic route in your rocket ship via the moon, you'd miss it by more than the diameter of the sun: 2,574,950 and a bit km, or 1.6million miles.

Pilots without navigational aids use a simple rule of thumb: one degree off over 60 nautical miles results in being one nautical mile off course. This is generally accurate, although over longer distances there is a wider error differential.

It's a useful calculation because it can be done in the pilot's head while flying so they can work out a corrected route to return to course at the next Way Point.

In life, sometimes we are too sure of ourselves. We cease to qualify our progress by checking to see we are still on the course we thought we were on.

Maintain a light touch.

In sailing terms, a 'sheet' is a line that controls the moveable corners of a sail. It looks like a rope to a landlubber – because it is.

Lightweight sheets give better control.

In life, relaxing control lets direction announce itself.

---

[2] *The White Hat Crew is the website of Antone Roundy, who shares his insights on internet marketing with a focus on doing so effectively and ethically.* www.whitehatcrew.com

Deploy a lightweight spinnaker.

A spinnaker is that wonderful triangular extra sail that billows colourfully from the mast from the mainsail and amplifies any wind that is there.

When the spinnaker fills, it is called flying, and because it resembles a parachute, the spinnaker is often called a kite or chute.

A well designed spinnaker has taut leading edges when filled. These form a smooth curve, with no bumps or depressions caused by inconsistent stretching.

In life you may wish to drift, but it is good to carry your spinnaker to catch an unexpected wind of opportunity.

For your spinnaker, choose the life tools that are simple and give an easy line to your travels, taking an alternate route from the things that cause depressions and bumps.

When you deploy your spinnaker, be as colourful as any you've admired as it paints the horizon with progress across the waves.

Reduce drag.

Drag is often caused by anything extra that breaks the aerodynamics of your vessel.

In life, when the winds haven't announced themselves, it's wise to jettison the extras that add nothing to your progress.

For a time it may be social media is the first to go, or the habit of letting TV fill the spaces where other activities may bring a better reward.

Negative people and negative input of any kind fall into this category. I found that once I ceased watching TV news I lost nothing but the negativity that featured. Radio gave me the news I needed.

Adjust your keel or rudder angle.

The force of the wind propels the boat, but the viscosity of the water slows her down and keeps her on course: a keel stops the wind blowing her sidewise.

The keel is a thin fin attached to the lower centre line of the boat. When it and the rudder– another fin-like device – are aligned, the boat keeps moving in a straight line.

Turn the rudder from that alignment, and the boat turns.

In life, sometimes you need to change your angle of perspective: it may help you see the opportunities offered by whatever winds are passing.

We often forget that we are the helmsman in our own lives and only we can adjust the rudder to change direction.

Check your 'Tell Tales'.

'Tell Tales' are the colourful strands of yarn or fabric tied to the stays that hold the mast in place. One is tied on each side of the jib, the small sail at the front – one to starboard, and one on the port side.

On large yachts they have two sets, the upper ones guide steering, and the lower ones giving the set of the sail: both should be in harmony.

'Tell Tales' on either side should both stream aft as you are pointed forward on your course.

In life, if you don't have Tell Tales, you should think about getting some. Otherwise how do you know if you are off course?

I once sat next to an executive from Boeing en route to Australia to discuss some problems about delays in component production at the local manufacturing plant. He told me he was pretty good at The Times Crossword. He always took a few of them with him when he crossed challenging time zones.

His measure of how much he was suffering jet lag was to see if he could finish the crossword in the time he would expect to do so at home.

This was his Tell Tale.

Once he had his Tell Tales flowing behind him he would start his negotiations, knowing he was mentally set, with sails trimmed to their optimum.

What are yours?

Adjusting your sails: Don't lower your sails when you have no sense of direction. Opportunity brings its own direction.

If you lower your sails you have announced to the universe that you don't expect to be able to catch the next wind.

There is a time for action and
a time to let the winds direction become known.

The Cuban Approach
is to make the most of the moments in between.

CHAPTER TWO

A month with no plan

means having NO PLAN

Being dedicated to having no plan did not mean being dedicated to having no idea about anything that is a possibility, so I bought a map of Cuba.

Without a map I felt I would be reflecting the quotation from the comedian Steven Wright when he said:

I have an existential map.

It has 'You are here' written all over it.

The lady in the kiosk where I went to purchase this invaluable guide to travel was convinced that I was buying the wrong map.

Unlike in our book stores where there is a smorgasbord of maps to choose from, in Havana there were two maps.

I had chosen one charmingly called a Geographical Map.

She was sure I had meant to buy the one for tourists called, oddly enough, a Tourist Map.

After a friendly exchange where I stuck to my selection – and had a lively discussion about the fact that she didn't have more than three of this postcard and four of that but would I like this one instead – we waved goodbye to each other and I rejoined my Cuban friends.

I explained about the lady in the kiosk and her dismay at my choice.

"You bought a map?"

Now they also looked concerned. They asked to see my map.

When it was produced and laid out on the table between the Bucaneros and Cristals, smiles lit up faces all around.

"Yes," they said. "You need a map of the roads. This is the right map ... a map of the roads".

It took two Cristals for me to assimilate that statement, as I pondered what a map without the roads would be like.

On our travels my map (with roads) proved useful:

- For indicating with a general wave of the hand the sort of general area that we might cover in our allotted time on the road.
- To give some concept of where we were in relationship to Havana when arriving in a given city.
- At the end of our travels, when we decided it would be fun to mark some of our routes for posterity.
- For my Cuban friends who liked to look over it thoughtfully as they discussed relatives and friends who lived here, or there.
- So that I didn't get a wet bottom when sitting on a stone wall.
- As a sunshade when my hat was left at the apartment and I was waiting for my horse to arrive for a day's riding.
- As a mat for resting the bunch of onions that we bought for the relatives we were visiting at our next stop after the village famous for its onions.

It wasn't any help at all in making a plan.

The No Plan was roughly based on a few principles:

- I am a tourist and want to see some of the things tourists generally want to see.
- I am not the usual tourist and so might want to see some things that require a great deal of acceptance of people the way they are – and an ability to 'blend' (as much as any tourist can 'blend' in Cuba).
- A plan is not a good idea as it might need changing and people might be disappointed. Instead, things should evolve as we go, allowing us to respond to opportunities as they appeared.

- The trip should include a few banks to refresh the money-pot – and a few fuel stops where fuel can be paid by credit card rather than cash.
- Accommodation should be original – and preferably not in hotels.
- The trip would take as long as funds would allow.

As you can see,
a map and
a route are not on the list.

At the time of our departure, I was unaware of this framework that later seemed so clearly to be the structure upon which our adventures hung. These were never stated as principles but in retrospect did seem to guide our travels.

My idea of a good trip is to let it unfold, like a story. I am severely against being told before a play or a film anything pertaining to the tale itself.

Just as I want to experience the unfolding of a story in the theatre, so it is with journeys of discovery.

I want to travel with the naïveté of the newcomer.

I want to be captivated by the sounds, the smells, the disasters and the delights of the journey itself. To me, the destination is secondary. Do I care if I get to some place with a label, a title, an expectation, if the journey itself has:

- coated me with the dust of the unexpected
- refreshed me with laughter
- fed me things I have never eaten before
- introduced me to people whose lives touched mine
- reframed my perspective
- given me a head full of ideas and new thoughts, and
- loaded my camera with images?

In this spirit, on our appointed departure day we set off out along the pothole-ridden roads of Havana to the city outskirts.

As we passed, in every street the everyday life of an overcrowded Cuban house was momentarily framed in open windows.

We passed a girl in a pedalo balancing on her lap a three-layered cake iced in coloured whipped cream.

On the next corner a wheelbarrow leant against a wall to showcase a meager stock of vegetables for sale.

In an abandoned yard there was a shooting range, with Cristal, Bucanero, and soda cans lined up as targets. An air rifle was tied to a big piece of wood on the firing bench. I couldn't see any prizes. Maybe showing skill was enough.

The jumble of electricity and telephone cables that festoon intersections never ceased to fascinate me.

My response was the same with the precarious electrical improvisations I had seen in local kitchens. These included taking a live electric coil and dunking it into a metal water container to act as an electric kettle - and bare wires that are just inserted into the mains when a connection is required.

I remembered that on my first few visits I was surprised to find a pig in residence within the inner courtyard of the home where my good friend Jorge lived.

It seemed not nearly as unusual now, after becoming a bit better acclimatised to the realities of Cuban home life, than it did then.

Then, finally we were at the suburban outskirts and ahead of us stretched the open road: as far as we could see into the distance here was a fantastic stretch of *Autopista Nacional*, or National Highway wide enough to accommodate an Italian rush hour.

The lanes are not marked so it would work well in Italy where they may as well be invisible anyway.

The quality of this main inter-city route was markedly different from any roads I had travelled within Havana. It was a highway in the real sense of the word.

In American English the term 'highway' usually refers just to a major route, but in British English it simply means any 'road open to the public'. It's interesting to note that, in either case, the definition makes no reference to what type of traffic 'the public' might employ – and on Cuban highways you see everything.

On our travels there were modern cars rented to tourists, an occasional relatively modern truck, classic cars and trucks from the 1950s and earlier, mule and ox carts, pony traps, vehicles of many varieties that had been made into buses, horse riders, people pushing wheelbarrows, and even a young man on roller skates.

Because the roads other than those that make up the National and Central Highway network are of what we might kindly call 'of variable quality', this can affect the rate of your progress.

The benefit of this is that it gives a chance to take advantage of roadside enterprises.

We stopped at one that showed the craftsmanship and ingenuity of the owners of the little house to which it was attached.

The roadside stall was cleverly made on a rather precarious trailer that obviously allowed it to be trundled in at dusk and out again in the morning.

The trailer was essentially a welded metal frame on which the stall would be constructed each day. On either side was a ledge. On these sat long sections of what appeared to have once been a balustrade of what looked like marble: an unlikely combination.

Another balustrade styled piece lay along the centre, creating a tiered market stall to which an extra shelf on either side at a lower level had been added.

One rested atop of a packing case and the other on a cleverly made metal shelf that was an extension of the trundle frame.

Arranged carefully on these shelves was an amazing array of tropical fruits, each variety sitting in old spring-form baking tins, frying pans, or metal baking tins of various other types and shapes and sizes.

An extra shelf that consisted of a board laid over the metal angular handles of the trundle base featured carefully arranged *El corazón de Bullock* or 'Bullock's Heart': known to most of us as 'Custard Apple'.

Branches of Snake Fruit, with grenade-like prickles emerging from bright orange skins, were leaned against the stall to tempt us for their flavour.

Just don't eat too many at a time – hard to resist, because they are really tasty. It's not something I've tested, but too many are reputed to bring on constipation.

Tropical fruits are tasty but in their enjoyment there's also a lesson in moderation to be had. Over-indulgence in many varieties may have cautionary side effects. For example, the lovely star fruits that were carefully arranged here make great jams and jellies, but due to their high oxalic acid content, too many eaten raw are hazardous to anyone with kidney issues.

The Custard Apple variant called 'Sour Sops' or 'Sweet Sops', sitting here in their horny green skins, were arranged on the handlebar shelf. These also have a payback for too many in the diet.

Over 70% of the Parkinson's disease in Guadeloupe has been attributed to an over representation of Custard Apple in the diet.

The culprit is found in the seeds and leaves: the compound within, called *Annonacin* is a neurotoxin.

The fruity part of Custard Apple might be a contributor to Parkinson's disease, but the seeds and bark have strong anti-tumour properties.

Custard Apples belong to the same family as the Papaya. As is so often in life, members of the same family can have quite different properties.

Papaya doesn't have a negative impact on health at all that we know of, and it also has been shown to have healing properties in cancer treatment.

Where chemotherapy poisons cancer cells - instead, papaya releases *Acetogenins* that starve them. At the same time, it reduces new cell growth around the cancer and helps reduce the duplication of cells already cancerous.

Papaya has also proven effective when the body rejects treatments: a condition called Multiple-Drug Resistance (MDR).

Our vendor had papayas aplenty, plus two pineapples, lots of oranges, lemons, and Chinese Gooseberries (now known better as Kiwi Fruit).

The story of how a fruit indigenous to China became claimed as the export fruit of a South Pacific Island nation is fascinating.

The US and England had both tried to cultivate the Chinese gooseberry but both were only able to propagate male plants. By contrast, the seeds of both sexes flourished when planted on a New Zealand farm in Wanganui after being brought there by a missionary.

The New Zealand Chinese Gooseberry crops thrived. They had the potential to become an important export crop until export agents identified a significant market impediment.

In the early 1950s, gooseberries were more common than now, but were not popular in any western market. The export agents felt that it would be too easy for a buyer to confuse the two quite dissimilar fruits. That would mean our much loved Chinese Gooseberry being tainted with the same label of being unremarkable, if not downright distasteful to the British palate as a regular gooseberry.

So this is why a new name was sought. It was mere pragmatism – and that is how the Chinese gooseberry became transformed to be named after the national bird of New Zealand.

It has been reported that nearly every Kiwi Fruit that we now eat can be traced back to that Wanganui farm.

I wondered if these Cuban fruits came from this, or from other stock.

The roadside market stall that had prompted these investigations into the character of the fruits displayed was finished by two tree branches.

The branches were anchored by weaving them through the structure. This gave the effect of two banana trees. This was due to the way that bunches of bananas were strung over stems left when the young branches had been cut off from the main one.

The effort and creativity that went into the stall attracted us to it.

Others nearby offered similar goods: some were constructed from shelves balanced over a wheelbarrow; others were made of packing boxes precariously balanced on wire frames.

None of the competitors' sales platforms were as imaginatively designed as the one where we made our purchases.

This quotation from John Ruskin summarised why, having passed several of these roadside stalls, we stopped at the stand we did:

> *We require from buildings two kinds of goodness:*
> *first, the doing their practical duty well,*
> *then, that they be graceful and pleasing in doing it.*

The little off-road shop built from branches and coconut thatch was another illustration of Cuban creativity in action.

Long pieces of bamboo were cleverly tied with raffia to make slotted shelves in which lemons were ripening on one side, coconuts, and snake fruit branches laden with pods, on the other.

Necklaces made from pods and gourds were hung from the top bamboo shelf. Beneath them were beautifully carved dried gourd maracas with wood-turned handles. Artistically woven straw hats hung across the back wall and colourful woven baskets were ranked across the corner. Unfortunate birds lived in small bamboo cages underneath the shelter. Their slightly luckier cousins lived in larger ones made from fishing seines hung from the roof. All had upturned recycled plastic water-bottle water feeders.

The little open-air shop and the cooking bench beside it were lit by energy saving light bulbs encased in shades made from cut-off plastic bottles.

On the main upright an insect catcher of the most basic kind was tied. It was a plastic bottle with the top cut off and reinserted to make a funnel. Insects get in, but as they seem programmed to climb the walls to get out, they never fly to the centre to find the open bottle neck that would make an easy exit.

A one-ring electric hot plate was plugged into an adaptor on an extension cord that was coiled on a shelf above the work surface.

I noticed that the wires for the light had been split off this. My brother went through a stage of collecting old Austin 7 cars and I recognised these twists of wire: you just touched the two wires together to start the car or in this case – the light!

It was raining, but our shop keeper just donned a plastic raincoat and patiently stood beside his stall with a bunch of bananas in each hand to tempt passing motorists. The commerce was vital to the support of the extended family.

Further on, we passed the official sales stall for the local agricultural cooperative.

Pork haunches and legs hung in the open air on hooks. An old scale sat ready to measure out a purchase. This was the sort that made me think it had once been used to weigh babies. Weights can be slid along a marked weight scale while the baby – or in this case the meat – rests in a curved tray.

A hand-painted sign on the front gave the Opening Hours: 8am – 6pm. Two ladies chatted inside the concrete structure until new customers arrived, the rain pattering comfortingly on the corrugated iron roof.

These are the benefits of a No Plan.

There is time to stop and gain a little insight into a different way of life. It was insight to lives far less privileged than ours.

With a No Plan you might find that you are stuck behind an ox-cart on a one-lane stretch of road.

This allows time to examine the makings of the cart itself and its improvised components: the cardboard under the ox harness to ease the pressure on the shoulders, and the rubber inner tube of a tyre that had been cut to make the back strap and the breeching straps. On one ox-cart a man's belt of plaited leather made the girth as it attached to the bellyband.

Along the way you might linger a long time mesmerised by the clarity of the water and the colourfulness of the fish in a flooded subterranean cavern.

In this context, making a plan to be anywhere at a particular time would be self-defeating.

This now seemed an evident truth.

For those of us who come from another world it is not easy to travel with no plan.

Our world of:

- appointments and meetings
- flights or trains to catch
- deadlines by which we must produce things
- morning and evening rush hour traffic to be avoided
- off-peak and advance purchase fares
- the need to check into accommodation by a certain time, and out by eleven in the morning.

All these thing blur our minds.

In this context, travel on a No Plan seems to be dangerously uncharted territory.

The key is to leave the 'What if..?' questions back in your previous world.

'What if there is nowhere to stay?'

Well, it is unlikely that there will be *nowhere*.

It might not be quite what you expected – but aren't you there for the adventure?

'What if we get lost?'

No. Not with a local.

You might take a circuitous route because that's the one your guide knows, or the one known by the person who was stopped and asked.

You may have a new destination because of misunderstanding, or convenience, or the sudden realisation of a hidden gem you may wish to see, but you won't be lost because you will be where you have been directed to: somewhere you never expected to be.

This begs the question: What IS 'lost' exactly, when you have no plan?

You will end up somewhere.

In my experience, in that somewhere, no matter how remote, someone will find you a place to stay.

It may well turn out to be one of the great memories of your trip.

Of course this can only be the case if you are not so busy obsessing over trying to make a plan that this causes you to ignore the alternatives available, or even not to recognise them when they appear.

What did the Cuban Approach accomplish?

My no plan allowed for a great deal of flexibility.

Without the constraints of having to check into a hotel by a certain hour or be at a certain tourist destination for an event at a particular time, we had the opportunity to let the trip inform our direction.

It allowed me time to just stand and stare, and in created a relaxed space uncluttered by day to day obligations and expectations of my usual life.

It allowed me to ponder the things that had coloured my time on earth.

It gave me space for peaceful introspection uninterrupted by social media, emails, work commitments, the input of others, or obligations of any sort.

All this effectively offered me a blank slate on which to draw. As I did so, each new encounter seemed to gently find a way to reveal something about myself.

Each insight became a different sort of compass to which I could refer in the future as I made my way forward from this time in my life.

Step 2 of the Cuban Approach: A month with no plan: When you have no plan, have no plan.

Reading the winds: There is no point in having no plan and then second guessing the person who is guiding your No Plan on maps of his own making, in geography you don't know.

With my No Plan I had many maps to guide me as I read the winds of adventure:

- There was the map (with roads) I bought from the friendly kiosk lady in Havana.
- There was the map in the memory of my Tour Director as he alternately followed routes taken to friends and family or diverted to new places heard of, but previously not visited.
- There was the map that was redrawn according to my disinclination to see this, but enthusiasm to see that.
- There was the map redrawn due to forgetting a crucial souvenir my Tour Director had bought and deciding to re-route to go back and collect it.

The most important of all maps was that which is etched into my memory.

This last one is a map of people, of tastes, of animals, of events and adventure, and of a period of freedom from the everyday constraints of my usual life.

It is a colourful map and one that will never be lost, because it is the map of memorable moments and wonderfully vivid sights.

Over this memory map, there are layers of all my later explorations into the history of things – like how a Chinese gooseberry transformed itself into a Kiwi Fruit, or to find out more about the wealthy sugar barons who created the wonderfully eclectic grand architecture of a once hugely wealthy and influential Cuba.

In this way, I balance the winds of the present against those as recorded in history – and of those as recorded in their own lands and their own languages.

This gives a sense of perspective and a wider context to the more common stories of the past.

Adjusting your sails: Just like the oceans, life has many swells and eddies. Riding them, or being taken by the tides, can depend upon how your sails are set, and by how accurately you view both sea and shore.

If you spend time wishing the seas were calmer, more welcoming, and kinder than those in which you find yourself, perhaps you need to take off your sunglasses and see reality.

The tides have a lunar pull.
So do you.
Both can be aligned
but only if you set a possible course.

Your route goes more safely by having combined several views taken from different perspectives to indicate the best way through.

As with all things tidal and with life, your view will be influenced by where you are in relation to the rest of the universe.

Fighting the tides is an unrewarding task.

If you fear losing your way
remember that your only obligation in this life
is to be true to yourself.

This is the compass
that keeps you aligned to true north.

If you use this compass
you will never go far off course.

My travels on the highways and unmarked tracks of the Cuban countryside gave me several fresh perspectives for my adventures after my No Plan month.

When I saw someone trudging in the rain with a heavy wheelbarrow load, or an exhausted hauler of a low, wooden tray with wobbly small wheels carrying four 50 kilo sacks of onions, it put issues in my own life into perspective.

Sights like this and many of my experiences of the everyday usual life of locals gave me a similar jolt of reality, just as did my best friend Linda when my partner died and everything went pear-shaped in my life.

Then, she looked me in the eye and said firmly.

"You can't change what is and let's be honest. When you think about it, who is more blessed than you?"

Perhaps your friends may apply the same tough love.

She was right of course.

Friends usually are.

It's aggravating at times, because it means you have to climb down your ladder or pick up your game.

Why was she right?

I have so many blessings.

I have the blessing of:

- good health
- a good education
- of having had a stable family life when growing up
- of having real friends who have lit my pathways with laughter and fun, and the way-finding lights of friendship that supported me when I faltered.

Who is more blessed than me?

CHAPTER THREE

Reversed Binoculars

Looking inwards

Not having a plan does not eliminate choice.

Accordingly, on Day One of my No Plan travel I declined the crocodile farm visit – having lived amongst them in tropical north Queensland, in Australia.

There, I used to walk the beach in the early morning.

Often the tell-tale tail track framed by clawed footmarks announced the happy fact that the local estuarine crocs had preceded me.

It made me more comfortable to see by these tracks that the local crocodiles had completed their dawn patrol. They would now be back in the reedy banks of the creek that flowed into the sea just above the sand hills.

With this experience indelible in my mind, spending time with crocodiles wasn't high on my list of preferred memories to capture in Cuba.

Instead, I opted for the launch trip to an island resort built to represent an original Taíno Indian village.

The Taíno were indigenous people of the Caribbean whose actual site of origin is variously attributed, but whose people themselves saw Hispaniola *(modern Haiti)* as the heart of their cultural heritage.

After Spanish colonisation in Cuba, the Taíno women frequently served the Spanish colonial men as wives – for in 1492 no European women were brought with the settlers.

The use of the term 'served' in the last sentence is no accident.

According to the diaries of Christopher Columbus, the original community of Taíno were lovely people, and very hospitable. They welcomed the newcomers to their island with gifts of sugar and tobacco – the latter a new luxury for the Spanish. However, their visitors didn't repay their generosity in kind. The Spanish quickly enslaved the locals to mine for precious metals and soon decimated the population.

If the Taíno didn't die from hard labour, they died from smallpox or other previously unknown diseases. Just fifty years after Spanish occupation, a third of the native population had died just of smallpox. Survivors were few.

Inter-racial mixing reduced bloodline purity further. According to official records, by 1514 – just two decades after their arrival – 40% of Spanish men had Taíno wives. Unreported liaisons would probably increase that percentage greatly.

It was therefore believed that the Taíno had disappeared as a precisely identifiable group, and that their legacy remained only in the cultural intermixture of Cuba today.

This belief was recently challenged by the studies of Robert M. Poole, who wrote in the Smithsonian[3] about his visit to Cuba to explore remnants of the Taíno.

During his explorations near Guantanamo Bay in the province of *Oriente*, Poole discovered 75-year old *Francisco 'Panchito' Ramírez Rojas*.

Panchito was a knowledgeable and respected tribal *cacique*, or leader. Poole's observations about him laid doubt to there being no direct line of inheritance of the Taíno, for it seemed that Panchito proved otherwise.

In the manner that had been recorded about his ancestors in the diaries of early Spanish settlers writing about the curiosities of Taíno culture, Panchito conversed with the plants, respecting them as

---

[3] *http://www.smithsonianmag.com/people-places/what-became-of-the-taino-73824867/?MobileOptOut=1&page=5*

'relatives'. This remarkable and learned man still lived by the same Taíno ways as those recorded at the time of the first Spanish settlement.

Panchito was a modern day example of these generous-hearted people who understood the world in which they lived and in a holistic way, their relationship to it.

As Poole writes, Panchito must have learned everything verbally just as it was passed down the generations by the elders, for he had no book learning. Poole believed that people like Panchito refute the previous belief of loss of the Taíno and their rich culture.

The Taíno give us something to think about in the way they respect the natural world.

They believe that if you want to get food from the earth you have to give something back.

At harvest they say a short prayer and bury a small stone or coin in the field as a little message to the earth, so she may help with production.

This respect reminds me of something I was once told:

> *There is no room for disrespect in life.*
> *Especially, never disrespect yourself.*

We remember the Taíno when we drowse in a 'hammock', attend a 'barbeque', take shelter from a 'hurricane', or smoke 'tobacco'.

These are all words the Taíno gave to us.

In fact it was the native population who showed the Spanish how to make cigars.

The resort village of Guamá where we were headed by launch is a simulation of what designers understood a Cuban Taíno village to have looked like. There are sketches of such villages from the time of Columbus. Even now, in some parts of Cuba the same construction is still being used.

This recreated village, with its palm frond and woven straw construction, was a mix of design based on sketches of original Taíno villages and the needs for accommodation deemed suitable for international tourists.

The Guamá setting is magical. It sits on ten artificial islands linked by arched bridges.

The resort was one of the first works appointed by Fidel Castro after the revolution. He named it after a Taíno chief who had also valiantly led a fight against Cuban colonisation, albeit unsuccessfully.

Previously the area was one of the most famous fishing and game reserves in Latin America. Before the Revolution it was in private ownership, and thus off-limits to Cubans.

When we got there, the whole Guamá resort was looking a bit weary. Certainly the brightly painted tourist boat artfully beached at a rakish angle and half underwater wasn't going anywhere any time soon.

But for a hideaway holiday together it would be lovely – if you brought your mosquito repellent along.

The construction began in 1959 but halted when the architect suddenly left the country.

Management of the project fell to *Celia Sanchez*, the influential former Revolutionary who had selflessly risked her life to supply and send messages to the Revolutionary army – herself assembling a combat squad.

In post-Revolution Cuba, physician *René Vallejo* and Sanchez became Fidel's closet companions. Celia was known to be the person to assess and deliver the practicalities to get a job done.

Knowing how important the project was to Castro, Celia needed a replacement who would not leave Cuba. This is why, for the continuation of a badly started project, she asked *Mario Girona*. He was a society architect who had never before worked in wood, but Sanchez knew his family from childhood and knew he would never leave Cuba.

Girona inherited a challenging job made easier by the fact that whatever he needed, he could ask Celia to arrange it. His work remains with us now and it has been enhanced. On the banks of the Guamá islands there are twenty-five life-size sculptures by Cuban sculptor *Rita Longa*.

Made from marble dust and cement, the sculptures depict what it may have been like when Taíno people went about their everyday life around the islands.

Rita Longa's style and art deco influences give grace and line to these tributes to a nation of the past. The sculptures alone draw global tourists, let alone the resort.

Rita Longa's wide collection of remarkable works includes the ballerina at the entrance to the famous Copacabana Night Club.

On my first visit I was deeply impressed by the exhilarating performances at the Copacabana – and especially by the statuesque human chandeliers – gorgeous, scantily-clad young women whose headwear consisted of lit chandeliers whose crystal drops tinkled as they moved.

Other Longa works include designing the first neon sign for that great central institution of Havana, Coppelia Ice Cream Parlour. This is in the form of a chubby legged ballerina in fishnet stockings and with the ice cream as her frothy tutu.

Perhaps that is where the collaboration between Rita and architect Mario Girona started, for she also contributed to the design of the Guamá resort.

Girona's works are also part of the fabric of Cuba and they include the once famous mob-run casino and art-deco-styled hotel, 'The Capri' was a favourite of Hollywood stars – especially Errol Flynn.

At the times of my visits The Capri was closed after being run down due to lack of maintenance, but since then, in 2014 The Capri was restored in collaboration between state run *Grupo Caribe* and the Spanish hotel chain *NH Hotelels SA*.

Another Girona work was the modernisation of the José *Martí* International Airport.

However, by far the most famous, and to locals the most meaningful contribution to the sense of place of post-revolution Havana, is Girona's elegant design of Coppelia Ice Cream Parlour.

The architecture of Coppelia responded to Fidel's desire for a meeting place in Havana where everyone could congregate irrespective of condition or class. With his dairy farm background, Fidel believed ice cream was the right of the populace. That meant that prices were kept low to ensure affordability.

What better reason to congregate as equals than over ice cream – that universal delight?

Ice cream diplomacy was once a key part of Cuban international relations. Diplomats travelled with the famous Coppelia Ice Cream in tubs stored in dry ice.

Ho Chi Minh received three different flavours as a gift from Fidel Castro: Salvador Allende only one – chocolate!

Senator Patrick Leahy from Vermont exchanged some Ben & Jerry's ice cream with Fidel because he said it tasted better.

In this way, ice cream opened new lines of communication in diplomatic circles. Then, there were more than fifty flavours, and Coppelia was the largest ice cream parlour in the world.

Coppelia ice cream was sought after by dignitaries and wealthy patrons throughout Europe and the Caribbean.

But that was then.
Times change.

In 2012, it was reported that nearly all of all Cuban ice cream is made of 30% soy milk.

Certainly, those who knew it in its early days lament the loss of varieties and reduction in quality.

Design of a tourist resort is quite different from a world icon ice cream parlour or an airport. One cannot but think that Guamá benefits from the influence of both architect and sculptor.

There is an affinity between the gracious curves of the planked walkways in Guamá, the sweep of the spirals in the interior of Coppelia, and the elegant flowing lines of Rita Longa's sculptures of the Taíno.

I wondered what was Fidel's vision for the Guamá resort. What had he wanted to create for the people of Cuba? It seemed when I was visiting that, as with other hotels in Cuba, the locals still couldn't stay here.

It had always seemed sad to me in my early visits to find that people who had celebrated their marriage before the revolution in the grand hotels of Havana like the *Hotel Nacional*, were now banned from entering those same hotels.

A stay at Guamá also offers the chance to explore the shores of Treasure Lake beyond the islands on which the village sits. This is the largest freshwater lake in Cuba – over 16 square km, or 6.17 sq miles. Its name reflects a popular story that the Taíno Chief had the village treasure thrown into the lake to stop it being seized by the Spanish.

Given the lack of treasure hunters seeking either to make their fortune or to disprove the legend, maybe the treasure has long since been found and removed.

Perhaps it never existed.

The story of treasure doesn't seem to be a part of the locally accepted folklore. I read it only in tourist documents and could find no references in other research – but may have missed it.

Perhaps those who write such stuff think that no lost village (even a recreated one) should be without its treasure story.

On our launch trip back from the short half-day outing, we paused before a giant anthill. Coming from Australia such a sight was not an unusual one for me.

Termite mounds like this are called termitariums and they pop up all over Australia: no building permits required. Their construction is complex and individual.

Termitariums are made from soil bound with saliva and excreta. This makes for differences in colour according to the variation of proportion and component makeup of each of both elements.

The combination is robust and forms a structure that can last over a hundred years.

There are over 2,000 types of termites and about 350 varieties make Australia their home.

In the tropical north, the termites eat spinifex – a coastal grass species that flourishes in sandy conditions.

The resulting mounds of this region can be 7 metres high *(almost 8')* and weigh around 10 tonnes *(22,046lbs)*.

Mankind is ever innovative, applying new uses to ordinary things. Early Australian settlers hollowed out termite mounds or anthills so there was space for an oven on one side and the chimney on the other.

Knowing the residents would seal up the opening as if closing a lid, before colonisation some indigenous Australian tribes dug out funeral tombs in the active mounds.

Because they protect their ancestors, many Aboriginal people still treat these termitariums with great reverence.

Geologists seeking minerals have recently discovered that some of these ant constructors of Australia are also expert gold miners.

After excavating from as deep as 4 metres *(13')* underground, when they bring material to the surface, they also retain within their bodies some of the gold of the deposits beneath.

Staring at the Cuban anthill, I wondered if the local termitarium residents could be harnessed to excavate for gold as a finished product instead of ore.

If so, then perhaps it would be they who would find the mythical treasures of the lake.

As others snapped photos of the anthill, my camera moved to a perched sea eagle that was watching a local fisherman setting out with hopes of a good catch: two fisher folk – one with feathers.

I wonder who did best that day.

As I watched them both, I thought of the observation of Henry David Thoreau:

Many men go fishing all their lives
without knowing that it is not fish they are after.

In a way, my No Plan journey was also a fishing trip.

This was not something I knew at the time, but something that is clear as I look back and relive the experiences.

Fishing is a chance to be alone with just yourself
– and possibly catch fish.

No Plan travel is a just such a chance to rediscover you.

The fish of those journeys sometimes appear in strange incarnations of the various selves of which we are all made. We are complex beings, showing only the face suitable for the environment of the moment, yet having other selves – some quite private. On a No Plan journey you have a chance to meet them all and assign them to their proper place in your history.

Our decision to take the boat trip was spontaneous and since the first boat had quickly filled, we had to await the next one. This delay in departure meant that by the time we got back from our visit it was twilight.

As is the way in the tropics, after about thirteen hours of an intense brightness that seems to etch landmarks with surgical precision, twilight goes to dark in one magnificent sweep of dying colour.

As we approached this night, the day ended with gold of its own: intense, fiery and molten. It burnished the coastal horizon with molten shades until fading to the colour of slightly tarnished brass. Then, it was if the brass was being polished for one last soft display.

The day hung tentatively on the edge of its watery stage, softening the twilight with pastels before a decisive curtain of darkness ended the show.

As we searched for a place to stay we drove through small hamlets, thin chickens fleeing from our headlights in a burst of indignant cackling, and small children watching our progress with curiosity from veranda steps.

After slow travel down narrow tracks we drew closer to a dim light in the middle of a wide range of brush-clumped meadows. As we grew closer, a guard house softly illuminated by an old fashioned hurricane lamp appeared from within the undergrowth.

Upon enquiry we discovered that we had arrived at the beach resort that my tour guide had been seeking by dead reckoning and a distant memory of having been here before.

The Hotel Playa Girón was as weary as the Guamá resort, but just as colourful.

Rooms are ranged in blocks of four, each with a small handkerchief-sized concrete patio.

Everything had that exhausted look so common in the older and often bypassed tourist hotels of Cuba, but in the lobby bar a small impromptu band played, and the rum was good.

Before this happy arrival, as dusk departed and wrapped us suddenly in the dark blanket of a tropical night I had suspended any thought about where we would stay.

This was not my domain but that of my Tour Director.

However, the later it got, the more I hoped he had some concept of where we were headed, if not an actual plan.

I was therefore relieved that there was a room for me, the linen was clean, and I was safe.

In fact I discovered I was overly safe. My Tour Director locked the door to my room so I would be so. There was no escape.

This incarceration was something I discovered when I thought I would open the door and have a wander around.

Finding it locked, I tried next to open a window. This was nailed shut, as were they all – and so too the sliding doors to the terrace.

I have an irrational dislike of being locked in, and sat down to calm my rising anxiety. It took some self-control.

Shortly there was a knock at the door and there stood a smiling Tour Director with a *Mojito* in hand. "They have a band and I thought you might like a drink".

I explained about my concern at being locked in, and we agreed that while concern for safety is one thing, locking people in is quite another.

We then repaired to the lobby bar.

So the No Plan had brought us safely and with minimal incident through Day One of our travels. It ended in hanging out with some locals and of course, a bit of salsa dancing with the staff.

The next day we had a late breakfast before I wandered about taking photos.

The location was unexpectedly lovely, perched on a postcard-worthy arc of white sand beach. Turquoise waters fringed the shore from emerald depths further out.

On the restaurant wall were fading photos of grander days when giant manatees frequented the shores. I wondered whether they are still as abundant as indicated when these photos were taken. Later, I discovered that the pressure for food has had devastating effects on these large sea mammals that were once thought to be the mermaids so entrancing to ancient mariners.

A blog called *Kobee* Manatee[4] reported in 2015 on the research of *Anmari Alvarez Aleman*, of the University of Havana.

From her ten years of study of Cuban manatees, her estimate of the population at that time was that there were only between 500 to 1,000 manatees still alive.

These hefty creatures are sometimes rather aptly called sea cows because they are placid plant eaters. They have no natural enemies but are often subject to ship or small boat strikes and, sadly, in Cuba they are hunted for food. It is illegal, but it happens.

In the huge restaurant of the *Hotel Playa Girón* where we were the only guests, the clever pottery with teapots and cups in the shape of crocodiles and manatees suggested that sea creatures were still making their mark at the resort – if only as life models.

The palm-frond thatch of the cabanas was patchy and the stacked chairs sagged in a way that seemed to indicate they had been unused for a season or so.

I imagined the colourful cabana bar active, tended by a barman with a flashing smile as he mixed *Mojitos* for visiting tourists.

It was but imagination.

The place was quite deserted, and just as my nailed up windows suggested, appeared to have been slowly drifting into that decayed tranquillity often seen when the spotlight of tourism is redirected to another site.

Having the massive restaurant to ourselves, we lazily discussed a general sense of direction over coffee, but I didn't bother to look at the Geographical Map for its roads. The previous day, by courtesy of that wonderful compass called 'Asking People' – something that might never catch on with the men folk of other lands –we had already travelled for considerable distance on roads not mapped.

---

[4] *http://www.kobeemanatee.com/cubas-endangered-manatee-is-a-rare-sight-indeed/*

We set off refreshed. After about an hour of driving, I saw that the road in the distance ahead was reduced to one lane. This was due to a long golden brown carpet being spread from a slow moving truck ahead of us.

As we drew closer I saw that this was rice slowly pouring from the truck tray onto the highway to dry.

A man stood by with a big wooden rake. His job of raking the runnels of rice into evenly distributed rows offered plenty of time to greet all passing travellers with a cheerful wave.

Our rice-raker stopped each car to talk. His enthusiasm was equal with those he knew and those he didn't but who were prepared to chat.

I discovered that in the afternoon, after the rice had absorbed the warmth of the asphalt, other men came to sweep it into large white sacks. These sacks would then be brought back to the warehouse overnight. This process would be repeated for three consecutive days.

Rice production in Cuba is sagging, at a time when the population's need for it as the staple of the government ration is increasing. It is estimated that each Cuban eats more than a kilo of rice a week, but with increasingly poor soil fertility, imported rice has been needed to maintain the supply.

Together with the Cuban government, the UN Food & Agriculture Organisation worked to develop a response to this growing challenge, by introducing a little known tropical nitrogen-fixing forage crop called *Sesbania*.

By planting as a companion crop in alleys or strips, *Sesbania* improves the soil quality better than with the use of fertilisers (which aren't available anyway).

Sesbania is a member of the pea family. Commonly called *'River Hemp'* it is found natively in Africa, Northern Australia, Hawaii, and South East Asia. Varieties include those commonly called *'Hummingbird Tree'*, *'Scarlet Wisteria'* and *'Corkwood Tree'*.

Sesbania can also be a good source of firewood and green manure. The bark releases substances good for tanning animal hides. The leaves and pods are used by many cultures for food flavouring, and a as medicine to treat a variety of ailments.

I didn't find out much about any of these uses in Cuba, but in a country with long use of herbal medicinal treatments, I expect this introduced crop with all its additional benefits is a valued commodity.

In 2016, an article by a Florida-based Doctor of Oriental Medicine, Dr J. E. Williams, listed some examples of unique treatments Cuba has developed:

- Blue scorpion venom for cancer,
- *Policosonal* extracted from sugar cane for high cholesterol
- Another extract as a type of Viagra, and
- Human placenta for correction of *Vitiligo* – the disease that destroys pigmentation of the skin and leaves white patches on any location in the body.

I was fascinated to discover that, with strict restriction on gluten rich wheat being imported or home grown, Cuba has almost no reported celiac disease.

We can learn a lot from the positives developed by a health care system starved of the medicines we take for granted.

At any rate, the rice crops have increased and levels of nutrition have hopefully followed. I was later to see miles of carefully raked rice along other roads and pondered how many conversations it takes to rake the straightest rows.

The thought occurred that it would be an interesting occupation to list on an official form in answer to the question: Occupation?

What would you put?

'Rice Raker'?

In our world it would probably be elevated to 'Food Processing Engineer'.

My favourite employment title comes from the great era of fine English china production in the potteries of the Midlands.

Before the china is fired it is placed in a protective ceramic cradle or *'sagger'* to protect it in the big kilns.

Colours and effects on the finished product can be artistically enhanced through placing particular substances within the sagger during firing.

Making the main body of the sagger to the specifications of the potter was always a skilled job requiring a craftsman.

However, the sagger bottom could be just knocked into shape by someone with not such advanced skills. His workplace title is the one that is my all time favourite:

'Sagger Maker's Bottom Knocker'.

Pondering such things of no real matter is a pleasant pastime we seldom get to indulge in our busy world full of plans.

As you travel the Cuban highway there is no shortage of things to capture your imagination.

Further along the road an array of beehives stitched a hillside with bright primary colours as they marked it into orderly rows.

We duly made a detour to see the honey being processed and refresh ourselves with some coconut milk drunk right from the coconut.

Cuban honey is the real thing: unheated, undiluted, and from bees that are reported not to have supplements of sugar water when local blooms cease.

Instead, Cuban bees are moved to fresh blooming areas – something easier in the tropics where the flowering sequence is rich and diverse. With this in mind, I was curious about the upturned plastic bottle attached to each hive, but discovered that bees need water – especially in hot climates. They need it to dilute or de-crystallise honey for larvae feeding – something especially important in times of intense brood rearing.

In a country where there have been no chemical imports since the Soviet Union collapsed in 1991 and where the subsequent American trade embargo has banned such importation for decades, the world of the Cuban bees is more pesticide-free than for their cousins in other lands. This is reflected in both the quality of the honey and the health of the bees.

I have read that Cuba takes honey Quality Assurance so seriously that every export lot is certified by Honey Lab of Bremen (QSI) in Germany.

Honey is still one of Cuba's key export products, although according to the 2016 listing of world top exports, Cuban honey had dropped to being the twelfth most valuable export – having once been fourth.

Some years ago there were plans to expand the Cuban honey business from the current 160,000 beehives that feed both private and state production. Total output appears to have stabilised however, at just over 7,000 tons exported, so I'm not sure how that translates into increased number of hives.

No matter what the quantity of the total output, there is no doubt that Cuba is a place of busy bees – and they are expected to get busier.

Whether anyone has communicated this to the bees or not, colourful hives can be expected to continue to embroider Cuban hillsides as this valuable export is encouraged. I was sorry that I only saw two on my travels.

Being fascinated by collective nouns, I had to look up the correct descriptive noun for a lot of bee hives. Apparently lots of hives make a bee yard, and you are only called an 'Apiarist' if you have several yards.

Keeping bees in a yard seems a bit of a stretch, although I was once present at a Local Government Council Meeting where a Councillor seriously proposed making a law that bee keepers had to keep their bees from crossing a neighbour's fence line.

Happily, the suggestion was treated with the disdain it deserved, but it doesn't give confidence in the competence and education of local elected authorities who make other local by-laws we must obey.

This incident falls into that repertoire of miscellaneous trivia one gathers on the journey through life and its many experiences.

It is the sort of thing that makes great entertainment around a good bottle of wine.

I usually follow recounting the proposed Bee Law story with that of another Local Government Council Meeting.

Here, there had been a decision to import some gondolas from Venice in order to enhance the visitor experience on a city lake – and thus create a unique tourism attraction.

After much discussion about how many gondolas to import, one Councillor expressed his frustration.

He wondered why there was a need to discuss this, as surely they should just import a breeding pair.

It's delightful to contemplate!

The city will remain nameless but it is recorded in Council Minutes.

But back to the bees: This Cuban bee yard was a family affair run from a big old ranch house with wide verandas.

Set amidst banana palms on the rise of the hills that sloped upwards from the highway, this gracious and well-shaded house seemed happily isolated from the rest of the world.

The sound of booted feet on well-worn veranda boards is one familiar to me from my Australian childhood, just as are the comforting sounds of rain on a corrugated iron roof and the taste of rainwater from a galvanized-iron water tank. Standing on the wooden veranda in the tropical heat, these memories added a layer of meaning to this quick glimpse into the solitary life of the bee farmers.

We took time to roam through the neat rows of hives and to be instructed with a practical demonstration of extraction – sampling both honey and comb. This method of production was a simple affair of a kind that had been operating here for decades. It reminded me of the reality I had discovered working in the field of technology:

It doesn't have to be the most modern.

It doesn't have to be the fanciest.

It doesn't have to do everything possible.

It just has to do the job it's there to do.

Rejoining the highway, the karst structure of the coastline visibly marked out the geological heritage of the island's formation.

The term '*karst*' has been used in various forms for centuries. Even early Roman documents use a variation of the term. It refers to the unique features formed from the uplifting of soluble carbonate rock (limestone, and sometimes dolomite).

These landforms can look like jagged saw-teeth, be twisted into fascinating shapes, or rise suddenly like great carbuncles on a pock-marked land surface. The effects that cause such strange topography are known to also create remarkable underground cave systems.

Karst country is most common in sub-tropical climates with plenty of rainfall, and this area of Cuba is like a living geography book illustrating its characteristics.

In some spots along the eastern coastal road, rocky landscapes fall directly into the ocean.

In others the coast is fringed with a ribbon of sand.

We wound languidly along as the road hugged the Bahía de Cochinos. This is more familiar to us by the name 'The Bay of Pigs'. It is famous as the site where a small island country successfully made a stand against insurgents funded by a rich neighbouring country whose intent was to overthrow the new government.

Named for the colourful and greedy Queen Triggerfish called *'cochinos'* in Cuba – and not for Miss Piggy's relatives – this is a beautiful stretch of tropical water painted deep shades of turquoise.

The bay now lay peacefully calm before us as we absorbed its beauty from high roadside view points and from quick beachside photo shoots.

I had read of a great migration here each year after the first spring rains. This is when black, red and yellow crabs that live nearby in the forests trek down to the coast to spawn. I can imagine the vivid contrast of colours that would make.

Like marine crabs, their land cousins breathe with gills that need moisture, so they usually live in tunnels in the damp forest floor. Once they mate, the lady crab carries a bulging pouch of eggs on a hazardous journey to the coast.

Having faced possible dehydration, run the risk of being picked off by other wildlife or being crushed by passing cars, these ladies have a delicate and life-threatening balancing act to perform at the water's edge. They have to deposit their eggs into the sea without being washed away by the waves. Having safely done so, they turn around and march back to the forest, sometimes up to 9 km away *(almost 6 miles)*.

Their babies will hatch almost immediately, and after a few weeks another army of crabs – this time in miniature – will make the same arduous journey back to the forest to start the cycle all over again.

Given the sheer quantity of adult crabs crossing the coastal road, it is not unexpected that many sharp crab pincers puncture passing car tyres. I was told that the consequent need for services of on-the-spot tyre repair forms another lucrative side trade for locals.

Condoms are the repair rubber of choice – easy to procure and effective.

Often, in Cuba, condoms take the place of balloons.

On an early trip I went to a baseball game in Havana and was fascinated to see elongated balloons floating above the stands.

My Cuban friends watched my face as I realised that what they were made from. They found it hilarious as realisation dawned on me.

I think that day watching the *Industriales* baseball team play endeared me to my Cuban friends.

Sometimes, such things form long-lasting bonds because they reveal a common passion and a willingness to throw decorum aside in favour of shared and unfettered enthusiasm.

With bases loaded I said to them: *"él bunt"* (He'll bunt). They shook their heads.

Like all those who watch competitive sports, they knew best what the player should or would do.

They engaged in a hearty and well-educated debate about how best to play the moment.

Bunting the ball is something that you can apply to life.

To bunt in baseball you hold the bat as if you want to strike the ball out of the baseball park.

As the ball is released from the pitcher's hand you step forward and slide your hand midway up to steady the bat with the thumb and index finger with the other hand.

The trick is to try to deaden the ball and have it roll to the hardest place to field, between first and third base, close to the foul line.

Then you run like the dickens
and hope for the best.

In bases loaded,
everyone runs like the dickens
and hopes for the best.

We've all been in positions when it is best to bunt and not play the tricky ball that circumstance has thrown our way.

We develop ways of deflecting curve balls and each of us has our own style in doing so.

Here is a typical curve ball: reading a letter or email designed to get you to respond emotionally and without thinking.

Don't.
Don't respond.
Bunt.

Deaden the incoming things that make it almost impossible to carry on with your game, by either parking them in a place hard for anyone else to field, or stopping them dead.

Play the game on your terms,
but don't place the ball behind the foul line!

Anyway, before this moment in the game I had been relatively quiet, but watching the game with the attention of someone who has a real interest in it.

I had been speaking quietly in my pigeon Spanish with my friends until the player up *did* bunt.

I then leaped onto the narrow bench on which we had been sitting, and waving both arms in the air as if to help push the runners home, in English I yelled: "Run. Run. Run".

To much jubilation throughout their home stadium the *Industriales* got all three players home.

More condom balloons appeared.

My friends laughed at me and recounted to themselves the complete abandonment of my instinctive encouragement of their team.

"You *really* like baseball Paquita!" they said.

Crabs, condoms and baseball games: it's amazing where your musings take you when you have no plan.

Now, as the road turned inland slightly at El Cenote on the edge of the Zapata Marshes, we came across an inconsequential hut with scuba tanks propped up against the wall.

Further off the road, a well-cared-for cabana of coconut thatch seemed to be a part of this scuba diving enterprise.

We parked and wandered along a winding trail of hole-riddled rock towards the cabana.

I was totally unprepared for what that lay before us at the end of the path.

We emerged on what looked like a beautiful miniature lake. In fact, it is a flooded cave that curves around to greet you at ground level as you approach from the road.

There are at least eleven diving sites in the Bay of Pigs area, and this one at El Cenote is the deepest one inland.

The cave has been explored to a depth of 70 metres *(229')* on the side fissure. A fissure is a crack that has formed a long and narrow opening.

The main cave is 25 metres *(82')* deep.

In summer people come here to swim in the refreshingly cold water: water so clear that the fish seem like 3D animations in an unrealistically turquoise opalescence.

El Cenote really is a little paradise, but it was not summer, so instead of swimming we stayed a long time just watching the brilliantly coloured fish that now ranged lazily below where we stood.

From above, the fish created the effect of a kaleidoscope that readjusted its colourful patterns in response to our movements.

The cave at El Cenote is a favourite for cave divers driven by a sense of adventure to explore the depths. They come to dive deep enough to find new fissures that make undersea gateways to the ocean. I'm sure it must be a real challenge for a diver, but now we had the beautiful spot all to ourselves.

El Cenote is the sort of place that makes you happy you have no plan. If you had one, you might be compelled to move on.

We didn't have a plan, so we had time to just stand and stare, watching the brightly coloured fish and certainly in my case, not thinking about anything.

At least I didn't consciously think about anything.

Perhaps it was the serenity and beauty of the place and its far removal from anything familiar that allowed my subconscious to think about things long forgotten, and bring the past to the present.

As I stared at the vibrantly coloured fish, I wondered why people risk something like cave-diving. It is as hazardous as rock climbing, but without the ready ability to be rescued if things go wrong. You cannot send a helicopter into a cave.

This is something that was demonstrated to the world with the rescue of a group of children by experienced cave divers in Thailand, just before this book went to press.

As an aside, what was also demonstrated to the world was the value of depending upon the combined experience and judgement of a team who had made hundreds, if not thousands of dives. This was selected as the method that ultimately brought the children safely out. It was chosen over untested technology enthusiastically brought to the site by someone believing in technology as the answer – possibly to most things.

The proposed technological solution consisted of what in Australian terms would be called a 'you beaut' mini submarine: clever perhaps – but no match for the responsive decision making of people drawing on a background of unique knowledge.

I know someone who had done some impressive cave dives but suddenly given up the sport. I asked why. He told me that one day he was about to enter a small 'press' requiring him to push his tanks in front of him as he squeezed through a narrow opening.

It was an entry he had undertaken many times before, but on that day, as he started to loosen his tanks from his shoulders he was filled with a black dread. He just secured his tanks again and surfaced to announce that he was done with the sport.

I asked him what it was that made him so definite as to quit like this. He replied that once that level of doubt enters your thinking you're dangerous: you're dangerous to yourself – and dangerous to those who accompany you.

The fish seemed to encourage my thoughts with their hypnotic choreography swirling below where I stood.

Why can one person accomplish something that others fear?

Why can we sometimes be instinctively successful in traversing territory that we have never seen before, even when we don't know where our chosen route will lead, whether it is a dead-end, or whether it houses something unfriendly or threatening?

I thought about this in context of my cave-diving friend. It had been his passion. He came to it from a background as a speleologist – a cave explorer – so exploring caves *not* underwater was already a competence. Diving into caves that are underwater was just an extension of a well-practised skill.

Caving is a sport that draws people with a particular approach to life. It seems to me that to be attracted to something like caving you need to be optimistic, self-assured, trusting of your travelling companions – and incredibly curious, wanting to be the first to discover something new and exciting.

For some things like this that stir your interest, you probably need to have also 'fallen into' the subject – in this case, hopefully not literally.

What chance does serendipity play?

I subscribe to the philosophy that says:

Coincidence is God's way of making thing happen.

I have never much believed in coincidence because my life seems to indicate that things tend to have a direction that is invisible to the individual.

These new directions offer a different set of opportunities from those planned.

It's not a better or worse equation.

They are just different.

I know many people who share the attributes I have noted in cave divers and cavers, yet none of them took up either sport.

It could be that they just never had the opportunity to be tempted by the concept of underground discoveries waiting to be made – or even beckoning from underwater.

Of all of the attributes that seem evident in those who take up cave diving, the one that seems to me to be important is self-confidence.

The self-confidence that says 'I am not doing this anymore' is as important as that that tempts you to partake in the first place.

Too many people in other sports would try to overthrow that instinctive warning in an effort to appear to be capable and competent, seeing such an admission of fear as weakness, or failure.

In cave diving, there are five accepted rules:

- Have specific cave-diving training.
- Always have a continuous guide-line tied tautly that leads back to open water.
- Never exceed the dive plan or maximum depth appropriate for the air mixture.
- Use air in the 'Rule of Thirds' that allows for one third on the way in, one third on the way out, and one third to assist a buddy. In a dive where there is no outflow to assist the return trip, provide more than the Rule of Thirds allows.
- Have three independent sources of light.

These are not bad guides for life in general:

- Spend the time learning from those with wider experience.
- Don't lose your way.

- Be adventurous, but don't foolishly push limits.
- Apply the Rule of Thirds: One third for you, one third for family and others, and one third for work – and be prepared to adjust the ratios as circumstances show the need.
- To see things clearly, use three different perspectives: yours, the person who objects to your interpretation, and an independent source who can shed a clear light on things.

I knew that my cave-diving friend had been an early cave cartographer – together with his mates he had mapped previously unexplored cave systems in Europe. When doing this the lives of all the exploration team rested with each other.

He explained that it's therefore vital to be strong enough to recognise what is a niggling problem of fear on a particular day and should be treated as such, and what is an overwhelming dark feeling that indicates something with greater implications.

It could be that something within you has changed.

Perhaps you no longer have the confidence you had before, or you subjectively feel risks that were previously only assessed objectively.

It could be that you are tuned to an inner early warning system that somehow previews something negative about to happen.

I remember stories told by a friend who used to schedule surgery in a busy American hospital.

She said that she had seen many people about to have relatively minor surgery who told her they didn't want to have it that day. They told her they had a 'bad feeling' about it.

Subsequently, unexpected complications peculiar to the day and not related to the individual's health itself, led to their death, or to severe and sometimes long-lasting health impacts.

From this, she deduced that we have some sort of inner radar that in times of intense focus of concentration seems to send very clear signals that should not be overlooked.

All this came from standing quietly beside the clear waters of the deepest cave in Cuba, and watching the coloured fish moving languidly below.

We were in no hurry and my 'thinking of nothing' carried on in my subconscious. My musing on the power of instinct brought to my mind an incident from my own life.

At that time I was living in Houston. I had a fascinating job recruiting top technical people, engineers, and senior management in the oil and gas industry and for large manufacturing plants and mills across the USA.

In my private life, I had been under almost constant tension for some time because I couldn't make sense of things that were happening.

I had been started to feel really dreadful and pretending I wasn't ill, thinking it just the difficult situation in which I found myself. To put this in context, I had been advised by people who cared about my welfare and were in a position to hear things that gave them concern, that my life was under threat from someone close to me whom I had previously trusted completely.

Finally, I went to hospital emergency and was promptly referred to a specialist for tests. I was clearly very unwell. The specialist said I should come back early the following week for the test results. I replied that I couldn't, because by then I would then be in Australia.

He looked at me in shock and asked if I was serious.

I replied that I knew I was really sick and despite having a residence locally, I had nowhere where I could 'crash'. Without a support system locally and since I was due to travel back to Australia for a school reunion, I said that if I had to crawl on the aircraft, I was going.

He shrugged, saying he could understand that, but thought that I was in no condition to make a fourteen hour flight.

I didn't.

I made a one hour flight within the US, a fifteen hour flight to Sydney and then another cross continent flight from Sydney to Perth – about five hours. That's like flying from New York to Los Angeles.

I then attended the school reunion.

Originally I had planned to spend a week there, but instead cut short the visit with old school friends to fly back to my family in Sydney.

In total I flew about twenty-six hours.

As I said, I was busy pretending that I was much better than I was, but inwardly really thought I might be dying.

I wasn't, but when the diagnosis came through, I was indeed very unwell. I had Pericarditis, which is the inflammation of the membrane around the heart – and infectious Hepatitis A. Either of these wasn't good, but together it was a bad cocktail.

I can't recall much of the ensuing six weeks of my life – just that my mother sat vigil, telling me stories of her childhood. My family slowly nurtured me to recovery.

Happily, I have never had a recurrence.

Recovery was slow. I had so little strength and my muscles needed to be rebuilt and trained after a few months of inertia when I was barely conscious.

After a while I could walk to the front door; then to the edge of the veranda.

A little later I got to the front of the drive, and eventually on one memorable day had the energy to walk behind the neighbouring houses and across the golf course which bordered our street, and then back home.

My Texan girlfriend told me that in my absence my dogs had fled our home and gone wild. She managed to retrieve the German Shepherd-Coyote cross, a gentle soul called Aggie, who was by then skin-and-bone but otherwise healthy.

It was a different case with my Chow Chow, Chuling. She could not be caught. She had found refuge in the undergrowth along the creek beside which we lived and had developed a deep suspicion of anyone who was not me.

Although the doctor's disagreed, I felt that I urgently needed to retrieve my furry friends. I was determined to go back and get them.

By then my lawyer had also advised that I was greatly at risk and should become invisible until a pending court case – a timeframe over which I had no control.

My father insisted on accompanying me to a safe refuge from where I could start a new life.

According to someone I met then and bumped into years later, it was apparently very obvious that I was still fragile in health. I had lost a great deal of weight and was slim to start with.

The impact of my illness was still visible but determination can get you a lot of places that your body would not otherwise be able to manage.

The day before we went to the house on the creek I slept in the shirt that my father would wear the next day, so he smelled of me.

I thought that should my Chow Chow turn up, the scared animal might then trust him.

We were loading the car when I saw movement in the bushes to the side of the driveway.

A very bedraggled, fur-matted Chow Chow was watching me.

I crouched down and called her.

Hesitating for just a moment, she then ran to sit between my open legs – and cried. She really cried. It was not a whine or a bark. It could only be described as a sort of sobbing. I was in the same state.

My father, who arrived shortly on the scene, quickly also had tears in his eyes as he watched the reunion.

We loaded the dogs and made a hasty retreat while the coast was clear, and headed a long way away to where I had friends.

My father had been in the Special Forces and before we set out he gave me clear instructions. We were to trust absolutely in our instincts as we travelled.

If one or the other thought we should take an alternative route direction than that on which we were headed, then that would be the route that would be taken: no questions asked.

He had learned in times of war and behind enemy lines that under intense concentration our senses are heightened. We over-ride them at our peril.

Eventually, we came safely to our destination but it was in a location where someone who knew me may have anticipated I would go.

I prayed for safety for us both and that no one would note my arrival with my distinctive two dogs and report that I had been seen in the area.

As we approached the town near to the ranch to which we were headed, a deep fog fell over the whole landscape. I had previously lived in that area for several years. There had never been any fog like this. In fact in that whole time the nearest thing had been occasional light mist.

This fog was so dense we had to creep down the back country roads peering before us to find the road ahead. Certainly, no one passing us would have seen inside a car with my tell-tale dogs inside.

Thank you, God.

Here at El Cenote, as I stared longer at the fish, this whole story replayed itself in my mind.

It was totally unexpected. I had thought that chapter of my life had been set to rest long ago.

Perhaps in the most part it had, but some of its lessons must have needed to be evaluated anew in the face of the new opportunities that working in Germany had offered me.

My life was now so positive, but I was in a role that saw me problem-solving critical contractual issues to restore client confidence.

Unravelling complex overlays of activity to find the elegantly simple is not easy, and my last few contracts had taken a lot of energy. It seemed that while I sought renewal of that energy, my soul was renewing my self-confidence.

I wondered if, at that time in the past, our few changes of direction had avoided anything untoward on that trip. It didn't matter. We had come without incident to our destination and will never know if our instincts were right.

We had travelled safely, and that is what mattered.

I was puzzled about why all this came to mind from the past, so uncalled for as I stood watching the swirling colour of the fish when I wasn't really thinking of anything.

It made me think that sometimes when we let go of our firmly-held convictions, it frees us to listen to other things our inner voices are trying to tell us. In my experience, our inner voices seem to be tuned to the emergency channel and can bring us safely through.

Not for the first time, and not for the last, I had then felt responsible that some events in my life had negatively affected those of people dear to me.

My father was not a young man at the time. My mother told me years later how proud they were of me for retaining my positive life attitude in spite of life's twists.

That meant a lot to me. She added that Dad had taken six months to recover from the anxiety of that trip.

Thank you, Papa.

Again I wondered why all this came flooding back now.

Perhaps again I was losing confidence in myself and my subconscious was reminding me of how far I had come from those precarious times, and what I had since achieved.

Perhaps it was suggesting that if I had come this far, I should hold to the course and keep going without losing confidence in my ability to create a positive future for myself.

These fish in a Cuban flooded cavern wove mesmerizing arcs of colour in transparent waters. Their movements, the purity of the lake, and the vividness of the colours within it, had set my mind adrift and led my thoughts to unexpected places.

The quiet beauty of the place soothed memories of a past I had thought had long since been dealt with but obviously hadn't quite been resolved.

Sometimes, the best healing takes place
in years distant from events
and in places geographically unconnected
to the circumstance of the cause of the hurt.

So it was for me at El Cenote in Zapata, Cuba.

We headed towards the refreshment of a cold canned drink, picking our way through the path and being ignored by the cabana staff.

We were obviously not divers and therefore inconsequential.

It's refreshing to be invisible after your work has placed you at the lead in major projects and you are now taking a well-earned rest from decision making.

Sauntering back to the car, I commented that you could be there all day staring at the fish or swimming with them.

They somehow seemed to release all the opportunities of life that are lying before you.

In later years it turned out that my Tour Director had been also entertaining his own thoughts – thoughts that framed plans for his future. He has since made a life outside Cuba and is busy stepping slowly towards dreams that at the time we were at El Cenote, was still just swirling in his head like the colourful fish that seemed to hypnotise us both.

The Roman poet Ovid wrote:

Chance is always powerful.
Let your hook always be cast.

In the pool where you least expect it,
there will be fish.

No wonder Ovid's writings influenced Chaucer, Shakespeare, Dante, and Milton.

We never know where our healing or our inspirational thoughts may come from. Unless we permit ourselves some time with No Plan, we may never allow ourselves the space to catch a fish.

We drove onward through Zapata which is the heartland of the Cuban Revolution. At the museum in *Girón* the relics of the revolution fought nearby are gathered for posterity. The building itself seemed once to have been a military one, but I later heard that it was formerly a school.

We arrived to see its low profile basking in a sandy space flanked by a former British Fleet Air Arm Hawker Sea Fury aircraft, and a Russian built T-34-85 tank of the type used by Fidel Castro during the battle of the Bay of Pigs.

Apart from us there were few visitors.

The quietness was broken only by the persistent sound of cicadas. It is a sound I associate with days in earlier years in outback Australia with my family where it was so crisply dry and still that it was impossible to bring to mind a verdant colour of green. My father was English but so loved the Australian countryside and this love passed to both his children.

By contrast, when I first drove into Austria over the *Grossglockner High Alpine Road* I commented that the mountains of Austria are so green they almost make your eyes hurt.

These are the mountains of the not historically accurate, but much loved film 'The Sound of Music'.

Agatha Whitehead, the mother of the Von Trapp children, married a much respected and well decorated naval commander in Von Trapp, but sadly died of scarlet fever. It was to nurse daughter Maria who was recovering from the same disease that the novice, also called Maria, came from the convent.

Agathe's father was my great, great uncle: Robert Whitehead. He worked with Italian Giovanni Lucas who had invented a prototype land-fired coastal defence missile launcher before changing it to a ship-born device: the torpedo.

Grand-daughter Agathe inherited the Whitehead fortune and lived to establish a kindergarten in Vermont and another later in Maryland. Agathe became a well-respected painter with one painting still displayed in the Austrian Embassy in Washington. She lived to be 94.

How strange to have such a comparison of heritage: one in a place so green and one in a place so arid.

Interesting to me also, that Robert left his home in Manchester to further his engineering experience by working at a shipyard in Toulon, then in Milan, and later moving to Trieste where the torpedo was developed, before again moving to manage a metal foundry in Fiume, then also in Austria, but now known as Rijeka, Croatia.

Perhaps my attitude of having the world as my back garden comes from a good genetic source.

Once inside the museum in *Girón*, I took time to read all the explanatory notes on the displays. These are relics of those revolutionary battles that changed the face of Cuba for generations to come.

Although they were in Spanish I could read enough to understand their meaning – my grasp of the language being good enough for that but no longer good enough to converse. That was useful, because the poor English translations were full of political polemic that often obscured the detail as written in Spanish.

This reminded me of the histrionic harangues of the highly filmed and televised Havana political rallies I had seen on earlier trips.

At those, the populace was so underwhelmed with the 'patriotic march' that we all saw on our TV screens as a thirty second grab in the news, that water trucks – *pipas* – sat on the streets that end at the *Malecón* and played recordings of crowds cheering.

The real crowds marched along the sea wall in bored groups, chatting with each other.

There was no need for polemic. The records of victory and of death deserve better.

Many locals had died in what proved to be the final victorious battle that took place in the area close by the museum at *Girón*.

Although they could not have guessed so at the time, it is a battle that would become known worldwide for generations to come.

The display cases are filled with the simple things left over on the battlefield with the dead. As such I found them particularly moving: a notebook here, a leather-bound photo of a lover there.

Under photos of those who died in that battle were small items that reflected their lives and the manner of their death, like the patch of uniform through which the fatal bullet travelled.

I stood before the black and white photos of these men whose love of their country and belief in a better world had sent them to war.

It was on their eyes that my own lingered. The photos revealed different emotions: defiance, sadness, warmth, kindness.

A wide range of human feelings was registered in those eyes, but they all shared one thing: Hope.

Hope for things to be better – and that their acts would force that improvement.

Many people had come and gone through the same space by the time I thoughtfully left. A non-Cuban fellow traveller would have been hovering, silently willing me to leave sooner, or actively trying to talk me into doing so – but that would only have been because they had a plan, and with plans come timetables.

We had none, and my thoughtfulness about those lives and who was left behind was allowed its space without conversational intrusion.

In fact, the length of time I took and my pensive response to the displays was seen as an appropriate response to the place, but one not common for a tourist. It led to deep discussions about what their sacrifice had achieved.

It was long past whatever time a midday meal should be when it is long gone midday and your stomach demands something, when we again headed off on roads unmarked on my Geographical Map (with roads).

After a short time we entered a small hamlet. The houses spread lazily along dusty tracks. A man on a bike looked at us with curiosity. Another on horseback barely glanced at us.

We asked a young girl for directions and she pointed to a house at the end of an undulating track.

Although my body was sending 'Please feed me' signals, I hadn't actually asked about when, or if we were going to eat.

Experience had taught me that we may or may not eat soon, but when we did it would be worth the wait.

I was reminded of a quote from Douglas Adams:

Time is an illusion:
Lunchtime doubly so.

I felt this illusion now, but had learned that if I asked about eating it would bring on a fluster of concern and possible redirection of a worthwhile plan that might have been formulating slowly as we travelled along.

As a result of my request, we would instead end up finding the nearest place to eat – and not necessarily the sort of place I loved to find.

As he headed for the house to which we had been directed by our 'Ask Someone' compass, my Tour Guide murmured. "I'm not sure she'll remember me".

Parking outside he sat for a moment, frowning as if to recall the image from past visits to verify that this was indeed the place he was looking for. Then, leaving me in the car he crossed the veranda, knocked on the door, and waited. I watched, Reggaeton blasting at full volume through the open car windows to an appreciative local audience.

A lady appeared on the front veranda, took one look, and with a face radiating delight threw her arms around her visitor.

It transpired that it was three years ago that he had last visited, guiding another tourist on his own personalised adventure.

I was duly beckoned in, and discovered a tiny restaurant on a concrete patio at the back of the house. Now that it was legal to do so, the restaurant flourished as an off-the-beaten-track treasure.

My stomach lay quietly expectant as I wandered about capturing photographic images of the house, the restaurant, and the memorial to the head of the local Postal Service, who had died just beyond the back yard during the revolutionary battles.

I regretted having forgotten my conversational Spanish when I was introduced to the local tortoise.

Poor thing, he has a hard life.

I decided he was a gentleman, and not a lady tortoise, because of his slightly notched 'V' in the carapace that allows two tortoise tails to sit comfortably – or at least without damage – during mating.

This poor gentleman was dropped suddenly and several times by the young lad showing him off, quickly pulling his head inside his shell each time.

It was not to the tortoise I would have spoken, but to the excited tortoise handler. His handling of the patient beast reminded me of the Dr. Seuss story of *Yertle the Turtle*. I suspect that Yertle was actually a tortoise, as his escapades took place on land.

Turtles are water creatures – but who wants to ruin a lovely alliteration like *'Yertle the Turtle'*?

For those not familiar with this wonderful tale, Yertle wanted to be the all-powerful turtle.

To elevate him to the right level to be king of a wider 'all you can see' he stacked turtles one atop the other to make a step pyramid. According to the story, unfortunately the founding turtle of the turtle tower (called Mack) emitted a burp just as the top turtle was positioned.

The burp was so resounding that it caused the stack of conscripted turtles to tumble down.

Yertle, who had perched on the top of the turtle stack, as the king of all he surveyed, was duly thrown deeply into the mud.

The result is described in traditional Dr. Seuss verse format:

'...and today the great Yertle,
that Marvelous he,
is King of the Mud,
that is all he can see,
and the turtles, of course...
all the turtles are free
as turtles and, maybe,
all creatures should be'.

Looking at the big tortoise who was my dinner companion, I smiled.

I could relate to Yertle the Turtle, trying to be King of a wider universe.

The moral of Dr. Seuss's tale holds true. Once you give up trying to have the high spot in your universe it releases not just you, but all those connected with you.

I was finding more and more that, as I let our trip slowly evolve with the Cuban Approach, things just seemed to click into place.

Within the general population of the Cuba I encountered I found there to be few Yertles, but of course they are present in all societies.

For most of the local inhabitants, apart from the few who have a seriously influential or political job, Cuba is not so much of a place of people wearing their titles to the extent that they do in other lands where identity is so closely tied to what you do for a living.

I found that generally in Cuba people are who they are. It seemed to me that here the 'window dressing' so familiar to us in our worlds is noticeably absent.

What you see is not always what you get – but on the whole and outside of the police, immigration officials, some banks and the Communist Party, personal interaction is based on relationships rather than organisational structures.

This has a contagious effect.

It also causes a visitor to rethink who he or she really is when not shielded by the many personas we adopt to deal with different facets of our non-Cuban life. I had pondered this over all my previous trips and now once again reconsidered my own identity in this context.

I was also discovering that, despite the fact that we often think that we are managing fine thank very much, sometimes our souls need space to regenerate, and unexpectedly we recognise a need to bandage the wounded places.

Having met the tortoise, I was then eagerly introduced to the next day's dinner – the baby crocodile whose relative had just provided us a delicious evening meal.

This feast had been of crocodile, lobster and reef fish, enjoyed with a Cristal amongst the bananas which were ripening beside us, while chickens roosted in the trees above and a mother hen by our feet gathered fluffy chicks into safe housing for the night.

Dinner was followed by a conversation about the crocodile bone earrings and necklaces made by a local villager. When I now wear them, they bring my spirit back to Zapata, a small dusty village, two small lads, and a tortoise.

I initiated a game with the tortoise handler. His friend with the patch over his eye had just come from the local clinic and stood shyly by, watching, and obviously wanting to join in.

One of the very real good effects of the revolution is that there *is* a local clinic.

My apparently not-so-forgotten Spanish allowed me to understand enough about the description of his eye treatment to think it quite severe for anyone, let alone a young lad. I was a bit concerned about what his next doctor's visit held in store.

Like many of the Cubans I had become friends with in the past, he was resigned to whatever it would be, there being few alternative options, if any.

He was a delightful but shy lad. At first he had stood by as an observer but he so obviously wanted to join the fun that I swooped him up into the air to be a part of the game. He erupted into fits of delighted giggles.

My tour guide was meanwhile catching up on all the news since the last time he had been here, recounting stories of his family and showing off photos of his partner and daughters.

All these things take time: time that wouldn't be available if you had a plan.

What did the Cuban Approach accomplish?

Not having a plan means really letting the No Plan work itself out. A No Plan needs room to expand from its original concepts.

This means that everyone on the No Plan trip has equal rights to suggest a detour, to request a photo stop, invite someone who needs a ride to hop in, or to make a stop to buy some onions.

It means accepting the choices of all, or being able to discuss options and point out that, while most people want to see that, you are not most people; and 'that' therefore has little appeal, while something else may.

In short, I came to the conclusion that a No Plan requires:

- The selection of the right travelling companion.
- A reliable form of transport.
- A map – a geographical map (with roads) to give general direction.
- The capacity to siphon money from your bank account when needed, and
- Music that makes your heart sing and your mind shut down from its usual expectations of how things (with a Plan) should be.

A No Plan gives you the space to think about the things you have seen, to think deeply about the lives of the people you encounter – and to give thanks for your own good fortune.

A No Plan triggers reconsideration of the jagged edged things you may not have quite smoothed out, so they can be stored more comfortably in your heart.

Once smoothed, these can then be reshaped into small bits of calm that, like the kaleidoscope of coloured fish, now shift into a different pattern that becomes part of the wider landscape of your life.

Now harmoniously set within the wider span of your experiences, these fragments of the past will no longer emerge unbidden to bring unexpected sadness to otherwise happy times.

A No Plan also awakens a wider sense of obligation to give back something of the generosity you encounter.

To undertake travel on a No Plan you must have two essential elements.

The first is trust.

The second is harder to define.

If I call it 'Patience', this implies the expectation of a particular outcome, and waiting for it to take place.

If I call it 'Endurance' it sounds as if the period of waiting is not to be enjoyed. So let's instead use the term 'Relaxed Anticipation'.

You might have to wait as events unfold.

You might have no idea what it is that you are waiting for.

But if you have a sense of anticipation, and you are relaxed enough to divert your thinking away from an obsession about controlling things, it's remarkable how many good things take place.

While you are in your state of relaxed anticipation, you may make new friends, touch someone's life with a smile, or engage a child in a simple game for which the language is universal.

You might savour the pleasures of a cold beer on a hot afternoon in a lovely environment and with good companionship (and I mean savour).

You might watch the peculiarities of brilliantly coloured fish as they swirl and mingle in translucent waters.

You might let music flow through you, and over you, and around you – and not just listen to it as if it was something separate from you.

You might eat things you've never eaten before.

Most of all, you might become part of the stories of the lives you touch along the way.

Step 3 of the Cuban Approach: Map Reading: When you decide to trust – trust.

Reversed Binoculars: Sometimes when you travel, the more you see looking outwards makes you see even more looking inwards.

Reading the winds: I had an idea of what I wanted to accomplish.

I had a guide.

I had a map (with roads). My geographical map was bought to give the framework for the No Plan – not to detail its structure.

I had seen local Havana living conditions so was under no illusions about the levels of comfort ahead of me. I knew that my No Plan did not offer the creature comforts of my parking place.

I made a judgment about whom to trust.

Ernest Hemingway, who loved Cuba, once commented astutely:

The only way to know whether to trust someone
is to trust someone.

Having made that judgment, I then allowed the trust to be employed by not checking and double checking and asking:

'Where to?'
 'Why?'
   'How?', and
     'How long?'

We had sat down and agreed a budget. I then passed the money across and trusted that it would be well employed – which it was.

When there was some question about whether something was a bit too much for our thin allowance, I was asked about it and doubly quizzed to make sure it was alright to spend on something out of the ordinary.

But before I transferred that trust, I had done my assessments of whether:

- To do so was a good idea.
- Enough was understood about me to make a good plan.
- I would be looked after.
- I would laugh a lot, and not just see the land over which we would pass, but experience its character.

My trust lay in someone who understood the landscape better than me. I trusted him to develop our No Plan – and that meant letting go. But I could only let go when, from my parking space I had read the wind.

Later, I found out that I was not the only wind-reader – for as I was assessing whether to trust, so was I being assessed.

Adjusting your sails: Aboard a yacht underway you must constantly trim the sails.

Even slight adjustments will influence how far and how fast you will travel, and in what direction.

Exactly when my No Plan started, I can't say.

Did it start when I spoke my dreams into reality by telling the world what I was dreaming and what I lacked to make it happen?

Did it start when my friends donated the flight points for the fare?

Did it start when I met Cuban friends of German friends – and I became their friend?

Did it start when we sat and ate together, laughed together, danced together, told stories of our lives, interacted with others around us in ways that revealed who we really were, and what we valued?

Did it start when we couldn't find some of my old friends – or when we visited the ones I could?

Did it start in the warmth of the Havana night when I woke from sleeping in the car to discuss elements of my No Plan?

All of my decisions and my 'letting go' trimmed my sails to catch the wind, but had I not passed the skipper's evaluation as being a worthwhile travelling companion I would never have left shore –

at least not on that ship –
and he had the map,
knew the Indians,
and had sailed the route before.

CHAPTER FOUR

Map reading

Trusting untried travel directors

We had set off from Havana with two small travelling bags, an empty chest cooler – something I didn't notice until it was used much later in the trip – a bottle of water, a small amount of cash and my one precious credit card, my map (with roads) and my camera – with spare batteries, SD cards to store lots of photos, and a battery charger with adaptor.

We were headed in the general direction of Cienfuegos. From there we would head onwards as long as money, tolerance, and travelling compatibility would stretch us – given that the enticement of photography often saw us stopping several times in a short stretch of road.

Apart from that, I had no plan, and none was forthcoming.

There is something quite freeing to head out on an uncharted course. There is just the stretch of road ahead, a general sense of anticipation and the idea that everything is possible.

In our case we also had the enhancement of loud Cuban music blasting lustily forth to fill our air-conditioned space.

Trust is a hard thing to define.

For me, it is the belief that a person will not do badly by you in return for your reliance on their integrity.

There are many reasons why they may not live up to the expectation implicit within your trust, not the least of which may be that your aspirations are unrealistic.

But for me, the trust relationship remains intact if the person on whom you rely does not cost you more than you can afford to pay – and I don't mean in money.

If a person makes every effort to respect your feelings and not damage either your image of yourself or of others towards you, but in other ways doesn't meet your expectations, then I still believe that when all things are considered, the bargain has been a good one.

In my month with no plan in Cuba I had plenty of time while waiting to ponder how one comes to trust. Some say it's based on a mix of rational and spontaneous thought.

My best decisions on trust have been made with inconclusive evidence of the worthiness of the person to be considered trustworthy.

I just felt they were trustworthy. So it was with choosing to accept my Tour Director.

There have been a few people in my life that I instantly distrusted. This was based on nothing they had done or said to me. In each of these cases all my instincts went immediately on high alert.

I had no ongoing contact with these people beyond introduction but their later actions with others proved the validity of that instant judgment.

In the course of my adult life there have been two people I have trusted implicitly only to find that it was a great mistake to do so. In each case I trusted in some of the best window-dressing possible – and so did my friends, those people who are usually the better judges than you about the trustworthiness of those with whom you form a relationship.

No one is perfect in the trust assessment business and in my two heart-searing cases I really did blame myself. This was mitigated a little following an incident where I encountered an explanation when I took a friend to a Women's Shelter for protection from an abusive spouse.

Upon arrival she asked why this had happened to her twice. What was she doing wrong and what was wrong with her to choose so poorly? The shelter worker held her hand and responded very softly: 'You don't pick them. They pick you. Your personality is of the type that will never see it coming. It's out of the realm of your attitudes and this leaves a blind spot they exploit.'

Sometimes when you help a friend, you help yourself a great deal more.

I have repeated this assessment to many people 'blaming' someone for their situation, as if they had any more insight than the victim in question.

Please remember it when your thoughts go in such a direction.

There are charlatans everywhere in life, and as the officer of the Fraud Squad in a major city told me:

"You'll never pick a good con man. They trick even the cleverest of people".

In this case he was referring to my inheritance of a franchise that proved to be fraudulent.

In this situation it wasn't me who had trusted: in fact, quite to the contrary. It was my partner who had made the purchase, believing the sales pitch despite my caution that I could find no validity of certain claims.

But I guess when your life has suddenly had a very definite end line drawn to it, you are extremely vulnerable. He had just been told he had eight weeks to live. It proved that he actually only had six.

In this case, my later research demonstrated that the person who was untrustworthy made something of a specialty in being unendingly supportive while one of the parties was facing death, in order to extract as much money as possible while alive.

Sadly in at least one such case, this had left a family with young children and a recently deceased parent homeless as a result.

The thoughts about trust and my own vulnerability haunted me after my No Plan trip.

Once back home I was eager to research wider thought on the subject of trust, and how one comes to place it with another.

In doing so, I read that trust entails:

- Elements of predictability,
- A value exchange,
- The expectation of some sort of reciprocal action in return in the future, and
- The exposure of your vulnerabilities.

That sounds a bit cut and dried and far too rational to me. The element of subconscious processing seems left out of that equation, and I definitely don't agree about expecting reciprocity.

Do I trust someone expecting that the transference of that trust will benefit me in the future?

Quite simply: No.

It is true that I pass an element of myself in all its vulnerabilities to any person I decide to trust.

In doing so I am displaying a faith that this will be not used against me – despite this having been the case in the past on some memorably heart-searing occasions.

To me, this is the triumph of trust:

Knowing that trust can have variable results,
the gains of trusting someone
still outweigh the risks.

Perhaps we make up our minds according to the map (both with and without roads) that we hold within us.

We each have such a map drawn from life experiences and prior conditioning. Perhaps, as in my case, just unfolding that inner map gives us courage and the determination that past betrayals will not destroy our ability to trust again.

The way I look at it is this: I can't fix the past but I can stop the past from influencing my future.

On balance, from the many thousands or more of trust relationships one forms in life – should the ones that resulted badly blind the rest of your life to the opportunities that the good decisions of trust bring to it?

There must have been some input from my sub-conscious for the sleepy decision to accept this person as a Tour Director in the little red car in Miramar on a warm Havana night.

What were the little things that went into my unconscious calculations?

A willing and amiable disposition
When we first met I had been looking for a special friend with no luck. When I recounted this story, help was immediately forthcoming without being sought.

The man who later became my Travel Director and his partner drove me to the area in Central Havana where I remembered the house was situated.

I had correct recall of the two parallel streets but not which cross-street or house number I needed. We crisscrossed each street asking people for the missing person, soon codenamed 'Nemo'.

Over the next three hours we met lots of friendly and helpful people but had not found Nemo.

Probably he had swum to another aquarium in the intervening nine years since I was last there.

In all that time there was never even a sigh of resignation at the task at hand. It certainly would have been quite understandable had there been some frustration shown, but it wasn't me who kept prolonging the search.

Several times I suggested we should stop, thinking that I had imposed enough. But my new friends were adamant that we should exhaust every opportunity to find my lost friend from long ago.

Attitude

I suppose also that the explanations of events that had caused the unending delays in collecting me after my two-hour wait also framed my opinion.

These matter-of-fact statements revealed a commitment to helping others sort out the dilemmas and small catastrophes of life, rather than reflecting a casual attitude to my welfare.

The delighted relaxation in the statement: "Well! Now everything is organised," with which I had been greeted after my two-hour wait was unexpected. There was such genuine satisfaction that things had been dealt with and that now we could set off uninterrupted by anything.

On hearing it said, I had chuckled a bit.

This seemed to be a really good attitude, instead of spending ages explaining and apologising.

It was apparent that my new friends all expected that I would understand that priorities need to be dealt with.

Context

What is interesting is that I had already switched to a Cuban context.

In my home environment would I have been as relaxed about such a wait, or such an explanation?

To be honest: no.

Should I?

This thought caused me to ponder my judgmental viewpoints in other contexts beyond Cuba.

I came to the conclusion that 'context' seems to filter the elements on which you decide to trust.

Example

It seems also that observation of how people deal with the obstacles in their own life helps frame a trust relationship as well.

Perhaps subconsciously I was assessing flexibility, resilience, capacity to resolve problems as they arose, as well as generosity of spirit and good humour.

During this assessment period we had travelled in the little red car over some distance around Havana, visiting my other friends from previous visits. Each trip was punctuated by stops at air-hoses to refill one or other of the tyres that were in a competition to lose air faster than each other.

Despite these precautions, we emerged from an apartment block in Boyeros on the outskirts of Havana to find that the rear passenger-side tyre was quite flat.

Off with the smart white shirt and it was hung on the open passenger door. Big smile, and the tyre was quickly changed – only to find that the front one was the tortoise in the race to deflate but was fast catching the now flat hare, which sat on the back seat ready to be treated for its inability to retain air.

Arriving at the service station – a back door in an alley – we had a conference over the tortoise tyre. The steel belting once within it had completely separated and now lay pathetically on the road behind the tyre, which was by now almost completely flat.

For a Cuban, it is opportune to have a tourist along at times like this – especially this tourist. The cost of a new tyre was quite beyond the scope of achievability without assistance. I volunteered, and a new tyre was duly ordered.

The tortoise tyre still had some distance to go before crossing the finish line, and so was administered a new ingestion of air so it could keep up the pace until the hare was renewed, for we were out of spares.

The little red car with its dented outside and rather gutted insides was a learning experience.

It was a learning experience in how much we take for granted the ease of our own non-Cuban lives. Most of us would never drive a vehicle in this condition. In fact a car in that condition wouldn't be permitted to be on our roads.

Since the little red car was our chariot and since it *was* on the road, I had an option. I could decline to ride in it or 'blend' with the local experience, knowing that my safe and good Cuban driver would take the utmost care.

Along the way, and through our many stops and starts to do so, I captured some great images with my camera – and even more in my mind, the latter quite inerasable.

The Cuban Approach educated me to evaluate the difference between what is important and what is window-dressing.

Familiarity

An additional and hugely balancing factor in my trust decision was that these people were not total strangers; they had been referred to me from friends of mine in Germany.

One of the things I had liked the most was the quiet assessment of any situation and lack of anger at the aggravation it caused. Oh – and the fact that I really respect a good driver. As I observed was the case with other Cuban drivers, my Tour Director was a really good (and safe) driver.

All these things add up.

It seems then, that trust is mapped by competence, reliability, integrity, and the personal interactions that consolidate all these, and then you make up your mind in a flash.

In the words of Malcolm Gladwell in his book 'Blink: The Power of thinking without thinking':

> *We need to respect the fact*
> *that it is possible to know*
> *without knowing why we know*
>
> *and accept that – sometimes*
> *we're better off that way.*

But, with all our non-Cuban conditioning, this is hard for us to do.

Ultimately it takes courage to trust.

What did the Cuban Approach accomplish?

I could either apply the 'Trust your mother, but cut the cards' approach or trust with a wholehearted belief in my own judgment.

This is an expression I adopted after hearing it when playing umpteen creative versions of poker on cold snowy nights in Iowa with my farm neighbours.

The delightful grandmother in her advanced years, who lived there with the family, was a very handy card player with a great sense of humour.

Had I tried to cut the cards in my favour, what would have been accomplished?

With a No Plan, I would have been trying to direct someone who had a vague sort of plan but was capable of adapting even this.

He could do so because he knew the terrain over which we must pass to achieve our desired end result.

His was a route constantly being improvised.

His was a route that hung as loosely as a circus balancing act slack-wire, pinned at intervals with relatives or local knowledge of something potentially fascinating for me.

It was a slack-wire over which I would be led – each of us balanced by confidence in the other.

What would have been the result had I tried to be the Travel Director?

Probably it would have been similar to outcomes at work when a colleague demanded a specified result, but allowed no deviation from the very methods that caused the thing to need repairing in the first place.

We have all been at the hands of those in command who expect people to use the same methods that brought no result before, and will not entertain alternative suggestions.

My two and half hours of people-watching while waiting to be collected could have left me all in a tizzwoz of frustration about my lack of control, when actually it was just was the way things were.

As it turned out, it meant that at the end of my wait the decks had been cleared so that the time we had to do the things planned for the evening (about which I also had no input) could be enjoyed without interruption.

I also would have been unable to:

- Conduct my mental tourism survey of the passing groups visiting the hotel that was my parking place.
- Think deeply about why we shy away from eye contact when confronted with someone from another country who might want to sell us something
- Buy two sets of calming clarinet-based CDs that I continue to enjoy and no doubt at the time the sellers appreciated the financial benefit from their sale
- Find myself in the presence of the Patron Saint of Cuba on her travels.

If I had thought my new friends to have been thoughtless about my welfare, or trying hard to extract funds from my wallet, I wouldn't have volunteered to purchase a new tyre for the little red car. Instead I would have decided it was what Douglas Adams in 'Life, The Universe, and Everything' called a 'SEP' – Someone Else's Problem.

Of course, had I not contributed to the repair this would have effectively dispensed with my free transport around Havana.

This transport came complete with curiosities such as passing the handles from one to another to wind windows up and down, having a commentary on what different coloured number plates on the Cuban vehicles indicated, and listening to the latest top Cuban hits en route.

Had the tyre not been paid for straight away, it would have meant that my Tour Director would have been preoccupied with having to find the extra money to buy one.

This would have translated into extra work of some sort, probably arranged through a friend of a friend. That would have consumed the time that would have been otherwise spent as my Tour Director.

But, most of all, it would have meant I stayed a tourist – someone outside the inner circle, someone with whom there was limited trust. Consequently everyone would have carefully screened what they said and did, in case it was unthinkingly the source of problems for them in the future.

This is no small consideration in a country where it is illegal to criticise the government, and where one lives with an ever-present police presence monitoring neighbourhood activity block by block.

This is why my Tour Director remains nameless throughout.

I don't give him even a fictitious name in case by doing so I inadvertently point authorities to someone else – someone of that name I don't even know, but who on the strength of such a mention might fall under suspicion of having been my guide.

I have quite a few good friends in Cuba, none of whom are unofficial tour guides – although some very dear friends work in the tourism business and that is how I met them.

On my second visit to Havana my Melbourne-based Argentinean Travel Agent recommended someone to help find an apartment to stay.

I became good friends with him and his lovely wife. The memory of their grand-daughter cuddling them while holding a Santa made around a bleach bottle still makes me smile.

They warm my soul with the continuity of our friendship.

My Tour Director was not officially entitled to guide a foreigner, let alone make the considerably larger amount of money from doing so than he would have done in his permanent job.

By sharing the challenges of a Cuban reality and contributing the one thing I could (money for the tyre), I contributed my bit to the relationship.

That important bit wasn't the money: it was the willingness to spend the money for someone just befriended.

In return, I benefited from all the particularly Cuban creativity that would go into planning all the little details of my No Plan trip.

This was all based on the mutual trust developed while I was in my parking place – and the spontaneous tyre replacement saga was one of those building blocks.

Step 4 of the Cuban Approach: Map reading: Trust your untried travel director

Reading the winds: How do you read an uncharted route?

As I have mentioned, my father was in the military when I was a child and in conflict zones was an Intelligence Officer often behind the lines gathering valuable reconnaissance on movements of the opposing forces. Amongst the many valuable things he taught me was that all good reconnaissance is ninety percent negative information.

It is only by identifying obstacles
that you find
the safest route through.

This is one of those 'blinding flashes of the obvious' – not obvious until stated.

Perhaps we are always scanning our inward maps for pattern recognition based upon the things that previously have set off alarms in our lives.

While there is a place for being careful, there is also a place for believing in your own judgment.

Believe that your own inner guide is already your best road map. It has stored all your life experiences. It even stores the spontaneous gifts of judgment that you had as a child.

It is commonly said that dogs and children tend to be good judges of character. So, since we were all children once and our past is stored within us, we must still have those same capabilities.

Trust your judgment.
Use it.
Practice trust.

I didn't know where our map was taking us – specifically. It was all in the head of my untried travel director.

Instead of trusting my map (with roads) that I had bought in the little kiosk in Havana, I decided to trust the brain map of my Tour Director, who was making it up as we went along.

I knew he had made some preliminary phone contacts with people along our intended route, but they were couched in the necessary vagueness of schedule that allows for the peculiarities of getting from one point to another in a country where this may be fraught with many unexpected delays.

As it turned out, even my Tour Director had his own version of No Plan. I was pretty sure he was going to bring me safely there and back – and to reveal things about life through Cuban eyes as well as seeing the things most tourists see.

But that decision to trust would have been no good if I then started Twenty Questions at every stop about "What Next?" and "When?" and "With Whom?"

Trust means to let go.

Adjusting your sails: To make memories on an uncharted course you may first have to trust an untried travel director.

On this trip I was the follower. As the trip unfolded I came to see that my Travel Director was assessing which new steps to introduce as we:

- climbed down mountains – me in shoes ill-suited to the job
- went horse riding in the same unsuitable shoes
- danced in unlikely places, and
- played with children with whom I had no common verbal language.

I have a physical geographic map (with roads) on which our travels were eventually mapped after the event.

However, the better map is the more vivid one.

This map sits in my memory and has the sum of our experiences engraved upon it.

It distils all that we learned from each other and from the land and its people as we travelled.

This is the sort of map my grandmother had in mind when she told me when I finished university and went off to travel:

Now as you travel, your education will begin.

You'll make memories
that no one can take away.

People can take away your possessions
but your memories are yours.

Make good ones.

CHAPTER FIVE

R-E-L-A-X

Leaving mindsets behind

Some wit once described volcanoes as being mountains with hiccups.

Cuba has no volcanoes, but because it sits along the Cayman Trough of the Caribbean Plate, it does have earthquakes.

The Cayman Trough is the tectonic plate beneath the ocean that covers over 3.2 million sq km *(1.2 million sq miles)* between North America and Venezuela.

The twelve most active faults along the plate are the *Cauto-Nipe*, the *Cochinos*, and the *Nortecubana*. Along these there has been a long history of earthquakes: in 1578 and 1678 in Santiago de Cuba at 6.8 on the Richter Scale, then at irregular intervals at about 4.5, until at a level of 7.6 in 1766.

Others of severe magnitude were spread across the subsequent years. In 1932, eighty percent of all buildings in Santiago de Cuba were damaged, and 1,500 people died.

In 1992, a 7.0 magnitude earthquake destroyed more than 100 homes in the south of the island just north of *Pilon* in Guantanamo province.

In 2017, earthquakes were reported at levels up to 5.8 on the Richter Scale in the area around Guamá on the southern edge of Cuba.

The European Macroseismic Scale (EMS) introduced in 1988 has a new way of measuring earthquake damage.

The EMS measures the intensity of an earthquake by the sorts of resulting damage. By this scale, it seems that fairly often Cuba has earthquakes at the 4th and 5th highest levels.

In short, Cuba seems to suffer from what might be called chronic hiccups of the tectonic variety.

Some people conjecture that thousands of years ago, in the course of a bad case of hiccups of the mountains along the Caribbean Plate, the mythical lost city of Atlantis was drowned.

There is always conjecture about Atlantis: Was it just a myth, just the way that Plato introduced it to us? Or does the myth pertain to some truth about an island consumed by neighbouring volcanic or earthquake induced hiccups?

Not having a specific location tied to the myth of Atlantis, everyone seems to want to claim it to be within their own geography.

In 2002, new oceanographic images led to suggestions that Atlantis just might have been found to be off the coast of Cuba[5].

Whether a city such as Atlantis could ever have been in these latitudes or not, Cuba seems able to create similar levels of myth and legend.

Although not formed in concentric rings of land and water that some people seem to think formed the unusual geography of the mythical Atlantis, Cuba does seem to engulf you with concentric rings of its own.

The first ring of Cuba will prod a jumble of questions that arise from your expectations of how things should be.

If you accept the challenge of leaving mindsets behind, this is followed soon afterwards by entering the second ring. Here, you plunge into refreshing waves of sound and dance.

When you climb back ashore you'll find that you no longer need the camouflage that you brought with you.

Instead, you can safely be you – the real you – the one that even you had forgotten existed.

---

[5] *http://www.latinamericanstudies.org/cuba/atlantis.htm*

Or perhaps you will discover a refreshing new version of the person you were previously.

When you meet that real self it will be a person you are happy to be, and whom you like!

It's easy to pre-judge things based on your own mindset.

For each of us, our mindset is constructed from a Lego-land of odd-shaped, character-building events and observations. These have come together over the span of our lifetime to imprint in our mind as 'the way things should be'.

A month in Cuba with no plan is a sure way to reassemble your Lego.

Waiting – that universal reality of Cuban life – is a good place to start.

On the previously mentioned two-hour wait in the lobby of my small hotel in the restored old city of Havana (my parking place before I set out on my No Plan) I had the chance to observe several hundred tourists.

The hotel *Los Frailes* (The Friars) that was my parking place in Havana is often, and apparently erroneously, thought to have been a monastery. This is because of its name and due to its décor influence that seems to be drawn from the church and former monastery of St. Francis that sits on the nearby corner.

However, I later read that the real provenance of *Los* Frailes is as one of the grand private homes that abounded as the wealth of early Havana grew.

This other version of history is not promoted but is equally evocative. According to this report, the hotel was built to be the Havana residence of the 4th *Marquis du Quesne*, Pierre Claude, who was born in Martinique and soon distinguished himself as a mariner, gaining his first command when only seventeen, and serving in both the Spanish and French navies.

Pierre Claude was a Marquis through inheritance of the title. He was also a member of the Spanish Order of Santiago. This was an order denoting generations of untainted noble blood and gives an obligation of honour to act like that of St. John – as both hospitaller, providing for the sick and wounded (like St John's ambulance today), and acting in a military capacity as Knight Defender.

By the time he settled in Havana and married Marie Ana *Roustan* de Estrada, who was from a noble Cuban family, Pierre Claude had won honours in his own right for his naval leadership.

Amongst these was the recommendation by Lafayette for the Marquis Du Quesne's victorious actions in getting the French General safely to America during the American War of Independence.

To give him his full title, *Marie-Joseph Paul Yves Roch Gilbert du Motier, Marquis de Lafayette* was a French aristocrat and military officer who commanded many battles of the American War of Independence.

How times change.

Lafayette came from a military family and was commissioned as an officer at the age of only thirteen. One dreads to think of the maturity of decision making of a thirteen-year old during battle.

Lafayette was against slavery and tried to convince George Washington to address the issue, but although writing that he was interested in the young man's ideas, Washington, a slave owner himself, declined to free his slaves.

Lafayette would later return to France and be embroiled in the bloody days of the French Revolution; his standing falling with the rabble when he was head of the National Guard and the King almost escaped the house arrest.

His later quelling of the 10,000 person strong gathering to demand either the abolishment of the monarchy or a referendum on its fate saw soldiers fire into the crowd in defence against their stoning by the crowd. He was duly labelled a royalist although he was constant in trying to defend constitutional law.

Lafayette had travelled to America on the French Concorde class 32 gun frigate, *Hermione*. Marquis de Quesne successfully defended the Hermione from two attacks en route. For this, he was accorded the Order of Cincinnati, awarded both to Americans and French officers who fought for the cause of American Independence.

The award does not relate to the American city of similar name. Instead the title comes from the name of a Roman hero, *Lucius Quinctius Cincinnatus,* who is famous for twice accepting the plea of the Senate to become Dictator.

Roman law made provision for appointing a Dictator in situations of extreme threat to the nation – but the key to selection was that such a person had to be impeccably honourable.

In both instances Cincinnatus proved the right man for the job – organising the military and civil population in successful actions that saved the nation – and then renouncing the role and returning to his civil life on his farm when order was restored.

The Order of Cincinnatus was instituted to perpetuate the memory of the sacrifice made by many during the American War of Independence.

The first President General was George Washington and its goals were to:

- maintain the fraternal bonds between the officers
- promote the ideals of the Revolution
- support members and their families in need
- distinguish its members as men of honour, and
- advocate for the compensation promised to the officers by Congress

The Order of Cincinnatus remains the longest hereditary social organisation in America. Today its works are largely educational and charitable but members must still be of the lineage of those who served during the Revolutionary War – both American and French.

I was later to visit the full sized working frigate replica *Hermione* at her home port of Rochefort, in the Charente-Maritime area of France, south of La Rochelle. She is a magnificent ship, and you get some sense of what it must have been like to be at sea with 32 guns blazing as they were when in battle en route to America, carrying Lafayette with his news of French support against the British.

So, although uncertain that it was so, it was rather exciting to know I may be staying in the noble house that was once that of the Marquis de Quesne.

The perception of my hotel as it is promoted, and the legitimacy of its factual base, in a way represents the enigma that is the Cuba of today.

This charming little hotel is an example of the history of a land as it is presented to the world and the history of it as it is lived. This often makes for a delicate unravelling to separate one from the other.

I think this is much like the lives we all lead.

We have our public face and our private selves and seldom are they even close to being the same image.

This is as it should be, for we need to shelter ourselves from displaying our frailties – but the balance is the tricky bit.

When we start believing our own press we do so at our peril.

We may not need to actually renounce the public cloak in the same way as Cincinnatus, but we should look into the mirror more honestly, to remind ourselves what a complex and delicate package a personality is.

The mirror that is the most honest is that held by our friends. As I told the Canadian tourist, this mirror can remind us who we are when we have lost our way.

It can also bring us back down to earth when success, or fame, or wealth threatens our true selves from shining.

No matter its true heritage, 'Los Frailes' is a lovely small hotel with a spacious rectangular central courtyard festooned with long vines that provide cool respite from the streets outside.

The one negative was the lack of a window in my room.

My mother always said:

Make every fault a fashion.

The presentation of 'Los Frailes' has done this well.

One had the impression – and I am not sure if this was actually written anywhere – that these were formerly monk's cells.

On this basis, one felt that the lack of a window added to authenticity rather than being an unusual and rather unwelcome feature of a tourist hotel.

Whichever story of its heritage is the real one, the building itself reflects the grandeur of colonial wealth.

From the 1500s onwards Havana had been a strategically important trading hub – and a critical assembly point for the silver fleets of the age.

Ships brought goods from all of 'The New World' *(The Americas and Caribbean islands like Bermuda)*: goods that were destined for Europe via Spain.

The city was first known as *San Cristóbal de la Habana* – a name that can be confusing in history due to there being another Cuban *San Cristóbal* near *Pinar del Rio*. To save our confusion today it is fortunate that the name was shortened to *la Habana* (in English 'Havana').

As the ability to export products grew, the Cuban trade in cigars, tobacco and sugar fed the desires of both the aristocracy and the growing bourgeoisie of continental Europe and Great Britain.

By the 1800s, Havana was a cosmopolitan city which drew wealthy merchants and scholars from around the world. With the arrival of this wealth, the city started to enhance its surroundings with grand buildings and fine public artworks.

With riches come two valuable things for a city: wealthy people and their wish to enjoy cultural activities, and with the time to do so.

Grand theatres were built. Parks and statues appeared. The city was growing. From a population of around 94,000 in 1811, by 1889 it would exceed 200, 000.

It was also growing in international stature. Good quality drinking water was necessary to support this growth, and in 1858 the *Albear Aqueduct* project was officially decreed to replace its more inefficient, open-channelled predecessor.

This new aqueduct drew water from the Vento Springs at an elevation of 12.5 metres (41') higher than the city.

Once completed, the new aqueduct placed Havana on a par with the infrastructure of Paris, London and Berlin, at the time considered to be the cultured cosmopolitan cities of Europe.

The complex new system was recognised as a real engineering marvel of its time.

At the 1876 International Centennial Exhibition in Philadelphia, and again in Paris in 1878, prestigious medals were awarded to the project's designer, *Francisco de Albear*. Sadly he died of malaria before the project was completed.

Over 100 years later his system still provides water to a section of Havana.

In 1837, the *Fuente de la India* (The fountain of the Indian Woman) was commissioned. Carved in marble by an Italian sculptor from Cararra, and poised with a quiver full of arrows, the Indian Woman holds the '*Cornucopea of Amalthea*' as she sits on a pedestal supported by four dolphins who pour water from their mouths onto shells below.

In Greek mythology *Almalthea* is the goat who succoured the infant God Zeus and whose horn he broke while he was playing as a child.

Legend says that by way of apology, Zeus blessed the broken horn to provide abundance forever – and so it has come down to us in artworks and mythology.

This Cuban 'Horn of Plenty' on the fountain was adapted from the traditional abundance of European flowers and fruits, to be filled with tropical fruit, topped by a pineapple.

The 'Fuente de la India' fountain has been relocated at least once but has returned to its original site where we now can see it, in the *Plaza de la Fraternidad*.

In 1856 the Havana *Hotel Inglaterra* stamped a new era of luxury on the growing city. It is now the oldest hotel in Cuba. Although it wasn't until 1901 that electricity, telephones and private bathrooms were added, even at its opening this was a hotel of great luxury.

In 1871 the *Gran Hotel Pasaje* opened, with its wonderfully colonnaded passageway between the *Paso de Prado* and *Zulueta*, where now you can see a colourful gathering of 50s American vehicles. The engines of most of these cars have been hybridised by decades of lack of official parts and by modifications made with creativity and ingenuity.

Unfortunately you can't see the hotel anymore as it is a thing of the past: it's now a series of apartments devoid of the style and elegance of the original. The gracious colonnades remain and are a refreshingly cool place to walk in the heat of the day.

These two grand old dames of a city that drew wealth and immigrants from all parts of the world still retain their grandeur – even if just in the colonnades in the case of the *Gran Hotel Pajere*, in the area of Havana we now know as *Habana Viejo* – the old city of Havana.

The *Ingleterre* was where the young War Correspondent Winston Churchill stayed when he was a military reporter on the Spanish-Cuban War in 1895.

The *Gran Hotel Pajere* was preferred by the Americans. Generals Grant and Eisenhower, former President Cleveland, and William K. Vanderbilt all made it their choice of residence when visiting Havana.

Havana is a port city and like all port cities always looked outwards to the world more than inwards. Port cities used to become home to some of the wealthiest of merchants as they oversaw their trade at close quarters. They also drew the rich, influential, and famous – both native and foreign. Havana was no exception. These wealthy immigrants helped to build the architectural grandeur of old Havana and their influence on the style of building echoes the best of that of other lands.

Walking around the old city of Havana and admiring this eclectic style made me realise how far people of every country travelled in the early 1800s; in fact it made me reflect on how far those of even earlier days travelled – Indonesians to Africa, Arabs to China.

The great Berber voyager *Ibn Battute* was possibly the greatest traveller of all time. Over 450 years before steam travel, his adventures in the 1300s are reported to have covered more than 121,000 km (75,000 miles).

China's famous Admiral *Cheng Ho*, or *Zheng He* as he is possibly better known, was also an amazing traveller. His 1405 expedition is reported to have consisted of 27,800 men and comprised a fleet of 62 treasure ships supported by approximately 190 smaller ships.

These ships would have dwarfed those of Christopher Columbus.

The fleet included:

- Treasure ships used by the commander of the fleet and his deputies: nine-masted and about 126.73 metres (416 ft) long and 51.84 metres (170 ft) wide
- Equine ships carrying horses, tribute goods and repair material for the fleet: eight-masted and about 103 m (339 ft) long and 42 m (138 ft) wide
- Supply ships containing supplies: seven-masted and about 78 m (257 ft) long and 35 m (115 ft) wide
- Troop transports: six-masted and about 67 m (220 ft) long and 25 m (83 ft) wide
- Warships: five-masted and about 50 m (165 ft) long
- Patrol boats: eight-oared and about 37 m (120 ft) long
- Water tankers with 1 month's supply of fresh water

Six more of his expeditions with fleets of comparable size took place between 1407 and 1433.

Thinking of these great navigational achievements reminded me of an old navy saying about holding your course.

Set your course by the stars,
not by the lights of every passing ship.

Havana's growth as an important international port brought wealth to the wider economy as well. All the visiting vessels needed servicing and provisioning.

This drove growth in skilled labour, agriculture, artisan craftsmanship, entertainment, as well as immigration.

As the city added architectural styles reflecting the diversity of these new wealthy citizens, the character of Havana evolved into the graciousness now restored in the UNESCO Heritage area of the old city.

This makes for a popular tourist destination for today's visitors.

My parking space in the tastefully restored 'Los Frailes' allowed me a unique view of the tourists exploring the old city of Havana.

From its lobby I came to the conclusion that my hotel must be a part of one of the Havana Walking Tours – or even of every walking tour in the city.

Certainly many tourists came and went in the period while I waited and people-watched. A gigantically proportioned leather chair in the lobby proved the ideal place to do so, and I moulded myself into it.

As with most hotels in that part of Havana, this one came with a band in the lobby bar. The music here was in keeping with the monastic theme promoted by the hotel, which has a sculpture of a mournful looking copper a monk in reception.

Unlike the relentless salsa of some bands, here they played a sonorous clarinet-based 'Ave Maria' and other gentle and wistful tunes to soothe the soul.

Participants on every one of these tours had to pass the band to get to their destination.

As is usual everywhere and not just in Cuba, the musicians had CDs to sell. One musician would lay down his instrument and stand hopefully on the return path of the camera-bearing crowd, holding his CDs and trying to catch the attention of the people seeing Cuba on a plan.

From my observation, these people fell into a few groups:

Those with a careful plan.

These visitors were very busy seeing Havana. Once they had mentally ticked off one site on their list of destinations, they hurried out into the street in search of the next.

In their explorations they made no eye contact with anyone, and generally seemed rather anxious, and certainly very busy.

Those whose plan made sure of no tainting by local contact.

This type of traveller headed through to the vine festooned arcades of the interior. They shuffled past the musicians in both directions, slowly enough to listen but not so slowly that they might have to have any sort of communication – verbal or otherwise.

These people took lots of pictures of the musicians – and many took videos of the performance. But when the CDs were proffered, they shrugged or grimaced as if insulted, shook their heads, and marched purposefully off to the next destination.

Those who had a plan
but responded to interest that might vary it.

These folk saw the sights, took their pictures, and then settled briefly in the lobby bar to listen.

Sometimes an aggravated Tour Director with a plan (non-Cuban) would huff back to the lobby to hurry them on.

To their credit, these people had obviously decided that Havana Viejo (the old city) on a broken plan was more interesting than one on a regimented plan.

Several thanked the tour guide with a firm refusal and ordered a few drinks. They usually either bought a CD or threw some money in the hat.

Not all stayed.

Some reluctantly succumbed to the sheep dog Tour Director's barking and sauntered back to their group with a heavy air of resignation.

All this challenged the philosophy of Mark Twain, who wrote:

> *Travel is fatal to prejudice,*
> *bigotry, and*
> *narrow-mindedness.*

From what I saw, this proved *not* to be a universal truth.

Watching these tourists from the leather chair in my parking place, I was fascinated by how some people in a new geographical location have scarcely travelled from home. They are so wrapped up in their own camouflage that they can't see the sights at all – just a sort of plasma-thin-screen-version of something remote from them.

To travel in this way is to lose the chance to renew yourself.

To renew yourself, you need to R-E-L-A-X.

To R-E-L-A-X means to let old mindsets rest.

There are mindsets – and there are mindsets. I am not immune in this regard. Further along in our No Plan trip when we were in Trindad de Cuba with a car full of cousins, a call on the mobile phone caused the driver, my Tour Director, to stop the car, get out, and answer the phone.

In most people's terms this is quite logical.

The fact that the car was stopped more or less at the place where the phone rang, on a street whose pot holes were so large that they could better be called small caverns, and that this spot was just in front of the local Fire Station, modified that logic – at least to me.

I had taken the opportunity to get out too and take photos of the fire engines when suddenly the Fire Alarm rang.

My Tour Director was talking loudly on his mobile phone.

This is a habit that seems common to many people. I have always thought they may as well not even bother with the phone: they could just as easily hang their heads out the window and expect to be heard at any distance.

It was useless to mention the high quality amplifiers in mobile phones.

He seemed to operate on the premise that, if you don't see someone close by, they must be far away. If they are far away, you had better yell.

At this time, he was looking in the opposite direction. With the car doors open and Reggaeton at full blast, he didn't hear the alarm.

I did.

    I yelled.

        The cousins laughed.

The firemen laughed – but they were laughing at me. They squeaked by the car by the narrowest of margins (Did I mention about good Cuban drivers?).

I felt rather foolish and then also laughed – a sort of dry "Oh dear I'm thinking I'm still in Germany" sort of laugh. Not to mention the fact that I quite sensibly could have moved the car myself.

The point was that there was actually no need to get excited. There was enough room for a driver who knew where his fire engine began and ended and could see there was no problem.

The cousins could see that.
The firemen could see that.

What I saw was a fire engine on a call peeling out of the fire station, and a stopped car – our car – in the road ahead of its passage.

Instant reaction: "Eek. We must get out of the way or we will be in deep trouble".

"R-E-L-A-X, Paquita", I was told by cousins and driver. "You are in Cuba – R-E-L-A-X".

At what point does 'R-E-L-A-X' *not* work?

I guess in a country where the electrical wiring arrangements are such that to the rest of us electrocution seems an ever-present threat, the non-Cuban definition of danger or threat is at variance with ours.

Sometimes a bit of caution is beneficial, but I guess it is a bit like how much spice you put in your cooking: too little you lose the desire to eat at all and too much and you wish you hadn't.

In this case it's a bit different.

Too much caution leads to an unchallenging life with definite levels of predictability: Too little can have terminal effects.

This was not the only time that what I had thought to be flexible mindsets of mine were challenged during my No Plan month in Cuba.

You get comfortable with some mindsets:
They come to feel more like facts than opinions.

An example of this was my firm belief that it takes at least a day to defrost a frozen solid turkey. This was also disproven in Cuba.

After returning from travels further afield I had announced a fiesta in my Havana apartment for my friends.

"How many should I cater for?" I asked my Tour Director. He looked thoughtful, obviously making a mental calculation. I added that of course his friend who was helping me cook should bring his girlfriend as well.

The total was summed with a wide smile: "Seventeen should be enough".

I laughed. *SEVENTEEN!* Well, I HAD asked.

My apartment had an oven with two temperatures: hot and even hotter.

There were lots of cooking pots, 4 forks, 2 knives, 3 spoons, 6 plates (of various characteristics) and 4 small soup bowls, 4 mugs, 10 glasses (priorities!) and 2 small serving dishes.

We agreed that the missing cutlery and crockery would be brought along by the guests.

This proved to be the case. The result was a sort of crazy tea-set with few matching parts.

Every dish and piece of cutlery was a precious commodity in a place where such things are costly, even though they are often of the equivalent quality of what we find in a one euro/pound/dollar shop.

I tried the oven.
It smoked.

When I say it smoked, this is really an understatement.

It was worthy of a wild fire blaze in my native Australia and, when lit (it was gas) smoke billowed out just as quickly as it did in a bush fire.

I peered inside. The bottom slide in the oven was caked with the leftovers of many hearty meals – fatty ones at that. These seemed welded on.

I couldn't un-wedge the bottom tray to remove it for cleaning. As a consequence, it seemed to me that the oven was dead – and dangerous.

I mentioned this small fact to my Cuban friends.

They investigated.

"R-E-L-A-X, Paquita.
    It just needs cleaning.
       We'll clean it."

With three days before the fiesta this seemed plausible.

Using the one decent knife in the place, the bottom tray was surgically removed and placed on the balcony.

The sharpness of the knife having been dulled in the process, it was brought to cutting edge again by sharpening on the balcony concrete.

This proved effective, if unconventional.

The tray then sat un-cleaned on the balcony for two and half days, during which I couldn't bake anything.

But there were other things to do.

Like to R-E-L-A-X.

We went shopping for food, which for us is a straightforward experience.

By contrast, in Cuba if you want butter, you have to go to the store that has butter today – not all supermarkets do; and if you want special sauces – a very rare commodity – you go over to *Miramar* to where the diplomatic set make their purchases.

For vegetables, you shop at a local market. That may also have some chicken or even a pig, freshly butchered and needing to be eaten that day, having been on the food stall unrefrigerated for some time. Otherwise you can get frozen chicken and some meats at the local supermarket.

All this is hungry and thirsty work, so three of us went up to the roof of one of the shopping centres and ordered some food. Food demanded an accompaniment of two Bucaneros and a Cristal.

We waited for the food, drank our drinks, and watched the world go by beneath us along the small area of beach.

Knowing of the housing shortage, I asked about the unfinished sea-front apartment block next door to where we were sitting.

I was advised that it wasn't for locals. It was for foreign workers but work had stopped some years ago. I thought it must date to the collapse of the Soviet Union and the fewer Russians in residence in Havana as a result. I have no way to verify that assumption.

This was the day we were to bake, but there seemed no urgency. I had dropped easily into Cuban time and so we sat and chatted.

I did R-E-L-A-X.

For the baking that the fiesta required, I had been loaned some precious baking implements. In listing them, I am still deeply moved by the fact that in another demonstration of trust they were lent to a stranger, for they were valuable to the owners and not easy to replace.

They included:

- a cake server formed from a piece of flattened metal welded onto a screwdriver handle
- a regular spatula
- a well-worn plastic bowl with indentations from years of good food being mixed within
- an even more worn electric hand-mixer
- two metal serving trays that served as cookie sheets.
- piping bags made from what looked like some sort of automotive repair material.
- These had metal piping tips in three different shapes – one seeming to have been hammered quite flat and then squeezed with pliers into shape.

All these lay in the kitchen awaiting our return. The wait was of no immediate avail because I couldn't use the oven until its tray was scoured, or otherwise separated from its tenacious coating.

In this context there was no alternative but to R-E-L-A-X. We had a leisurely late lunch – or early dinner – and discussed the recipe book that had been produced at the table for review.

This was a small notepad about the size of a mobile smart phone. In it were handwritten recipes passed down from one generation to another. To me this handwritten recipe book seemed a very poignant object. It was filled with recipes and hints on improvisations, all carefully written in pencil.

This little book showed the desire to make meals that offered hospitality and not just food, despite the challenges of scant supply of ingredients.

We laughed a lot, talked about things in general and nothing in particular, and decided it was time to get going.

By the time we had unloaded the shopping and attended to the necessary renovations so that at last there was a working (hotter and hottest) oven, it was quite late.

My friends departed and I was on my own. It would probably have been sensible to at least start the meal or do some more preparation. However, I decided I couldn't face an inferno and promised myself that early tomorrow I would start on what would prove to be a bake-athon.

For now, I took the Cuban Approach and settled down with a Cristal and a book.

Over the previous three days I had lightly cooked chicken, bought frozen in plastic bags. Once cooked these pieces were stored in the fridge in saucepans. The following day I would skim off all the fat and pull off the bones what little meat there was to be had.

It was a labour of love but the result was not attractive.

I came to the conclusion that Cuban chickens had all been to the health spa after running consecutive marathons and then pigging out on McDonald's burgers. They were thin and wiry, but yet covered in a deep layer of fat.

By staging my preparations, I figured that by the day of the fiesta I would have enough to make a decent Coq-au-Vin to be finished off in the oven – now it was in working order.

Wine is a hard to come by commodity in Cuba but I had found some to cook with, and some to drink.

The day before the fiesta I looked doubtfully at the results. Not enough for seventeen people – even with the tuna and rice dish to complement. Then I remembered that I had seen a turkey in one of the supermarkets.

When my friends returned I explained the need to supplement the menu and off we set in pursuit of a turkey. I was staring at the turkeys in the frozen food section with some perplexity when my Cuban friends joined me.

"Do you think that one will fit in my oven?" I asked.

"Don't worry Paquita, my friend will cook it in his oven".

"But it takes a day to defrost a turkey", I said doubtfully.

"Paquita R-E-L-A-X. You are in Cuba. We will bring it to you fully cooked and stuffed by 10 o'clock tomorrow" (the day of the fiesta).

Of course we all knew that this was 10 o'clock Cuban time, so it was not surprising that it wasn't until 1:30pm that they arrived proudly bearing a beautiful looking cooked bird.

It is hard to R-E-L-A-X when seventeen people are about to arrive and your main dish is not there at 1pm – but I did.

I stood on the balcony and took photos of the life of a Cuban street.

Things were sort of ready.

I had baked a chocolate cake.

Remember the oven temperatures?

I should have started with something other than a cake so I could find a workaround for the temperature. The chocolate cake was black on the top and the bottom but once these were removed was quite tasty in the middle.

I decided I had better try to find some ice cream at the local shop and happily found some whipped cream in a vacuum spray can to cover the evidence of a much trimmed exterior.

I drank another Cristal and stared at the oven. Cookies would suffer an even worse fate and couldn't be so trimmed. I decided I would insulate.

This required designing a sort of swinging bridge type structure of trays and lids on which I perched the cookie tray (very carefully). It worked, for the cookies were nicely brown having been saved from the inferno beneath.

On the arrival of the turkey we started to do the baking of the Cuban recipes that we had selected from the handwritten notebook the day before.

The results were terrific. This was a man who knew how to tame an inferno. His creations came out unscathed, golden and delicious.

Meanwhile, I was making the tuna dish.

Having lived in America I had succumbed to the creativity of Mid-Western farm cooks who can marry a bunch of things in tins with things not in tins to create fabulous tasty dishes – enough for the whole seven-county area. It was good training for creating food for a fiesta for seventeen in a Cuban kitchen.

But in conceiving this plan I had goofed.

I had several cans but no can-opener. I stared at them sadly.

"R-E-L-A-X, Paquita".

The same sturdy knife that had doubled as a scalpel to remove the oven tray was now employed as a tin opener.

It pierced the top and quickly travelled around the can leaving a rather serrated, jagged lid but releasing the contents.

The knife was then again sharpened on the balcony concrete and returned to its rightful place in the kitchen.

It was hot work sharing the kitchen with another person and a gas oven that knew no moderation.

Covered in perspiration that rolled down my face and back, I asked when the guests would arrive.

"I have no idea", responded the Tour Director from the doorway.

It was a truthful answer, though not the one I would have preferred. As it happened, the first guests arrived about an hour later, some thirty minutes after he had left to collect his family.

This arrival was about two hours earlier than I would have expected for dinner guests.

"Oh dear", I said as I wiped damp hair from my face. I was told not to worry – to R-E-L-A-X. The man of that newly arrived family was a chef. He had come early because he wanted to cook some Cuban-style rice for us all – to contribute.

That made three of us in the kitchen that was like an incinerator, and really just had room for one.

In between various other activities to do with the arrival of a borrowed CD player and two large speakers, I finished the tuna and rice and went to set it on the table.

There before me sat our beautiful turkey being decorated with a piped mayonnaise greeting:

'*Felicidades* (Congratulations) *Paquita*'.   Awww.

I pondered upon what I was actually being congratulated. There were several options, not the least of which was on finding this happy group of people eager to show me the best of what they knew of their home country.

By then it seemed possible that others might soon arrive, so I headed off to the bathroom to make myself presentable. Emerging from the quickest of showers, I started to dry my hair. Within moments my hair dryer shorted the electrics, and the whole apartment went dark – and quiet.

It was my turn to say it: R-E-L-A-X.

Everyone laughed.

I groped my way to the fuse box and reset the fuse. I knew how to, because I had shorted it out the previous night resulting in absolutely no electricity to the whole apartment.

That meant a call to my landlady and a struggle with my long-since forgotten Spanish to explain. Shortly afterwards, her son arrived and fixed the problem at the fuse box. When he left, I had the false impression that this was a fix of a permanent nature and that it wouldn't happen again.

So, in the photos of me at the fiesta, my hair is – shall we say – creatively between native curls and my efforts to lay them into a smoother order.

I had given up.

I knew that in Cuba people see who you are, not what you look like at that moment, but they are quick to compliment you when it is deserved. This predilection to compliments is a mindset that could be imitated elsewhere with positive results.

My provision of drinking wine proved to be the cause for another cultural disconnect.

I wanted to provide something I presumed to be a welcome luxury. This proved to be not so.

I love a good wine, so secured the best I could for my friends.

They weren't used to drinking wine and found a crisp dry white unpleasing – so added several teaspoons of sugar to each glass.

By now it was getting quite late and the children were starving, so we decided we should all eat and not wait for my Tour Director and his family.

When they arrived a bit more than an hour later I was a bit cross that they were so late.

Remember what I said about mindsets?

I was to feel yet again that humbling realisation that you have made a judgment based on insufficient information, and have now been proved to be very unjust in doing so.

It wasn't until the whole group entered the apartment that I saw the reason for the increased numbers in calculations about how many guests were coming.

From his tour directing earnings, my Travel Director had employed two musicians. They arrived with guitars on their backs and singing voices at the ready.

This was the cause of the delay.

The logistics of the simple addition of live music to the fiesta went something like this:

- First you have to go about and find musicians who are good, but available.
- You then negotiate a price.
- You then rush home and make sure you and the family are all in your best party clothes.
- Once you have your family together and ready, you go back and collect the musicians, and then bring the whole group to the destination, looking terribly proud of what you have accomplished.

It was a lovely gesture of generosity and made for a memorable evening of listening to live music and dancing to CDs.

Given this context, how does it put into perspective a late arrival to a dinner that has been three days in the making?

If you take the Cuban Approach – well, you just R-E-L-A-X and enjoy.

Over the course of our travels and in return for the openness I had received, I had opened my heart to this lovely family and its extended range of cousins. This led to me being a guest in many different apartments and houses. It also saw me experience some interesting situations.

On one occasion when we were travelling I needed to go to the toilet in the home of one of the rural cousins. I could see there was consternation caused by my enquiry of where the toilet was, and asked if I had said something wrong.

My Tour Director told me they were ashamed.

The toilet was an external one – what in Australia is fondly known as a 'long-drop' because it is essentially a moveable shed that sits over a deeply dug pit.

This one had no door.

I went to the toilet and when I came back I asked my Tour Director to tell them that when I was a little girl in a sparsely settled area of Australia, we had just such a toilet – but with a door.

Before going to bed at night my brother and I used to be escorted outside to the toilet by our half–Labrador, half–Blue Heeler cattle dog, a big black dog whose shoulders were at chest level of a little girl.

All three of us had to cram in the small outhouse together because we children were afraid of the dark outside and needed the dog for company.

I asked him to tell his relatives about the similar toilet in my childhood and compliment them that, with no door and no big brother and no big dog, this toilet seemed very comfortable.

Everyone laughed.

No shame should be felt!

I had already had a prior experience in Havana where the same request produced equal consternation.

In that case the toilet was just a hole in the floor and no light. It was late at night. I slipped and fell over and was very glad for the backpack type handbag that saved me falling directly onto the floor.

When the tale was told on my return to the living room, everyone laughed– especially me, for I had a mental image of what I must have looked like!

In a country where the infrastructure is crumbling and toilet paper mustn't go down the toilet but should be placed in containers beside, you have to re-adjust your mindset rather radically, for old habits die hard.

What did the Cuban Approach accomplish?

What is worse? An oven that doubles as an incinerator stopping you cooking for your friends?

OR you making less-than-perfect home-cooked goodies to show that you care enough to cook them yourself?

Putting pressure on friends who already have enough pressure in their lives, by insisting on timetables – even those in your head – when they know the end result you want to achieve and are actually doing everything to accomplish it in their own way (often a very creative one)?

OR responding positively to their admonitions to R-E-L-A-X?

Being perfectly groomed for the fiesta?

OR having a bit of a creative coiffure but also having electricity in the apartment?

Shrieking at the use of your only sharp knife as a tin opener?

OR appreciating the inventiveness of how it was used, and courtesy of being sure to re-sharpen on the balcony concrete before returning it to the kitchen?

Fussing and fuming over a long wait in the lobby?

OR using the time to listen to the music and to think about the lives of the musicians in comparison to those of the tourists who passed by them in that time (and of course giving you time to absorb the music and buy some CDs)?

You, feeling discomfort at toilet facilities not everywhere to the standard of your home country?

OR the shame that your hosts feel that what they must accept daily as the norm, is less than ideal for a visitor?

It is not until we leave our mindsets behind us
that we can R-E-L-A-X.

When we do, we find a new side of ourselves.

I think it's a nicer side:
less judgmental and seeing the plus side
rather than the minus of the situation.

It's a choice. Either you can hold your own frame of reference and try to cram reality of a foreign place into it, even though things are sticking out and don't fit, leaving you in a constant fuss for trying to make them do so,

OR you can R-E-L-A-X and reorient yourself to someone else's reality of life.

The Cuban Approach has taught me that even when I think I have let go, there is still some of my expectation of how life should be organised that can be positively realigned to a different reality.

It usually leaves me a bit humble, often laughing. It always leaves me with the warmth of having connected with my fellow human beings on a much more genuine level.

As Kahlil Gibran said:

If your heart is a volcano,
how do you expect the flowers to bloom?

Step 5 of the Cuban Approach: R-E-L-A-X: When you relax enough to leave mindsets behind you, the world is full of new possibilities.

Reading the winds: When you have a commitment to no plan, you have thrown yourself on the wind.

The wind brings on it both dreams and specks that can get in your eye.

The trick is to let the dreams get caught in your sails and drive you onwards towards their realisation –and to keep the specks out of your eyes by wearing goggles or sunglasses, or carrying a real fabric hanky to extract them.

On my one month with no plan in Cuba I was a dream hunter.

I had a dream of a special sort: to recapture the passion that Cuba brought to me in the past – and to come home with the stories and photos for a book.

To do that, and to have authentic experiences to relate, meant accepting that things would probably not be quite as anticipated. It also meant being prepared to accept that the most flexible component of all would probably have to be me.

Most of us believe ourselves to be able to be accommodating of other points of view – of different lifestyles.

Sometimes, it takes falling on your back in a toilet of a sort you can't even see in the dark to teach you that everything is relative.

Sometimes, we need to have a reality shock to adjust our viewpoints and expectations.

When they happen, these reality shocks cause our views to be readjusted more substantially than we ever expected.

Dream your dreams and set your sails.
A speck in the eye is a small price to pay.

Adjusting your sails:

The Cuban Approach identifies the objective that is sought and keeps that as a sole focus.

The objective might get enhanced – as with a turkey stuffed with ham – or unexpected live musicians at your fiesta.

The timeframe might elongate or shorten:

- by your driver having to take someone from one town to another on a family emergency and therefore you having to wait to be collected
- or your dinner guests arriving two hours earlier than planned.

But, if what we seek in life are end results that exceed expectations in levels of quality, then I go with 'The Cuban Approach'.

From toilets to turkeys, Cuba had me adjusting the sails of my mindsets to steer me on new winds to a much nicer me.

CHAPTER SIX

En route photo stops

Things to capture along the way

From the outset, I had explained that I would be making lots of stops to take photographs. My Tour Director assured me with his wonderful smile that he was used to tourists.

But I was no ordinary tourist.

When we were en route to the island cays of the coral reef-lined coastline of the *Jardines de la Reina* or 'Gardens of the Queen' (named to honour Queen Isabella of Spain) we made many photo stops – often quite close together. The scenery was spectacular.

The first European to record the beauty of the area was Christopher Columbus in May 1494. He thought he had discovered a continent.

It wasn't until the 1508 explorations of the Galician *Sebastián de Ocampo* that the *Doce Leguas* or Labyrinth of the Twelve Leagues, as it is known in English, that the fact that Cuba was proven to be an island.

There are more than 600 small islands and cays – small, low lying sandy coral reef outcrops that parallel the coast for some 150 km (*93 miles*).

Because of my many photo stops, the uncle travelling with us commented drily that, at this rate, we might be there by dark.

My Tour Director laughed and explained that this was his job.

I explained that taking the photos was *MY* job.

But photographs were not all that I captured along the way. I also captured vignettes of how life is lived beyond the realm of tourism.

Outside of Havana, we had travelled on an unspecified route that would be spontaneously charted as the occasion demanded.

The route was punctuated by the opportunity for visits to relatives who had not been seen for some years.

From such a basis our day-trip forays were always in the company of one of the cousins – for it is a rare chance for a local to live on a tourist's penny. This lets them see things that tourists see, and not just the everyday, sometimes harsh Cuban reality.

One of our stops en route was at the home of the furniture-maker cousins.

The house was on a small hill. It was a roomy place and in former times must have held some standing in the small hamlet.

The veranda looked out over the road beneath and some meadows, where children rode bareback on horses.

A lazy creek trickled through the reeds at the bottom of the valley.

We came to it without a map – even one with roads. Instead, when we got to a small town nearby we decided to stop to buy some bottled drinks.

My Tour Director was unsure where to turn off. The myriad tracks off the main highway were unmarked. Since he hadn't been there for over three years his mystification was unsurprising. He decided to use the 'Ask Directions Compass' at the shop when we found one.

We had been driving slowly through the town, peering ahead for a shop when suddenly the car took a swerving detour and pulled suddenly to a stop beside a truck.

My Tour Director leaped out and called a name. A dust-stained face turned in surprise and then, with a shout of delighted greeting, the person to whom it belonged embraced my driver.

Here was yet another cousin, and by that happy serendipity that often redirects life's plans, this was the man who could direct us through the maze of smaller roads to the house of the cousin we were seeking.

As they conversed, I watched the local bus pull in and fill with passengers. This 'camione' was typical of transport between the smaller towns and hamlets of Cuba. It was actually a big flatbed lorry.

Some of the camiones have a canvas top laced over metal frames to keep the rain and cold out on long stormy rides or give protection from the unrelenting summer sun.

Some are enclosed in brightly painted metal with tiny windows, so the huddle of warm bodies inside forces inhalation of each other's breath and perspiration.

Sometimes there are welded seats or wooden planked benches.

We often passed camiones with the people standing, holding onto the roof bars with arms that must have ached after several miles.

The camione transport is cheap and supposedly there are schedules, but they seem to be not especially reliable.

This form of transport is not supposed to be for non-Cubans, but even they seem to have trouble in finding the bus stop in any town for the particular bus route they want.

In the countryside the bus stops seem incongruous. They sprout up along otherwise uninhabited stretches of road to have you wonder where the passengers come from.

The alternative to bus travel is to hail a ride with a passing motorist. It was not uncommon to see an 'Amarillo' – a person in a dusty-yellow-coloured uniform whose job is to arrange paid hitchhiking rides from the drivers of passing government vehicles on behalf of those waiting in the long queue for the next camione. The money paid goes straight to the government.

I come from a background where you form an orderly queue and diligently stay there until your turn comes.

The Cuban system is far more practical and I love it.

Now, I watched it in action as I waited for the conversation between cousins to finish so we could get on our way.

The Cuban queuing system goes like this:

- When you arrive at the departure point of bus or camione or ferry you just call out, *"¿Último?"* ("Who's last?")
- The last person to arrive responds. You make a mental note of who that person is. When the bus loads, you follow behind.
- Once you know who's last, it's polite to wait until the next person arrives so you can say that it's you who is the last.
- However, if you make an error in etiquette and depart, someone will point at you, so all is not lost!
- Once you have made that announcement you can now depart the immediate spot.

This means:

- you can wander off to sit in the shade
- have a chat with the person selling tomatoes on the corner
- window shop
- go off and get a cup of coffee or a cone full of deep fried chips of sweet- potato.

Your place in the 'queue' is secure without you having to stand in line.

For those not used to this system it comes as a surprise when your transport arrives and people appear from nowhere to board in orderly sequence.

What I was now watching seemed to be a queue for a local camione route rather than one that was inter-city. Some people looked to be returning from work, others travelling with small children carefully lifted them up onto the tray of the lorry.

It made me realise how much we take for granted.

We frequently passed people with no Amarillo nearby who just waved local currency at us to entice us to stop. Once we did stop to collect a lady and her little girl waiting in the middle of nowhere in the blistering heat. They hadn't waved money and we didn't expect any.

The ride was gratefully accepted – in equal measure because they didn't have to ride the camione and because the car had air conditioning.

As our travels continued, we often travelled in a crammed car, transporting goodies collected along the way for the family in Havana, plus cousins, or neighbours of cousins, or friends of cousins.

On one occasion we rescued a chap whose every day was spent in anxiety about getting to work as a Night Security Guard at a school in a city many miles away from his home. He had to leave really early in the day to make sure that, if the expected camione didn't turn up, he could catch the next one.

His job depended upon regular and timely attendance. This resulted in a sort of terminal tiredness and if he was ever caught napping on the job it was instant dismissal.

Consider doing this every day but Sunday for less than $18 a month – and again thank your lucky stars.

On another trip, neighbours hastily showered and changed into best fiesta gear to attend a birthday party in a local city.

They had thought they couldn't go because of the distance and cost but one-way air-conditioned transport made it possible, enjoyable, and getting back could take whatever time it took.

My No Plan had no 'must see' destinations within it, however as with the way of No Plans, one that was on my general list of places to see one day was *Trinidad de Cuba*, and without any reference to this wish, it turned out that we were destined to go there.

Most tourists to Havana try to visit both *Pinar* in the beautiful *Viñales* valley, and Trinidad.

I had done the first part. We visited Pinar on my first trip with the group of dancing students: two and a half hours in a minibus to get there after a long night of dancing.

My photos show everyone with their heads back against the seats and cucumber slices on their eyes.

It had been a many-mojito-night after the dancing stopped the night before.

We had gone with Cuban friends through the tunnel to close out the night – or more appropriately to welcome the dawn – at the foot of the iconic two forts of the *Morro-Cabaña* Military Historic Park.

The original fort was built of soft stone that was easy to work, but this same feature proved its undoing in making it an effective fortification. It would not have repelled cannon balls and it was so porous that water seeped through it like a sponge.

The history of its construction carried on for years in the late 1500s, as successive disastrous efforts followed one upon the other, ruining the reputations of the many who were put in charge.

In the rainy season pools of water stood in the magazine, making the gunpowder unusable, so a wooden shed had to be built for its storage.

The reservoir was made of the same porous stone and was therefore completely unable to store the water to supply the fort and the city.

There was a saying in the city that as the powder magazine was always wet and the reservoir always dry, the two should be exchanged for their purposes.

Add to this the fact that the construction was not robust. It was thought that if all cannons were fired simultaneously, the reverberating shock would collapse the walls on which they stood.

The fort we visit these days was built in the 1800s.

There is just one cannon that fires at 9pm and 9am. These used to signify the closing and opening of the city gates.

It wasn't until a later trip that I saw the ceremonial firing of the fort cannon. With no city gates to close, now the 9pm cannon just marks that hour and I certainly had heard it before when walking in Havana.

We were a bit earlier than the morning cannon when we settled on the terrace of *El Mirador Bar* below the forts and beside the *La Divina Pastora* restaurant.

From here the city of Havana lay across the water, hiding its secrets and its beauty under a cloak of soft sea mist. City lights glittered in the darkness like crystal beads on a velvet ball gown.

It is one of the treasured memories of my first encounter with Cuba.

No doubt for my fellow students it was well worth the cucumber slices on eyes during the bus trip.

My eyes never got that respite. I couldn't spare a moment of photo opportunity and spent the trip capturing with my camera the roadside cameos that such a route offers.

Pinar del Rio was at first known under Spanish colonisation as *Nueve Filipinas* due to the fact that it soon became populated by Filipinos from the Manila galleons that sailed past on their Acapulco – Manila trade route.

They dropped off this new labour force in Cuba for the tobacco plantations, and brought back some precious tobacco plant seeds to Manila. It was from this source that the tobacco industry of the Philippines grew – perfecting their export product in the globally appreciated *Flor de Isabella* cigars, still sought after, worldwide.

Later, some Filipinos jumped ship to Louisiana, others moved to *Barrio China* in Havana, some intermarried throughout Cuba, and those with money either went to Spain or back to the Philippines.

The new immigrants introduced to Cuba their cotton undershirts, the spice tamarind, and a particular type of rice that is good for soups.

Our first stop in Pinar was at one of the most famous hotels outside of Havana, the *Horizontes Los Jazmines Hotel*.

Here, my fellow travellers woke to stunning views.

Standing in the hallway of this great hotel you can almost feel the presence of the many famous people who have stayed here over the centuries. Its current state is not of this standing but the views are amazing.

The pool is located at the best point to not miss any of the beauty of the valley below while swimming. It is a remarkable vista.

'*Mogotes*' – isolated haystack shaped karst limestone outcrops with imposing sheer rock faces –stand like errant carbuncles on the knotted tapestry of green below.

I have a photo of this panorama framed through a doorway of the hotel. There are glass panels of bright yellow, cobalt blue, and ruby that frame the opening.

It is a striking image – but the view remains vivid in my memory without the photo.

We didn't stay long: the food was nondescript and staff disinterested.

On the terrace at street level, coconut palm baskets and hats were laid out for sale: they made a green and gold mosaic of beautiful proportions. I thought the artwork on the hoardings alongside didn't compare.

Our next stop had been a tobacco farm and our host was genial, of a great age, fit as could be, and witty. He said his good health was due to good cigars, good rum, and good women. Having recently remarried, he said this was keeping him fit. I remember him drawing on his cigar with a smile as he watched our fascination with the big old wooden accordion player processing its music punched into a continuous stream of folded cardboard.

We had then taken a short dinghy cruise through some spectacular caves.

Of course we took the almost mandatory photo of the fellow who waited beside the ticket kiosk for that purpose together with his extremely tame and docile, but massive water buffalo in a straw hat.

So, while in the past I had explored the tiny town of *Pinar del Rio*, one of the two 'must see' points of a tourist agenda in Cuba, I had never made it to *Trinidad de Cuba*. Now, at last, I was about to visit.

I wasn't disappointed
    – but it wasn't totally as expected.

Life seldom is.

Trinidad de Cuba is a little postcard of contrasts between the tourist scene and real life: vivid colour, vivid personalities, and great photo opportunities – and in the back streets the crumbling apartment blocks common in today's Cuba.

My memory holds small cameos that give a constant reminder of how hard life can be without the opportunities we take for granted.

The colourful houses of Trinidad are a photographer's delight.

There was the musician with the cockerel on his hat, the lady in her exquisite cotton lace shawls sitting resplendent to read fortunes, the fellow with his bicycle decorated like a piece of retro art with beer can sculptures, or the clever little beer-can cameras or exquisitely hand tooled leather saddles laid out for sale – two extremes of artisan creativity.

However, there is another side to the town that gives some balance. These scenes tell of the reality of the Cuban over-crowding of existing accommodation and unemployment.

At the edge of town there is a corner that seems to be the gathering spot for men to sit and idle away the time. They were of all ages and the resignation in their posture seemed to indicate a sense of hopelessness about the future.

As we walked through the back streets of Trinidad, a man sat smoking on a doorstep behind his hand-made wheelbarrow – a large box on metal frame. I imagine he must carry the garden produce in the box when he cycles, but now it was neatly arranged for sale on the box top: two yoghurt tubs of fat tomatoes, two smaller ones of chillies, a few bananas, some leafy greens, and some spring onions.

Just over a dozen mangoes sat on a carefully smoothed paper flour bag with jute stitching, whose edge was raised to make a backdrop by resting against the nearby fire hydrant.

Further along, there was an ingenious tricycle that was a mobile produce stall. It was made from modified cycle parts. The chain went to the single back wheel above which was the saddle.

The two front wheels supported a red welded produce-frame with two shelves, the top filled with green peppers and tomatoes, and underneath ten huge papayas.

On the same street of colourfully painted houses, a chap in a well worn straw cowboy hat was buying some fresh pork from a stall on the street at the front door of one of the houses.

Cuts of meat lay in the open. They sat on a table top of wood resting on thin rods that looked to be concrete reinforcing rods. Above the meat hung a wooden plank on which slats of wood had been nailed to make slanting shelves for rolls of plastic bags. You could select one into which to stow your purchase.

Around the corner a man was painting his house. Paint being a scarce commodity, it seemed that a bit had been spared for sharing. His neighbour was on the tiled roof of the house adjacent so he could paint the same burnt sienna colour onto his house on the side that projected above the roof on which he stood.

In the back streets of Trinidad where tourists seldom go, decaying apartment blocks sit on streets that have cavernous breaks – too large to be called potholes. This makes a long route around a better choice than trying to drive through and dropping into road subsidence the size of your car.

I stayed in an apartment recently established as a tourist residence by a friend of the extended cousin group whose hospitality and generosity of spirit had framed our travels so far. It was airy, roomy, comfortable, and the catering was delicious.

By contrast, the cousins who lived in the world-weary apartment block had a different life.

I discovered that they had no bathing facilities when the two lads appeared with broad smiles asking if two good-looking chaps could take a shower in my apartment.

One cousin, a strapping lad with wide shoulders and a lovely spontaneous smile, to whom I will give the name José, had managed recently to find work. This was what amounted to hard labour. It was in the brickworks and it caused him some local ridicule.

The locals called these workers 'donkeys' because they carry heavy loads in a back-breaking regime likened to the heavy loads of mules.

José persevered despite the hard work and the derision of his friends, because he was dreaming of a new set of sneakers: literally dreaming of them each night.

On the few days that there was work available, despite the conditions he grabbed the opportunity because it was a chance to earn a few dollars. This had gone on for months and the day of purchase seemed tortuously slow in arriving as funds slowly accumulated.

The brand-name sneakers in question were on display in a store in town. José had been there several times to try them on. This made them even more vivid in his dreams. We had to go with him to see them and his expression as he handled them was one of longing.

Together with the contribution of a few hard-earned dollars from his mother, by the time I learned of his dream, José had saved almost $30. The sneakers cost $60.

It was his 19th birthday the day afterwards, so off we went to the store once more and I provided the balance. The delight on his face was something to behold.

We were about to leave the shop when there was some sort of remonstration between my Tour Guide and José.

I enquired what the problem was. It turned out that José had been about to carry the new dreamed-of sneakers out of the shop in their box.

My Tour Guide proved to share my philosophy of life when he asked why. He pointed out that should the world end while José was carrying the sneakers in a shoe box, he would have never worn them. He should put them on from the moment they were his: 'Just in case.'

I concurred.

In life, seize the moment and relish its delight.

We never know what the future may bring but we can be in control of the moment.

My photo stops are not of the pre-planned type. Many of my best images are of the inerasable type that stays in your memory to bring a smile to a grey wintery day, or one that has tested your patience or worn out your emotions.

I tend to take things as they come when travelling and not pre-plan, even when on a plan (of sorts). That isn't to say that there aren't things that I have thought I would like to see or do.

It is useful to have an idea about things you would like to do or see, or places you want to live, or performances you would love to enjoy. These 'Christmas Wish Lists', as I call them, are not written down lists for me but memoranda that I keep in my head.

I had always wanted to live in a loft apartment, so when I went to New Orleans I spent a great deal of money in rent to do so, in I what was the Old Cotton Mill. Here, I lived in an apartment with four huge windows - 4.25 metres *(14')* high and about 3meters across *(almost 10')*. Downstairs was an open plan room with a guest room under the loft and just inside the entrance – with my loft bedroom above.

Some legendary parties took place there and I was told by the then Head of the Gene Therapy Research Centre that it was the 'A List' who attended – mostly people he had never met in New Orleans, despite having lived there for more than 14 years.

Perhaps it is the way they were invited.

They all shared three attributes that I had given as prerequisites for an invitation.

144

They must:

- demonstrate generosity of spirit
- not take themselves too seriously, and
- have a sense of occasion.

Apropos the last quality of a sense of occasion, we may drink some quantity of alcohol, but it was not what one call a 'booze-up' and therefore people should behave accordingly.

Who was invited?

I had found that many of the people who parked your car in the underground parking of the city of New Orleans while you went to a meeting had two very active lives.

One was that of parking cars (they often washed mine for nothing and refused to take payment), and a night job that as profession musicians, a job that reflecting their passions while the steady day job helped pay rent.

As is my habit, I always chatted with these people and they told some fascinating tales. Each was generous with his great big welcoming smile.

I invited my favourites.

At the time, in an Economic Development role, I was working with helping competing companies in different sectors to decide on what things they could do together to help all ships rise on an improved tide of opportunity for their industry sector.

My job was to guide them in developing the trust to do so, and then develop the frameworks so these interfaces with each other worked for both sides.

I invited the most interesting of these leaders.

I was also leading the development of the Film and Music Strategy for New Orleans upon which the amazing growth of both sectors over the intervening years has been based. Our strategy saw the state Tax Laws changed to make Louisiana a more film friendly location.

It is one thing to change the law and quite another to know how it will be enacted.

We had a film company from California pose a $1.5million test case and got rulings on all of the points that needed clarification within the act – in just six weeks. I reckon that has to be a record. But that is what happens where there is a will to do so and people work together, as they do in Louisiana – and especially in New Orleans.

Because from the outset we had involved everyone relevant who we could find, including full and part-time musicians, instrument repairers, amateur and professional film-makers, music and film industry lawyers, agents, promoters, sound technicians, representatives of the Music Business Program at Loyola University, and relevant State Departments, they all understood what needed to be achieved.

When we held an event called 'The Future of New Orleans Music', the musicians told me it was the first time they had ever come together as a group.

It is a tribute to the people of the region what was, and still is being accomplished by them.

Some of the people from this group were also invited.

I dance Argentine Tango, so I invited my Tango friends.

My girlfriend Myra was at the time a University Professor. She invited the most interesting academics and her salsa dancing friends.

I have another wonderful girlfriend called Lisa – the original rock chic. She has been a journeyman backup singer for the big names – Springsteen and Bon Jovi – and boy when she sings she can stop a bar of noisy people! Lisa is also a great cook and makes terrific Cajun Food.

Lisa invited her favourite musician friends, including a really fascinating member of a UK band visiting the city. He was heavily stapled, tattooed, and with a reversed Mohawk style to his fire-engine-red hair. He was a delightful, well-mannered, and very interesting person.

We called these parties the 'Chix Parties' and they were well lubricated by two types of sangria made in big picnic coolers.

I invited a very talented guitarist to undertake a paid gig at the first of these.

I had met Frank at one of the best dancing bars in New Orleans.

I usually arrived there about 2:30 in the morning. I never knew when it opened because I went there only after exhausting all the best places down Frenchmen Street, often called the New Orleans Capital of Live Music. The music styles here range from the blues, to jazz and soul, to country, to Latin. It's a local's favourite.

When I first saw Frank he was dancing salsa with a gorgeous Brazilian girl. I was mesmerised. They made a hypnotic pair on the dance floor but what was the most puzzling was that Frank has blue eyes and blonde hair but his hips did that thing that seems to come with Latin genes (not jeans).

There is a fluidity of movement that non-Latinos usually just can't quite imitate – but here was this blonde person who was obviously not Latino whose dancing was as magically fluid as the best of them.

When the dance finished I turned back to the bar but Frank caught me as I turned and displayed that he really had adopted Latino practice. He asked me if I "Would like to try".

I had long since learned that good dancers are wary of asking someone to dance if they are unsure of their level of dance capability, and this superior approach made me grin. Suppressing my instinct to smirk, I replied that I could 'try'.

After a few minutes, he said as we danced: "You can dance!"

I replied slightly sarcastically: "What a surprise".

It was an unlikely start to an enduring friendship.

Although Frank is German, he has long lived in Mexico. He is a brilliant guitarist and good singer. He was studying jazz guitar in New Orleans after doing a similar stint in Madrid to learn Flamenco.

Years later en route to visiting family he visited me in Germany. I then learned then that he is adding to his artistic repertoire. He is now on the way to a new career as an actor.

Good friends are a delight to find. I am glad he asked me if I 'could try'.

So, we had Frank playing and people dancing and lots of talk over the sorts of wide ranging subjects to be expected of a group of people who cross all socio-economic sectors of society.

It was an unusual mix of people who may otherwise never have met but for my three criteria for being invited.

I loved my time in New Orleans. I always felt it was a lot like Cuba – but obviously it is. It was under the same governor under Spanish rule.

When I win the lottery I am going to buy an apartment in the French Quarter of New Orleans so I can visit whenever I want.

Until then I have my memories.

It is a wonderful, vibrant place to live and I am very lucky to be able to tick off my list the full experience of loft living in one of the best cities in the world.

Another thing on my not written-down list of things to do I accomplished after living three years in Germany.

I had always rather fancied living in a castle.

I mean, who doesn't?

Having to move from my city apartment a few blocks back from the Rhine in the heart of Mainz – one of my other most beloved cities – I managed to rent an apartment in a very gracious and picturesque

Schloss. A 'Schloss' is what in England would qualify as a stately home. In France it would be called a 'Chateaux'.

Ours was on the edge of the vineyards on the steep banks along the Rhine and sat above the largest labyrinth in Europe.

My apartment of the five there, was where they used to drive the trucks in to load the wine. It had been beautifully restored.

The tree in the courtyard was over 400 years old and the house was of the same vintage. It even came with a little tower with room for two cosy seats where you could look out down to the Rhine.

Some of the best and most character filled restaurants of the region were just steps from my door.

I had a great landlord and wonderful neighbours.

Balu, my Chow Chow, arrived there as a puppy and quickly found a furry friend in our neighbour and co-Schloss resident, a chocolate Labrador called Odile – Odi for short.

It was a great game for two-year-old Odi to do laps at labrador pace around the tree in the courtyard with puppy Balu just leaping out at her as she passed on each lap.

Balu then would look at Odi's owner and me as if to say: 'This is fun but she's geared to run and hasn't worked out yet that I am not – either geared up to – or running'.

When he was tiny, Balu came to work with me and slept in my laptop bag on my desk. His snoring caused smiles all down the office and some people came and took photos to prove to clients on the other end of the phone that it was Balu and not a colleague who was responsible for the snores.

Balu was still working out how the world worked when a visiting dog called Carlos arrived in our courtyard.

Like most Chow Chows, Balu is interested in other dogs in a mildly dismissive way, but Carlos fascinated him.

Carlos is as high as my hips and is a proud and friendly chap – however, when puppy Balu wandered underneath him and saw some things hanging down, he was fascinated.

Little paws reached up and used the tempting features of Carlos's anatomy as punching bags, pummelling them as neatly as would any champion boxer.

Carlos went vertical in one almighty leap.

His owner was taken unawares and wondered what had happened. My friend and I were helpless with laughter and could scarcely describe the pantomime that had taken place.

Balu and I loved living there, and we both loved the peacocks that used to drop feathers for us in the courtyard.

I have a friend who is part Cherokee and she always told me that such a feather is the bird telling you that you, too, can fly. Perhaps that is so.

As a reminder of this peacock encouragement, I have our peacock feathers (not those with the eye) gracing a vase in our home in England as I write.

It was a great place to live. There was a train to the airport at Frankfurt and good access to the autobahn for work. I could have a glass or two of wine as I visited my friends in Mainz and then catch a train home.

I thought I might stay there forever. (Remember what I said about making plans?)

But nevertheless that was my castle for several years.

Tick!

Years before, I had returned to my home city of Sydney and went looking for a place to rent.

I wanted a terrace house with iron lacework decoration, plus an open fireplace and a balcony with a view over Sydney Harbour.

Most importantly I wanted it a pretty regular rent as I was anything but wealthy.

Everyone laughed at me.

Scoffed would be a better term.

However another of my amazing friends called Karen, the mother of the children whose lives were so short, had the answer. When we both worked for an airline, she had demonstrated the knack of always finding some quirky and character-filled place to rent.

When I asked her how she did it, she imparted this wisdom that I have found to be true, and so pass it on.

There is always the type of place you want
at the price you can afford.

You just have to find it.

Find it I did, under the most unusual circumstances.

I had been gone from Australia so long that it did not occur to me after several weeks of plodding round estate agents that this particular day was Melbourne Cup Day.

Now, every Australian knows that this horse race is not for nothing called 'The Race that Stops a Nation'.

It was on that date that I found a tiny estate agent on a corner on one of the hills in McMahons Point, just across the harbour from Circular Quay – the main ferry terminus in Sydney – but on the other side of the Harbour Bridge.

Once inside I stood for a moment. There seemed to be no one there. I shuffled around a bit in case someone was in the back attending to paperwork only to find that they were: all of them.

They were attending to the Sweep paperwork in which you draw lots for the running horses of the race.It is a tradition that you all throw a few dollars into the kitty which one lucky person will win from their winning stead breaking the line first. On that day there is no more important paperwork to attend to.

I realised at once that I had been a nitwit to forget how commerce ground to a halt at this time. I therefore made apologetic noises and made to leave, but was hastily and warmly gestured into the back.

Here, everyone was watching a TV commentator prepare the nation for its biggest horse race.

Within a moment the horses were off and minutes later celebrations were due.

We all chatted happily about the race and its traditions, gave due congratulations to the Sweep winner and then they turned to me and said they supposed that I had come to look for a property.

I suggested that I go outside and come inside again and we could start again. This we did and laughingly we turned to my much scoffed at request. There was a small pause. One lass looked at another.

"What about 29 Bayview Street?"

There was a quiet discussion and they said that they knew this was due to come to market but it hadn't yet been listed.

However, since by now we were all friends they promised to pop down and speak with the then tenant to ascertain exact dates and details.

The next day I had a phone call to tell me I could have it if I took it sight unseen, but to stop it being advertised I must bring down my cash deposit payment before the following day.

Unfortunately, they couldn't actually show it to me as the resident was going to be away.

As described to me, it was a charming house and it fit my description perfectly – even having no obstructions to a wide harbour view in front, with just a boathouse between me and the harbour.

They explained that the house looked out over a little bay on the banks of which was Luna Park, the historic fun fair that sits beside the Harbour Bridge.

To the right of that, behind the Meccano-set-style bridge arches rose the sails of the Opera House.

It sounded wonderful and after our Melbourne Cup festivities bonding I trusted them, so sight-unseen, I paid the money and took it.

Once viewed, it proved even better than advertised. It needed some decorating and I stripped four layers of full gloss from the ancient staircase and refinished the natural wood. I repapered over wallpaper that was holding the wall plaster on, and invited friends for a series of dinner parties to celebrate.

Our neighbours at my parents' home further up the North Shore of Sydney were Sir David and Lady Jean Griffin. Sir David was quite a music and art aficionado, and their son Edward and I were great mates.

I was often at their place and enjoyed watching a giant koi in their fish pond. They called him Hudson. He was so named because he was the biggest fish in the pond, so was named after Hudson Fysh. This Hudson was also the biggest fish in his pond, having been one of the three co-founders and later Managing Director of Qantas.

As you can see, the two families shared a similar sense of humour.

Sir David thought I could benefit from some decent artwork, so he lent me an original Sidney Nolan of the Ned Kelly series. Before it returned to their own lovely home, for a while it hung in my tiny dining room.

Perhaps that started my love of original works, although anything like a Nolan is out of my league.

I have been fortunate to be attracted to some works of then relatively unknown artists whose creations have later become highly sought after. These works have travelled with me around the world and make wherever I am to be always 'home'.

I am still collecting. (My friends say I live in a cross between an art gallery and a library).

The Jazz Boat used to make a loop inside my little bay on its weekend cruises, and I still can recreate in memory the magical sounds of clinking of glasses, laughter and fine jazz drifting over the sparkling dark waters of the harbour.

So, some of my not written down list of 'Things to Do' have been accomplished.

I have other aspirations on my checklist of fascinations to explore in the world while still on this earth, and going to *Trinidad de Cuba* was certainly on my Cuban list.

Was it happenstance that this emerged as a destination on the wandering No Plan trip?

Or had I communicated this desire to the Universe who was complicit with my subconscious in arranging it?

No matter, I did get to tick off Trinidad from the list.

What did the Cuban Approach accomplish?

Had I not taken The Cuban Approach with a No Plan adventure I may never have been able to do so.

More than that, I got to understand Trinidad a lot more than I would have done had I just seen it as a tourist.

Most people visiting are called here for the colour and the creativity, the history of the nearby sugar cane valleys, and the music. They only see the obvious parts that are so colourfully attractive to tourists.

For me it was a different experience and was made up of the layers of viewpoint that travelling with locals enables you to identify.

This meant that I saw all of the fantastic things that one should see, and then got to balance that with some local realities. By being genuinely interested in the people of my travels I was able to understand so much more of what life holds for them.

In turn this put my own small concerns into perspective.

The trip also put me in a position to share some of the very great benefits in this life to make someone's 19th birthday dream come true. It's not every day you answer a dream – even if it means it's a dream of new sneakers.

My photo stops have left me with a repertoire of photos that when I look at them again; recreate the memories of a trip with no plan. It was a trip made easy in a country where there were no expectations of you.

Step 6 of the Cuban Approach: En- route photo stops: Capture the valuable and package the rest in humour.

It is possible for you to record memories with no camera – memories so vivid that they include all the emotions and senses of that moment in time.

Adjusting your sails: Whenever you set out on an adventure, it is important to prepare yourself so that, wherever you are you will actually *be* there.

That is not as trite as it sounds. In this era of electronic dependency most people are either looking at their phone or plugged into earphones.

The moment and its gifts pass by unnoticed, and therefore unappreciated.

I have found that as I sit and watch I learn so much about context.

It is often the sort of context that comes from watching something and thinking: "Why did they do that?" or "How do they think they are going to get that to work?" or "I wonder why...?"

It has often been the case that as I watch the answer unfolds. Sometimes it doesn't. I discover the answer later because my curiosity was piqued and I looked for the answer(s).

In this way my understanding of the world and its interactions is constantly being expanded.

If I was instead focused on passive engagement with my phone, or locked away from the world in a musical world of my own with earplugs connected, I would not be doing so.

Not that each doesn't have its place - I am just struck by the imbalance I see around me.

Many of my photos come from having had the time to wander about. In those wanderings I have the eyes of a curious person.

I believe they are also the eyes of a friendly person as it doesn't matter in what non-Asian or Middle-Eastern city I find myself, people ask me for directions. I have been flattered at being thought of as 'Parisienne' in Paris, a New Yorker, and 'Madrileña' in Madrid, German in any German city, and of course rightly thought a *Sydney-sider* in Sydney, Australia.

My curiosity has me taking in the sights as widely as I can, seeing:

- The magical coloured replica of a stained glass window cascading down an internal staircase in Havana Viejo
- A creative bunting across a road in a Bavarian village announcing the arrival home of a baby boy.
- A Rhine barge called 'Passion' near my home in Oppenheim.
- A quirky bumper sticker announcing that a classic Lada car lives on as *'el Immortal* in Havana.
- The reflection of the State Premier and the company owner in a shiny brass plaque announcing the company as proud builder of the trailers for the Prancing Horse Ferrari racing team.
- People living under bridges that a bus passed over quickly in what were then the 'New Territories' of Hong Kong.

My wanderings give me a chance to see things from a different perspective. This results in different types of photo to the traditional snaps of others hoping to capture a visual memory of a place.

My photo taking requires a bit of thoughtfulness, the time to look up, and down, and underneath and on top of things, and an ever-present readiness of the camera to capture the unexpected.

It's like life really.

Often the most rewarding things
are those that at first glance seem inconsequential
but later mark out that moment as special.

Photographs are images that are not always fully understandable without their fuller context. What they appear to reveal may be something quite different from the actual atmosphere of the moment at which the photo was taken. They can be framed in such a way as to tell a story different from reality.

It wasn't until I was back in Havana that I came upon the images that made this point clear to me.

The cousin I have called José loved to dance.
I love to dance.
My Tour Guide doesn't.

The photos he took of young José and I dancing were framed as if there was much more going on than dancing as they captured our mutual delight in dance. I was not in the market for any relationship – let alone one with a 19 year old.

In this context, I can't help but think that for some reason it suited my Tour Guide to insinuate something not there, for had I not actually been there myself, perhaps looking at the photos I may have come to other conclusions.

Again: like life really.

Depending on how you view something,
your conclusions can be coloured
by your own expectations...

and then you see what you think you see
rather than what you do.

My trip was one with enough solitude to have my mind roam into the philosophical.

Many of my stories arise from having had the time to 'stand and stare' and to absorb the environment – whether it is an internal discussion regarding the nature of fear – or long thoughts before discussion with my tour guide about the nature of this last Cuban Revolution.

In our unhurried travels we had time to talk about the revolutionaries whose eyes looked back at me across the ages in a Zapata museum.

This museum is dedicated not just to them and their sacrifice, but to the whole concept of what this revolution was supposed to mean.

We had time to ponder what that was, and then to discuss how the reality compared with that hope.

Reading the winds: Some things are self-evident.

It was evident that the daily allowance for our travel was assumed to include purchase of CDs of Reggaeton, Son, or Mambo from whatever street corner they were being sold.

THAT was self evident to my Cuban tour guide – and so it became self-evident to me.

Relative to the cost of the car rental and fuel, the CD costs were insignificant. It seemed appropriate that, since I had elected to travel in a more Cuban than tourist manner, I should accept the inevitability of such extras.

In the end these CDs came home with me.

They carry with them many vivid memories. They recreate the feeling of exhilaration of being on the road with a good companion to somewhere new and unexplored.

Often it is that which others hardly notice that gives the opportunity to capture the images that reveal the soul of a place.

That has always been self-evident to me – and became so to my Cuban tour guide.

His forward planning of what our 'No Plan' plan might comprise was therefore in constant need of adjustment, as his estimation of the time required and mine of the same became more closely aligned.

Had we not both been rather agreeable sorts such self-evident truths, each not so evident to the other, might have significantly reduced our enjoyment of the trip.

Had we a plan, we wouldn't have had the time to let the Museum of Revolution work on our thought on the subject.

I had heard all the rhetoric from official tour guides about Cuba being a revolutionary success.

I had also observed the benefit of good Cuban education and of good (though formerly much better) medical care.

On a former trip I had personally enjoyed the benefits of herbal remedies secured from a marvellous apothecary shop in Havana.

This wonderful store seems frozen in a past and more gracious era. Mahogany shelves are filled with jars of potions or their component parts. The polished wood, glass cabinets and mirrors on which gold script has remained intact for many decades, send a visitor far into the past the moment they step inside.

However, although appreciating the amazing progress made in post-Revolutionary Cuba where people are generally much better off than most were in the past, I also had seen enough of Cuban life to balance both the rhetoric and the reality.

The conclusion I came to was that Cuban society is very complex and no one single person seems to have its map. Everyone seems to have a piece of the story of how to get from here to there. Together, they weave their parts to make a semblance of the bigger picture.

This helps to understand how to achieve the final outcome to remedy whatever situation they are facing.

In all my travels there, I never met anyone who had more than a ragged and well-worn corner of this map of the whole. Perhaps it is because it is a map that is constantly evolving, but, whatever the cause, it made everyday life strikingly different from the sometimes over-regulated society of much of our world where such routes are clearly dictated.

In previous trips I had heard stories that described some of the Cuban routes. Let's together explore a few:

How to get to prison without trying:
Be in the wrong group at the wrong time when others decide you will be the patsy.

How to respond to prison life:
When in prison remain calm and get through the ordeal. If you don't and panic you'll be treated harshly. Keep a low profile.

Watch carefully and read the moment to know how to respond to the situation as things happen.

How you are supplied and fed:
If you have no family to bring to the prison your food, toothbrush, bedding, toiletries – or no one who cares to do so, you do without. As long as you have water, after a day the body adjusts and starts taking its needed glucose from your liver and muscles, but by day five the abdominal pain can be debilitating.

How to get through the endlessly boring days:
Read.
It doesn't matter what.
Just read anything you can find.

How to get out of jail:
If the Red Cross is inspecting – after being cautioned to do so and if you are lucky enough to be asked – give the right answers (that: 'of course you have enough food, and are well cared for').

This can get you out of jail faster than telling the truth and getting out (maybe, if you live long enough) via the Red Cross.

Another example of a route on the Cuban map of life is how to get a particular type of job that gives you opportunities to work elsewhere than in Cuba.

How to get the job you really want:
Follow the stated process and wait (and wait, and wait).

Buy someone a $350 camera/microwave/ or something else of different but substantial value - that puts you in a favourable light to advance up the queue (It's called 'encouragement').

Every country has its own variations of these unmapped routes.

Cuba is no exception.

Rhetoric is useful. It is the marketing mask under which lies the reality that is often at variance with descriptions of historical events.

Every country has a particular image it wants to present to the world, and to its own people, and Cuba is no different.

However the 'official story of Cuba' and the one you can witness for yourself, quickly illustrates the contrast.

As a traveller on the non-tourist routes of Cuba I saw much of this, and kept my opinions to myself when confronted by statements of revolutionary zeal that contradicted what I had seen.

I think that Mark Twain was right, and I wish some business leaders, as well as political ones speaking empty rhetoric, would also take his advice:

Don't tell fish stories
where the people know you;

but particularly,
don't tell them where they know the fish.

CHAPTER SEVEN

Unexpected routes

Detours and discoveries

Trusting my instincts, I felt sure that the wind that blew towards the open road was not one that foretold anything but an interesting trip, wherever it might take us. However, no route is a certainty and no simple task is always able to be accomplished as planned.

Detours are everywhere in life.

Therefore, my No Plan was not devoid of the underpinning framework – the slack wire I previously mentioned – on which to hang it safely. That way, no matter where the route led, the basics were in place.

Like many people, I generally work on the basis that if you take an umbrella the likelihood of rain diminishes.

This extended reasoning – that a little pre-planning for when your detour takes you into danger or extreme inconvenience –may mean you will never have resort to that trustiest, and most loved of all companions of the experienced traveller: Plan B.

First, I believe it is important that people know where you are, in general terms –and how you can be reached.

It is equally important that you know how to contact the world with which you are familiar should you really need to.

In my case I had a good reason for also thinking about the medical side of things. I have allergies to certain insects, spices, moulds and medications and wear a Medic Alert bracelet. This gives a toll-free number to call 24/7 to get detailed advice. It was therefore important that my tour leader knew what to do in a medical emergency.

Going into anaphylactic shock is never a pleasant experience, but in a remote part of Cuba it could be more serious, especially if no one knew that I had antidote medication with me.

Plan B is useful if you suddenly find yourself unable to withdraw money.

This happened to me at one bank in Havana when I was still in my parking place, my hotel.

I lived at the time in Germany where cash transactions are common. There, as with other European countries, many small enterprises accept no payment other than cash.

Cash is always a good idea.

However, most people don't want to carry a sock-full of cash with them (one of my favourite friends being the exception). Jane's sock of folded banknotes is a delightful illustration of her personality.

The sock has joined us on many fantastic international explorations. It has each day's allocation of funds bound with elastic bands, and anything left over goes into the next day's allocation. It's a sock version of a rollover bingo.

Many a memorable activity has been enjoyed because we had available cash in local currency.

In view of this. I had therefore armed myself with a certain amount of dollars as a small fund that could be supplemented before I left Havana on my No Plan adventure.

On this occasion, when I tried to undertake what had formerly been a simple transaction at a Cuban bank, the bank teller shook his head.

This card won't work, he said. I blanched. If I couldn't withdraw money from my credit card (the usual thing to do in Cuba) what to do?

I remembered that you can transfer money by Caribbean Transfers from outside countries into Cuba to a Cuban. I had Cuban friends who could perhaps receive it for me. Perhaps my friends in Germany could wire the money and I could pay them back on my return.

Having this Plan B calmed the initial concern, which appeared first in a level of anxiety approaching panic.

As it turned out, this was a Plan B not needed, but it was comforting to think I had one. Whether or not it would have worked is a mute point, but it soothed jangled nerves at the time.

I walked to another bank and underwent the exact same procedure. With a signature and a smile money passed across the counter.

It pays to have grown up believing that although there might be one answer given, there may be others that are equally valid.

I was to have a similar experience right at the end of the trip when I needed to increase my overdraft again by securing cash locally.

This time it was not a bank in a main city but in the suburbs of Havana at Miramar.

The procedure went through smoothly but this branch required the finished transaction (which, by reading upside down, I had seen had been already approved by my bank) to be signed off by a bank officer.

This was a young woman who wore her authority with the full seriousness of the party machine.

First of all the teller had to wait.

It was not that the young woman in authority was visibly doing anything.

Waiting seemed merely a function of putting other people into a state of due appreciation of the importance of her position. After about five minutes, she finally deigned to handle the paperwork.

It is important not to respond to deliberate antagonism when you are a visitor in another culture. Fortunately, I grew up being teased to distraction to entice me to lash out.

The secret is not to ever let such a person know how successful they are being and to maintain supreme composure – at all costs.

I have a big brother.
He trained me!

To my tourist eye it seemed apparent that there would be some mistake before Miss 'I-am-in-charge-here' even glanced at the documents.

Finding none, she looked at me with supreme indifference and asked for my Immigration Visa.

It was stored safely in my apartment in Havana. In all my seven trips to Cuba I had experienced its use merely to get into and out of the country. It had never been required for anything else.

I said I didn't have it with me.

She shrugged and told me in the tones of one speaking to a very silly child that it was very important to show it.

With supreme satisfaction she declared that she could not authorise the withdrawal without it.

With very penetrating eye contact, I responded that in the last four weeks of money transactions it had never been necessary.

She told the teller it was impossible.

I repeated my stand. It was obvious I was not leaving without the money that had already been processed by my bank.

The teller was not slow on the uptake. In confirmation he gestured to the approval documents. His point was clear but unstated. It would take an impossible amount of paperwork to undo an already cleared financial transaction on a nicety of her choosing. She stared at the documents again and found a small error in the way he had written something. With delight she pointed it out, sternly lecturing him in front of me.

He was obviously used to it and it made absolutely no impact. As she departed he made a friendly comment to her.

She made no response except to turn and tell me in future it was essential to have my visa
> – which of course it isn't
> –unless the supervisor says it is!

165

It is not just in foreign lands that what should easily achievable turns out to be quite the opposite.

Some years before my one month in Cuba with no plan, my partner died while we were on holiday in Mexico.

Knowing that he would not be emerging from the hospital alive, and knowing also that I did not have very much money, when he realised the imminent nature of his departure from this world, he told me to take $500 per day from his American Express card.

He had given me instructions about how to find his English family and how to handle his ashes. These activities would require some funds.

To enact these wishes meant travelling on to London as we had planned, meeting a family I did not know, and arranging events according to his last wishes.

It also meant travelling with my carry-on bag, his carry-on bag, my winter coat, his winter coat, and both our suitcases – plus the container with his ashes.

As if this was not enough challenge, I had been also entrusted with the container with his mother's ashes.

He had procrastinated about interring them as promised some years beforehand, and this had been part of the reason for our trip. That duty now also fell to me.

At this point, niceties went out the window.

Mother went in the suitcase.

I arrived with this excessive baggage at London Heathrow. Before collecting my rental car (which I could pay for with my credit card) I went to the Currency Exchange with my supply of Mexican money.

London Heathrow, the busiest airport in the world, could not exchange pesetas: not at any of the two agencies to which I pushed my overloaded trolley. I was therefore credit-worthy but cash disabled.

A day later, I went to the corner bank in a small Shropshire village. They changed the pesetas with a smile, no service charge, and no preamble.

Sometimes you need to make your own detours.

'Around'
is often the quickest way through.

Now, the further inland we travelled on my no plan we met few rental cars like ours. Instead, the vehicles and their loads were more varied.

We passed a man riding a four stroke motorbike towing a sturdy metal trailer that was a piglet transporter.

Four pigs were uncomfortable crammed into the space, one lying atop the three below. Two were facing forward and two back.

Little curly tails poked out at each end under a worn piece of rubber tarpaulin, and as we passed my heart went out to them.

A young woman drove an ox cart carrying her and a young man in jeans and rubber Wellington boots, both perched above a load of solid tree roots that had been cut into chunks.

The tray on which they and their load travelled was a roughly-made wooden platform. Rope mesh held the load. It was attached to two rough-hewn poles lashed to each side of the tray. This was in turn tied to a perpendicular upright at each corner.

In a small hamlet, a horse-drawn cart on rubber wheels had pulled into a roadside filling station where air was what was on offer, not fuel.

The young piebald horse wore a heavy-duty hame, or collar, to which the shafts of the wagon behind were attached.

Hames for a horse shouldn't be the same as those for oxen because the gait of each animal is so different. However, I learned that for people with few resources that made it challenging to have hames for each animal, sometimes an ox hame was turned upside down for a horse – and in this case it seemed they had done so. This upside-down fitting is fine for light loads such as the wagon, but for heavy field work, or pulling heavy loads, it would cause a great deal of chafing and wear.

A young man with an air hose strode out into the heat and checked both tyres, filling the failing one first while the young woman who was passenger leaned over the cart edge to watch.

The driver sat pensively facing forward, hand on chin. I wondered where his thoughts were travelling.

I noticed that they had strung a hessian sack as a poo collector behind the horse and understood the value of not wasting such valuable compost.

We passed several ox carts. One had stopped so the driver could talk to a cowboy on horseback and it gave me a chance to look at how carefully the individual yokes had been cushioned by rolled fabric to protect against chafing the neck.

Mostly ox yokes are hand carved from wood to fit the individual animal. These two had metal nose rings attached to the yoke to keep the oxen head in place. The oxen were pulling what looked like a recycled tractor wagon, still with its heavy-duty mud tyres and a sturdy tray.

The tray had metal holders along the side into which thin saplings had been inserted to hold in place the load of similarly cut wooden staves.

The roadside cattle looked to be Zebu or hybrids of the breed. Their floppy ears, big flapping fold of skin under the neck and fatty hump are distinctive. They are well suited to high temperatures and I was familiar with them from the similar climate of tropical northern Australia.

Further along several gentle calves with huge carved wooden nose rings came to investigate our car and have their photos taken.

They were brindle brown and on one there was a trace of blood where the wooden ring attached to the nose.

Putting a wooden ring on an animal must be a painful process, and unlike the metal nose rings put in by vets where I had lived, I thought this must have indeed been an ordeal.

My thoughts wandered back to the happy times when I lived on a small farm in Iowa.

My neighbours Keith and Jeanette Loney had Santa Gertrudas cattle that Keith fondly called 'them floppy-eared bastards'.

Santa Gertrudas come from a crossbreed of Texas Longhorns, and Herefords that were then cross-bred with Zebu – hence the floppy ears. Their name comes from *Los Cerros de Santa Gertrdudis* which was the Spanish property where they were bred. This later became the famous Texas 'King Ranch'.

Whenever Keith and Jeanette bought a bull, they named him after the person from whom it was purchased.

One day I called Keith to tell him that from my farmhouse atop the hill I could see that his bull called Edward was in the neighbour's corn field.

Edward has previously stopped all traffic on our switchback track that travelled over the hills past both our houses en route to the small hamlet of Haverhill that had once been a thriving railway freight hub for local farmers.

The general store cum diner cum gas station that was the main focal point of the little town stood beside the grain silo. These two were about the summation of the town's remaining commerce. There probably hadn't been much that had changed in decades.

I loved this wonderful store. You could buy all sorts of things inside and lick an ice cream as you did.

A hand-drawn picture of Haverhill graces the locally created recipe book that is still well-used in my kitchen wherever my current residence is located. In this way I am always connected with the wonderful people who filled my life at this time.

169

At the time when he blocked the whole route to and from this thriving metropolis, Edward just lay down on the small bridge in the valley between our farms and declined to move for some time, despite having his genealogy described in colourful terms by a frustrated Keith.

Now, Keith arrived to return Edward from the corn to our field where he cohabited with my two Quarter Horses and a Pinto that was on recuperative leave, having been found tethered to an empty water trough.

When found, this poor horse was no more than skin and bone. I had agreed that he could stay in our field free of charge on the basis a farrier came the next day to deal with his terribly overgrown and probably very painful unkempt hoofs.

The farrier came and gradually the horse fattened up and realised life could be quite fine after all.

When he first arrived, I had asked his name.

No one knew it. They said I could name him.

To everyone's horror I called him 'Catastrophe', but as I explained, it was only on the basis that when he was back in form we could drop the first part and just call him 'Trophy'.

He was in Trophy condition now and watched curiously as events unfolded.

Keith was a solid Iowa farmer whose gruffness had scared me when I first moved there. It hadn't taken long to find that under his tough exterior he was a kind and gentle soul but one who didn't suffer fools gladly. I now met him in the yard and we headed off towards where Edward had escaped.

Keith turned to me.

"I'll get him back in the field and if he comes up towards you just shoo him back down again".

I weigh 58 kilos, *or 127 lbs.*

A mature Santa Gertrudas bull weighs around 907 kilos, *or just short of 2,000 lbs.*

I stared at Keith.

"Look at me Keith!" I held my arms out and gestured down my body. "How am I going to scare a fully grown bull?"

Keith glared back, muttered, "Just do it" and stomped off down the hill.

It was a hot summer day and I always loved the view from where I was now standing, so I stared of into the distance and then looked across at my large vegetable garden.

The neighbours on the other side of the road had calves that were also escape artists and their recent adventure had led them right across my vegetable patch. Looking at my reconstructed garden now, I could see that the plants were well recovered. It gave me satisfaction to know that despite their best efforts to the contrary I would have lots to bottle for the winter.

It was a delight to me in the snowy winters to open my large basement larder cupboard and see neat rows of bottled, jewel-like vegetables.

We also had an apple tree that was a favourite of my two horses. The filly had learned at a young age how to jiggle the gate catch with her leg so she could dine alfresco under the tree.

Several times I returned home from work to find her lying contentedly beneath fewer apples on the branches than when I had left. Now, in the quiet of the summer day, I did a quick check to see if she had relieved the branches of any more.

A bit lower down the hill was the cherry tree. Seeing it reminded me that I would soon have to start amassing bottles for my famous cherry brandy that was a Christmas present much sought after by my friends.

These reveries had taken a while, and I wondered how Keith and Edward were getting on.

As I set out in their direction to find out, suddenly the whole horizon below the hill crest where I stood started to be filled by an emerging image of a very big Santa Gertrudas bull.

Edward was plodding steadily towards me, head down and making loud exhalations of breath. He had evidently been scolded roundly by a very cross Keith and was headed away from him as fast as he could.

Not knowing anything about dealing with bulls, except that one preferred not to, I stood straight up, raised my hand at Edward and yelled indignantly:

"You stop right there and go back".

A startled Santa Gertrudas bull stopped in his tracks, stared at me apologetically as if to excuse himself, and then turned and trotted back down out of sight.

I think that was a tribute to the good nature of the breed and not to my abilities at cattle handling.

Here in Cuba, these young bull calves looked equally docile as would a Santa Gertrudas – but it was not something I wanted to test in trying to be sure of their breed.

Nevertheless, thinking back to Edward, I thought it was a bit of a life lesson.

As the Willie Nelson song says:

Know when to hold 'em,
know when to fold 'em,
know when to walk away
and when to run.

In the case of Edward the bull on that particular day, standing your ground was the right thing.

It just as easily may not have been – and on that occasion I hadn't even thought of Plan B.

Passing these Cuban bull calves, further on we saw a group of six cowboys herding some cows. They were escorted by eager dogs that were obviously well-trained to keep out of the way unless needed.

Not all transport we saw en route was by domestic animal, unless man is also so classified.

Twice, we passed men pushing heavily laden wheelbarrows: one in the rain with no raincoat had a load of onions in two large, worn, plastic fertiliser bags – the other in a location equally distant from any housing, with a heavy load of bamboo still in leaf.

In each case this seemed like long distance haulage.

We passed many different types and makes of tractor – none of them new, and some with really peculiar looking improvised additions.

One was a bright blue metal box that looked as if it was a sort of bus with air cooled sides – or perhaps a mobile office that would be plopped down on site on a state-owned cooperative farm.

On one horse-drawn wagon two young men sat – one with his bike tucked in behind him having hitched a ride in the heat.

I had seen a bicycle tied onto the side of a steam roller in Trinidad and wondered if that was in case they ran out of fuel – an ever present risk.

These hardships make for colourful photos but reveal a life devoid of the niceties we take for granted.

I thought back to the eyes of the dead freedom fighters and their hope.

Hope is a mysterious thing.

It keeps us going against awful odds.

But as General Gordon Sullivan so rightly expressed in his book of the same name that records his philosophy in restructuring the US Army in times of reduced budget and changed adversaries:

Hope is not a method.

In the case of the Cuban revolution there was much 'method' employed in its immediate aftermath: new housing for poor rural people, literacy for all, improved public health – much was achieved.

I saw now the fraying of that fabric under the winds of change that saw a US Trade embargo, the loss of aid following the breakup of the Soviet Union, and the ambivalence that China's interventionist 'help'.

I thought of the 'Method' of the Chinese fan saga.

Everyone who can have a fan in Cuba has a fan.

It's hot.
    It's muggy.
        A fan helps.

For those who are ill, or for newborns, a fan helps a lot.

However, Cuban fans were all of a certain age.

China pointed this out.
    They offered to supply brand new fans.
        Free.

The catch? *Free always has a catch.*

I have been known to frequently decline free, because I have learned it can prove to be very expensive.

In this case, the catch was that all old fans were banned from use and had to be handed in.

Great we think. Good deal.

Yes – as long as the new fans work.
    Work they did, but not for long.

Now the fan repair shops are even busier than before.

The new fans have not been built as hardily as the old ones.

Not all can be fixed.

Now lots of people
      who truly *need* a fan
         haven't got a fan.

Lots more people
      who would just really *appreciate* a fan
         haven't got a fan.

It is an example of the paradox of the poor everywhere who are 'helped' by those whose interest is only marginally that of helping.

It is like the paradox of being without funds and not being able to buy food in economical packages because the cash flow doesn't allow a big purchase. This way, one is constantly hand-to-mouth, living week by week within the slimmest of budgets.

This had happened to me: twice.

Most recently I recall not being able to afford a big bag of dog kibble for Balu. The big bags were cheaper, but totally out of reach on an income that had me save for months so I could go out to a country pub for my birthday and afford a hot chocolate.

The history of why I found myself in that situation is summarised in the fact that I had left my previous residence with a suitcase and a dog. Anyone can connect the dots as to why one would do that.

I had real empathy for those caught in the fan debacle.

The 'Method' seems to have failed on many levels: sugar is another. Dependence on sugar made the nation's economy to draw upon a major single source of revenue.

This single market was first in Spain, then after independence from Spain, to the United Sates until 1959, and later, with subsidised prices until its collapse, in the Soviet Union.

In 2002, with the closure of sugar mills, around 60,000 people were laid off. The associated push for self-employment has had variable results.

Ostensibly there is the right for *paladares* (in-home restaurants) to operate, but in fact in many cases it has been reported that the officials limit their licensing approvals to operation only in 'out of season' periods.

This ensures no competition to state-run beach cafés from which the profits provide local benefit – but possibly mostly to those who implement the rules.

Another 'Method' is property transfers.

The previous restrictions on property transfers meant that the way around getting a new house was often marriage and divorce.

This is apparently how it worked.

The property owner would marry the purchaser. After some period they would legally become divorced. Then, the buyer would get legal title and the seller would get the cash.

In the case of not being able to own more than one property, at least one person I met had got divorced so the house of a parent could be owned by the other partner and rented out as a *'casa particular'*.

Hope may not be a method, but where the 'Method' provided fails – innovative alternatives are usually able to be found in some way.

Seeing the myriad transport challenges on the back roads of Cuba, and visiting people whose livelihood was minimal, gave me some insight into another aspect of living in a country where hope has taken a new and different form.

One of my friends from an early visit described this to me. He had been a young and active participant in the Revolution. He asked me about the changes I had seen over my many visits.

My reply was as positive and diplomatic as I could be.

He responded that he believed that the Revolution had brought improvements: particularly in education and health care.

What saddened him was that in the worn fabric of a hoped for future, where even these improvements were degrading, the young of his country now saw their future not in Cuba but in other lands. His own son was in Chile.

It was in this context that I was happy for my detours to be based on the wish of my Tour Director to use our travels to supplement the lifestyle of his extended family. To this end, at the end of our travels, we loaded the car with a range of goods to take back to Havana.

This involved so many detours that I almost lost count. It was like a major military manouevre to collect all the treasures my tour guide was bringing home with the proceeds of his fees.

We stopped to get real coffee from the growers. This meant another detour back to another cousin who had managed to get some from a friend of a friend.

The coffee grown in Cuba – a coffee that in the past was of very high quality – is an important part of the Cuban ration. However, these days it is reputedly diluted with whatever beans are available on the day, with ensuing degradation of flavour.

The result is that sadly, in a country where the coffee itself is premium quality, the locals don't get to enjoy it as such.

My friends treasured the Dallmayr coffee I had brought with me from Germany due to the trouble of getting decent coffee on previous trips. After I returned home from this trip, before I also fell on difficult times, they e loved receiving their Christmas packages with spices, coffee, and good quality chocolates.

While this best quality coffee was being procured from the grower, I watched a local bar set up in what at first looked like a shipping container on an empty plot of land between the grey apartment blocks of the Trinidad most tourists don't see. On closer inspection it was a clever construction of sheets of steel, planked wood and corrugated iron: a sort of imitation version of a container.

This was on a road that was formed of large irregular shaped slabs that had broken loose and were creeping down the hill at competing paces, leaving great gashes of clay beneath. The resulting hollows could engulf a small car.

The grey apartment blocks on each side of the street were of decaying concrete that seemed to have an advanced form of blistering eczema.

The 'container' bar obviously had a good local customer base. People gathered, chatting together as the proprietor of this unlikely establishment served coffee and beer (on tap). I wondered about their lives. It was a long way from the tourist places in the heart of town.

In fact, the heart of town seemed sad to me for the grandeur it had once boasted, and the vestiges that are left.

Trinidad has always been colourful – for its style of architecture and for its personalities.

Visitors usually explore the *Palacio Cantero* just off the central square. It is now the general Municipal Museum of the town but was once the extravagant home of Justo *Germán Cantero*.

Although Cantero had arrived in Trinidad under a cloud of speculation about his past, he had a winning personality and was soon within the inner circle of the three most powerful men of the city: *Don Pedro Iznaga, Jean Guillaume Bequer*, and *Don Jose Mariano Borrell*, who was Count of *Guáimaro*, a city in *Camagüey* province about one third of the way from the most southerly tip of Cuba.

Bequer was actually born John William Baker in Philadelphia. He changed his name when taking Spanish citizenship in 1819.

If you wonder why, new settlements could be very lucrative for Europeans.

To give some idea of the sort of wealth the slave trade supported, Bequer had intended to inlay gold doubloons in the floor of his new mansion. He wisely didn't because he was advised by the authorities that this would mean improperly walking on the Spanish Coat of Arms.

However, of the three it is he who contributed most to the civic organisation and infrastructure of the town. The investment to build the long-lasting cobbled streets of Trinidad we still walk upon is attributed to him.

They were indeed a colourful trio now joined by another colourful personality. By 'colourful', I allude to the many stories of local history and one such gives us some insight.

Apparently Don *Pedro Iznaga* liked to dine nude on the rooftop patio entertained by dancing and singing slaves. According to records he was rather grossly over-weight.

Possibly understandably, his young wife fell in love with Cantero.

Upon the death of Don Pedro, rumours suggested that the two lovers had poisoned him so they could live together and enjoy his fortune.

It makes a fine story.

Despite Don Pedro's oddities, at least one person felt he had some merit, even if it were just that he 'deserved to be rich because he knew how to enjoy his wealth'. This view was expressed by another personality of the city in that era, the Spanish Galician *Ramón de la Sagra*, who was a Professor of History at the time he wrote this summation.

Perhaps he shared the love of excess that Don Pedro demonstrated. Sagra travelled extensively in the Americas before settling in Paris, where he wrote and published copiously.

His interests were varied and he wrote of:

- His travels in America and extensive investigations into primary school education.
- Health care and prisons in Belgium and the Netherlands.
- The History of Cuba – a massive volume.

Sagra also started the first-ever recorded Anarchist Journal in 1845 (quickly shut down by the Duke of Galicia).

In a sort of yo-yo of: 'We don't want him, you have him'

- he was first expelled to Spain in 1849 by France for spreading socialist ideas, and then
- in 1856 by Spain to France for spreading 'radical' ideas.

In Paris he worked as the Consul General for Uruguay and at that time met Karl Marx and Friedrich Engels. It is unclear whose thinking influenced whose – but one could assume it was a lively intellectual swap meet.

Ramón de la Sagra came again to Cuba briefly, but then returned to Switzerland where he died aged 73. It had been a rich and influential life.

With the death of Don Pedro Iznaga, his fortune enabled Cantero to renovate the house now known as Palacio Cantero. It had originally been the home of Maria Fernandez de Lara Monserrate and Borrell.

As you see, the stories of these men are closely intertwined.

Apart from the beauty we now see, Cantero reputedly installed a marble bathtub with cherubs from whose mouths came gin for the men and cologne for the women *(in other words both for the benefit of the men!)*.

For a while it was Camelot,
but Justo Germán Cantero lost it all.

Given the level his extravagances, even the fortune Cantero inherited and managed couldn't last.

But he did go out in style. As a final shrug against his impending penury (his survival of same being something of which I cannot find a record), he threw one last magnificent feast with lots of dancing and extravagant food.

Apart from the legacy of the architectural magnificence that the wealth of his sugar plantations enabled Justo Germán Cantero to bestow on Trinidad, he left a rich and enduring literary heritage. His books 'The Book of the Sugar Mills' and 'The Book of Inventions' are treasures now kept in vaults for the lucky researchers who can appreciate them.

These books were illustrated with lithographic plates illustrated by the talented *Eduardo Laplante,* a Frenchman who came to Cuba aged about 30 in 1848. His lithographs now number but a handful, and they are worth a great deal of money.

According to two artists retracing the lost patrimony of the valley of the sugar mills, two original editions of Cantero's book 'mysteriously disappeared' from the Palacio de Junco in the Museum of Matanzas in 1993'.

There is always a trade in fine art – and often it is an illicit one that steals the patrimony of its home country.

Cantero was indeed an extravagant man who indulged his senses and those of his friends with great events and fine dining.

In the words of Jennie Churchill:

We owe something to extravagance,
for thrift and adventure seldom go hand in hand.

The more I read about the guests who frequented Palacio Cantero, I can't help but think about what it would have been like to be present amongst such amazing thinkers and creative people as those who attended the grand and lavish dinners and festivities hosted there.

It is a sad contrast to the back streets of Trinidad now.

Two young girls appeared: one on brand new roller skates. She wobbled down the only piece of footpath smooth enough to do so in a three-block area, her friend watching carefully. I knew that in Cuba most likely the girlfriend would soon be borrowing the skates herself – property there being considered to be communal rather than in our countries where such things belong to one person.

When my Tour Director returned, I was smiling as I recalled the many girlfriends who had helped me wobble along life's sometimes pot-holed pathways.

I think it to be true that 'we have some friends for a reason, some friends for a season, and some friends for a lifetime'. To me, all three types of friends are precious for the moments we have shared, the way our hearts buoyed the other in times of doubt, and how they added sparkle to the great times.

My friends have coloured my life and kept my heart singing.

When the coffee arrived back at the car carefully wrapped in a miscellany of paper, it had to travel inside the car.

An empty fish cooler was taking up most of the room in the boot/trunk – so that the onions for which we had made another detour got stacked on top of the cooler.

The next detour was to a small hamlet where the woodworkers had been busy making a TV stand that my Tour Director had ordered some days before.

When we were first there, they had been busy trying to design it without benefit of a measure.

I suddenly came into my own when I was able to produce my paper IKEA tape measure.

I keep it folded in my wallet on the basis that one never knows when one might need such a thing.

Mary Poppins and her magic bag can compete fairly with me, and mine.

This was the family whose toilet conditions had caused some embarrassment by being somewhat primitive.

The house was quite large and accommodated an extended family in residence, including grandmamma who was undergoing chemotherapy for cancer. She was thrilled with the booty of bread and fruit that we had brought with us from our last lodging.

En route, my Tour Director had told me that he had been visiting this house sporadically over his whole lifetime and it had never changed.

As we drew up outside on our very first visit he repeated in a sort of bewildered tone but one tinged with resignation: "Nothing has changed, Paquita".

He stared at the house for a few minutes and repeated, "In thirty years, nothing has changed".

He later told me how determined he was to pursue his dream of a different future, better than one where he felt you could hope for no change for the better.

I hope he is on the way to developing it for himself.

I believe we all should have dreams of a better future, and my last words at the airport were those of the Dalai Lama: "You must never give up".

On this return trip to the woodworking cousins, the kitchen had been stripped bare. All the pots had been scrubbed with sand and a worn bit of steel wool until they gleamed. They now stood to dry in the sunshine outside.

The unpainted concrete kitchen was next. It was in the process of being scoured, top to bottom.

The house pig lay pensively in his dusty hollow, tied by a thin rope. His upturned and rather battered empty food dish lay tilted at the last angle he had created while emptying the contents.

The two-ring burner also stood outside while the cleaning operation took place. Beside it was the Cristal can filled with petrol that had served as a lamp when all the power went out for the second time on the day of our first visit. The power outage was such a regular occurrence for them that this unusual lantern scarcely caused comment.

On the wide wooden veranda, beautifully made chairs waited for their new owners to collect them. Having seen the extremely rudimentary workshop, complete with thin paper templates carefully stored on a nail driven into the central support post, I was impressed with the quality of the end product. Tall backed and beautifully carved, the chairs stood as sentinels, guarding the busy doorway.

In the front room was a telephone and above it a sign that said that if you don't have the money to pay for the call, please don't ask for credit. Perhaps it was the only 'public' phone in the hamlet. It certainly was getting regular use from the various people who arrived on the doorstep.

The finished TV stand my Tour Director had ordered on our first visit came 'flat-packed'. We gathered about as all the parts were duly assembled.

There were lots of approving nods and comments as wooden dowels fitted into perfectly accurate holes and then it was all disassembled again before being stored in what limited spare space was left in the car.

Our bags now had to be moved to the back seat and then stacked high to allow for the two cousins who had heard we were going back to Trinidad. They were in their best party clothes because our transportation had made a big night out possible.

Delivering them in Trinidad at their destination, we then made another short detour to collect a special type of fish, freshly caught. It was to be stored on ice in the cooler that had travelled with us in anticipation.

This detour was to a back coastal section nearby where someone supposedly knew someone who had a catch and would spare a fish for cash – and so we went from house to house.

I hadn't realised that the coast was so near to Trinidad, but La Boca – literally 'the mouth'– is where the *Cañas* River empties into the Caribbean after tumbling a short distance from the nearby mountain range.

La Boca is just 7km (nearly 4 ½ miles) from Trinidad. My reason for thinking the coast was further away was that I hadn't consulted my map.

Instead I was judging on the length of time it took to get to *Playa Ancon*, where we had gone a few days before with our bathing suits and towels and with a cousin in tow.

Playa Ancon is double the distance and has lovely white sand beaches.

Here you can rent a sun lounger under a *palapa*, the palm-thatched open-sided sunshade common on South American beaches.

We lay at the far end of the beach away from ghetto blasters and the small crowd closer to the resort.

The big drawback of *Ancon* was the really awful toilets: too many people using a tiny facility.

However, there were cold drinks available and you could buy a coconut from a beach vendor if you wanted.

We were divided from the main tourist area by a long sort of fence – except it was lying flat and not upright. Where it terminated at the shore-end it formed a cover for a pile of hole-pitted rocks cemented together and sheltered under the resulting flat topped triangle.

Like so many things in Cuba I had no idea what purpose the whole thing served and neither did anyone else.

I was pretty much shaded under my hat, long having given up being a sun-baby having learned the lessons of too much sunshine in my native Australia. The lads revelled in the whole experience as we sat at the water's edge sipping our drinks and soaking up the beauty of the place.

Leaving the beach, we drove along the road that hugged the coastline. Here, we passed another example of creativity in action and backed up to explore it.

On a stretch of what looked like tidal plain, fiercely jagged and twisted forms of the karst coastline had made a sort of moonlike crater edge between land and sea.

One small inlet still had large pools of brackish water that would lie under the hot sun until refreshed by the next high tide. Here, there was a very small section of pure white, sandy beach. This sat above the dark pocked rocks that must have made a great habitat for all sorts of sea creatures that rode out the tides.

At the ocean edge before a low drop off it was as if the ocean mermaids had arranged a frill of white coral to soften the panorama. This bank of coral revealed that a reef shielded the bay from the worst storms.

I knew from living in a coastal hurricane zone in both Galveston, Texas, and in the Whitsundays of north eastern Australia, when a hurricane hits, the oceans get turned upside down: complete reefs suddenly empty their content onto exposed land.

In the midst of this coastline of weirdly contorted aerated, grey rock, the tiny inlet had captured all the purest white sand onto which past storms had heaped loads of stark white coral onto the only clear area of shoreline.

Walking onto the sand it proved to be not as fine as that of the beach we had just left. It was gritty and flecked with bits of the twisted rocks and coral – but had no trace of any small shells.

The way this little beach area sat in a forbidding coastline was one of those oddities of nature and reminded me of life generally.

In the middle
of the least prepossessing circumstances
there is often beauty to be found.

Sandy beaches under a Cuban sun reflect the sunshine with blinding intensity. This was made even more remarkable by the lush green coastal vegetation which flanked this one on either side.

An enterprising chap had decided to possess this area as his personal art gallery of 'found art'. His bike lay against a bush with succulent fat leaves of dark green, so perhaps he commuted all the way from Trinidad. His art gallery was marked out by a wall of stacked coral.

The walkway from the road was made in the same way, to escort travellers 'inside'.

Beside this pathway of sand, the artist had placed several evenly-spaced long-leafed coastal plants.

I wasn't sure if these were actually planted, or just leaves stuck in the sand, but the fact that they hadn't wilted suggested they were permanent.

Within the flat, gritty crescent boundary coral fence to his gallery, our artist had stacked rocks and coral into a series of unrecognizable shapes that to him each told a story.

As with many Cubans, the stories wound the beliefs of Santería, the religion brought with slaves from Nigeria and Benin and that frequently merged into hybridised Christian tales.

On several of these mounds, he had positioned truly magnificent large Queen Conch shells, their distinctive blood-orange colour blushing pink in the interior lips. These were sometimes linked with vine leaves. The contrast of green against the pearly white was distinctive.

Apparently, our artist dived for the conches and he supplemented with some that appeared on the beach after storms. He assured us that the shells he took never had a snail in residence. However, I know conches sometimes supplement the Cuban diet and they also very occasionally produce a wonderful pink gem-quality pearl. I hoped they had occasionally produced one to reward his artistic aspirations.

Like much modern art, his meaning was obscured to each of us, despite him discussing the stories of a few of these curious mounds. These were created from worn out marine bits: coral so washed against the abrasive rock coast as to seem polished, stones equally so, and great lumps of geometrically pocked stone broken off from the egg-box landscape, with its odd shaped haystacks of twisted aerated rock.

Having made our artist a donation, we returned to the heavily-baked sandy track and soon had to slow down for a drove of unsupervised goats escorted by snowy white egrets.

The contrast of colour against the lush roadside vegetation was striking.

The white of the egrets seemed more notable against the multi-coloured brown and black of the goats. Many were red tan or a softer brown.

Blobs of lighter shades made each distinctive: one was a rather smart brindle. Several of the others looked like miniature Belted Galloway cows, with the same types of black and white markings.

In Australia we called them Collingwood cows because their black and white markings seemed replicated in the Victorian Aussie Rules shirts of Collingwood football team...or was it the other way around?

The egrets fluttered alongside the drove or strode beside an individual goat, watching intently as the animal munched its way down the roadside. As quickly as grasshoppers or other insects were disturbed during the goat's meal, they were quickly harvested by a darting yellow beak.

We had earlier made a short stop at another cousin's house to drop off a fish before going horse-riding. When we returned there later in the day we found a feast.

The fish had been baked and was surrounded by salads, vegetables and rice dishes.

The banquet was laid out as if for some great celebration and I was touched by the care that it showed, and impressed by the artistic presentation of each dish.

The house was simple, with wide veranda and tiled floors. Their Grandmamma was also in residence. She was making cotton lace as we chatted (me not saying much).

At an old vintage treadle sewing machine, off cuts from garments recently made were carefully stored in a tin can. Nothing much is wasted here.

The little granddaughter was wearing a smart white dress recently made on this machine and decorated with nanny's cotton lace. Heavy crocheting cotton of the same type that formed the bodice of her dress had been wound around a long wooden spindle that now lay beside the sewing machine.

Carrying on after our fish collection, we made several abortive small detours before being successful in the procurement of a special type of handmade cheese that had been requested by my Tour Director's brother.

As a chef he had used cheese from that region, and from the flashing juke box mobile phone came his suggestions on its source.

These detours into the general area he thought the cheese to be made were slow and punctuated by roadside queries about who made cheese locally.

We were directed first here, and then there. Each tiny rural hamlet was as poor as the other, but as friendly as could be. In the yards there seemed to be endless different varieties of chickens, guinea fowls, and crossbreeds.

Eventually a man on horseback directed us to a house further along. After a short while a lady cheese-maker slowly emerged after deployment of the usual 'doorbell' of Cuba.

This method is to stand outside and call out loudly the person's name until answered by either the appearance of the person being called, or someone else who will tell you where to find the person you seek.

This lady had a lovely shy smile. She must have had many years experience at her cheese-making but looked worn out by the harshness of existence. It seemed to be a pleasure for her to be greeted by someone other than those of the local area. She chatted quietly, smiling as she told stories of her cheese and its curious supply chain of local cow owners.

I was told that, contrary to popular tourist belief, the Cuban food ration is limited to those in the cities.

Those who live in the country are said to be fortunate in that they have land – and therefore a wider richness – something easily disproven by visiting any one of the small hamlets where we stopped. Life without the ration is therefore not easy in these places.

It amazed me some days later when a Cuban girl living in Havana recited this party line to me a second time. I knew that she had travelled to some of the same desperately poor houses that I had. It therefore surprised me that she happily repeated the Official Version of 'Life in the Country' when she had seen with her own eyes to the contrary.

Perhaps it is easier not to think too deeply when confronted with everyday life when so much of it is controlled, as is it in Cuba.

Finally we seemed ready to set out on our return drive.

We had agreed that we would return via Santa Clara and in making the decision it was the one time we actually did consult the map.

As I mentioned previously, the map proved useful only in so far as it instructed me as to where Santa Clara sits in relationship to Trinidad and Havana.

Again, a map proved to not be useful in getting me to a destination – for we never did make it.

We were just about to set out, when a telephone call came from the aunt who had not been at home when we collected the furniture. She told us we had forgotten to collect the lamp.

The lamp: what a story. It appears in detail in the chapter OOPSA: Improvisation.

It being the only fragile possession that travelled with us, we had left the lamp for safe-keeping, knowing that the carpenter's house would be one of the last stops en route back to Havana.

Now we found that, in the fascination of the assembly and disassembly of the TV stand, we had totally forgotten to collect this prize possession – and it was over an hour's drive away.

My Tour Director looked dismayed as he explained that we had left the lamp behind.

Then with that big smile and no plea to change direction he told me to R-E-L-A-X for our agreed route meant we wouldn't be going that way.

He said he would collect it 'on the next trip'.

Given that the last trip was three years before, this didn't seem practical.

I suggested we alter our route, go back to get the lamp and then on back through Trinidad – rather than returning via Santa Clara as planned.

This is the benefit of a 'No Plan'.

It gives flexibility.

It also opened up a chance to:

- Go horse riding.
- Climb the Manaca Iznaga tower in Cuba's *Valle de los Ingenios*.
- Trek through a lush rainforest in the *Topes de Collantes* to the *Salto de Caburni*, the Caburni Waterfalls, and
- Browse more extensively the treasures on sale in Trinidad.

So it was that we drove back to the carpenter, collected the lamp, and balanced it carefully on top of our bags on the back seat.

At the last minute we collected another passenger who was off to work in Sancti Spiritus, and unexpectedly could have a comfortable ride there. We then set off. This change of plans – even of no plan plans – proved once again that one man's detour is another man's good fortune.

What did the Cuban Approach accomplish?

A mental Plan B proved useful when I was faced with the possibility of not being able to access my bank account from a bank in Havana.

I had learned from my Cuban friends that there are more ways to get a result than the first one you try.

Their tenacity to achieve the outcome they want is to be admired.

Just look at the impossibility of keeping a big American 1950s-era vehicle on the road with no spare parts dealer, service garage, or body-work shop.

So when the bank teller declined to process my transaction and made serious 'tut tut' noises while frowning a lot to show the severity of the situation, I tried another bank – with completely contrary results that saw me emerge triumphant with cash in hand.

I was to have no further bank troubles in Sancti Spiritus or Trinidad. The tourist industry is too important to Cuba not to address these details.

However, there is little more daunting than being stranded without money in any land, let alone one in which your competence with the language has deserted you and you don't understand the system. Having the ability to calm myself with Plan B saved me from panic.

Cubans seem not to stop at Plan B. They have alternative plans B, C, D, and F ... ad infinitum through the whole alphabet. These are all based on their own experience and that of others, creatively thinking through what they have in their toolkit to address the situation, plus a lot of determination and in the case of most, the charm to pull it off.

It could be interpreted that given the amount and nature of the detours at the end of our road trip, that it had turned into nothing more than a convenience for my Tour Director, rather than being for my benefit. It was true that throughout the trip most of our detours centred around the desire of my Tour Director to be the village telegraph, bringing news and photos from Havana to relatives not seen for some years.

However, this routing meant that we met warm and welcoming people who created magnificent meals beautifully presented with the art of a master painter.

They opened their homes to me, and in our short time together shared something of themselves.

They told me their stories, and as we moved through their homes I became aware of the things that had been left unsaid – and were later discussed in the privacy of the car when we travelled on.

The routes we took – whether to *Managua*, to the island peninsulas, horse riding, or to the beach – nearly always had the addition of one cousin or another.

It was not without prior agreement, for as had been explained to those who travelled with us, we thought it was important that they take the chance when it appeared. The appearance of a tourist prepared to include others doesn't come along every day.

However, the last day our detours saw the culmination of gathering together all the goodies for the Havana family that my tour fees had made possible.

These detours were certainly not done for my benefit, as I didn't even get a fish for my Havana apartment – although to be fair I did have the fish feast beside the antique sewing machine in Trinidad.

Instead, I got musicians at my big fiesta and many small lovely acts of thoughtfulness that really touched me, for I knew the cost in terms of available funds.

What affected me most was that they signified that someone had really been thinking about what would make me happy.

Seen in context, the detours greatly enhanced my trip, for it was through these many delays that I was exposed to the small, telling details of everyday Cuban life.

Step 7 of the Cuban Approach: Unexpected routes: Make your detours to be adventures, and when you decide to trust - trust.

Unexpected routes: Every detour and potential distress offers some discoveries – mostly about yourself.

Adjusting your sails: The bank story demonstrated what I already knew: that the wind around one island – though it be the same wind – might be harnessed differently to give a different outcome.

All it takes sometimes is the discipline not to panic, the ability to balance the apparent looming catastrophe with a quick mental review of what is the worst that can happen, and then the ability to think creatively about how to respond *in case* the worst happens.

It is surprising how seldom the worst *does* happen.

Reading the winds: Although I was prepared to trust the winds and the tides I wasn't reckless.

I believed that eventually they would bring me to shore – and how safely I got there would depend on my own resilience.

I know that any trip – even those carefully planned and regulated *(in fact especially a trip that is so planned)* produces many unexpected detours and alternative destinations. These emerge due to the unforeseen *(or overlooked)* details that life is very good at producing, just when you think everything is going well.

I may have had no plan, but I did have the sense to make sure relevant people knew where I was – and how to contact me. That was a starting point from which I could be found should things go astray en route in a detour of significant relevance.

I had also taken the precaution of educating my Tour Director about my drug allergies, and where to find the hospital letter and remedial medications should it be necessary to do so.

That way, I was less likely to detour to the next world ahead of schedule *(assuming that my allotted schedule was not during my month with no plan).*

The financial impasse of being refused funds at the bank caused me to find my own intellectual detour.

When confronted by the definite inability to withdraw money from my credit card I was able to calm rising consternation by slowly evolving Plan B.

In fact by the time I got the money I realised that there were other alternatives besides 'B'... I was up to 'D' by that time.

In the case of the physical detours along the route, there was not one that, while delaying our concept of the daily itinerary *(such as it was)*, didn't offer compensatory rewards that far outweighed any need to have – let alone stick to – a plan.

Detours teach you a lot about yourself
and when you rejoin the main road
it is never the same as before.

CHAPTER EIGHT

Unmade roads

Rough terrain

One of the most noticeable changes in the nine years since I was last in Cuba – apart from the opening up of commerce to locals – was the quality of the local roads. They had degraded significantly.

The one exception was the National Highway system. It was still remarkably good, wide enough to accommodate significantly more traffic than it does – though happily this does not seem an imminent option – and has sufficient en route fuel stations, all of which accept credit cards (as long as their machine is working).

When you are navigating the streets of Havana it is a different story. You have to be vigilant, for the terrain can hold surprises not just pertinent to the road surface.

On the street of my Havana apartment I watched a sort of pantomime that demonstrated the benefits of such caution.

On this day, at the end of my road, a bus was parked very close to a truck, making the road totally impassable. There seemed to be a complicated battery exchange taking place.

This meant that the bus snuggled up as close as possible to the truck, a battery-holding device was extended, and people disappeared under the truck, calling directions to the men on the bus side.

It was a curious operation, the likes of which I had never seen. It took perhaps forty minutes from start to finish. Ten of those minutes were spent in greeting, discussing, pondering, suggesting, disagreeing, and coming to some sort of mutually accepted methodology.

While all this was taking place, several vehicles tried to use the street because it was the through route between two major roads in Central Havana.

Some drivers, already used to delays, settled in to wait for the operation to be completed so they could enjoy the through access as usual.

After a while they realised this was going to be a long job and reversed to the junction to take an alternative route.

Some drivers looked far enough ahead to see there was something happening within the next block and paused at the intersection, made a snap judgment, and turned off to join the next parallel street.

Some just waited.

Never once from any of the inconvenienced travellers did I hear a horn blast.

There was some discussion by one driver. It was obviously along the lines of: "Fine place to do your truck maintenance".

This drew what from a distance seemed to be akin to: "If you have a better suggestion for getting the truck going, go right ahead".

The frustrated driver then backed down the street to the intersection to take an alternative route.

I noted that this was done without the sort of piqued rapidity that is so often seen in such circumstances in my world. He had had his say, been answered, shrugged, muttered to himself, and drove away at normal speed, having no need to announce his frustration more widely by driving like an idiot.

I wondered what it is that causes us, in the busy complexity of modern society to react in a more extreme fashion. Are we already so tense that small frustration like this is like lighter fluid poured on smouldering ash – creating a 'flash point' from which a wild fire of irrational behaviour follows?

With tyres that were competing with each other to be the next to deflate, we literally picked our way through the streets of Havana, mindful of every pothole and crater.

In so doing we crept down many back streets and I had the chance to see into the houses and shops and back alleys and get a better insight into realities of the city's life.

When we hired our rental car and headed out on our No Plan adventure, there was a notable contrast between the good quality National Highway and the roads over which we had crawled in the days before.

There was also a contrast also in the huge variety of transportation using the National Highway.

There were fairly modern Chinese trucks – most were employed on state business – something I learned from the colour of the number plates.

I am always fascinated by number plates as it was a game when a child to try to guess what the city of registration to which the first letter designator referred.

At the time this was before Federal Standardisation and it was peculiar to Western Australia. That difference was typical.

The Western Australians have historically had their own way of doing things and discard any solution that worked in 'The Eastern States' as unworthy.

The distance from Perth to the nearest other capital city of Adelaide, is 2693 km *(about 1673miles)* away. It is a 28 hour drive. But the real Easterners are in Melbourne a 36 hour drive over a distance of 3406 km *(or 2116 miles)*, and Sydney , a drive of 41 hours over a distance of 3,934 km *(or 2,444 miles)*.

You can see why those in Perth think they live in a different land!

In Germany I also loved guessing the registration area. It tested my newly learned German and my capability to develop a mental map of Germany.

My early inability to have such a map of Germany in my head resulted in autobahn detours making no sense to me when they gave alternatives by city name. I was so glad to eventually employ an electronic navigation system.

German licence-plate-spotting has traps for young players because of the anomalies caused with reunification of East and West.

Normally, the bigger cities have a one letter prefix, but as reunification was for some time deemed unlikely, single letters were assigned to small regional areas – like 'L' which Leipzig eventually claimed back, which was initially issued for the rural area of *Lahn-Dill Kreis*.

Hamburg is HH – because that stands for the *Hansastadt Hamburg*.

Bremen and Bremerhafen (Bremen Port) both also have the 'H' to designate their hanseatic status, sharing the letters HB.

I was fascinated with the designation and researched the history of the Hanseatic League.

The Hansa has one modern global heritage that is immediately recognisable: Lufthansa – the airline with whom I am a frequent flyer and so is my Chow Chow Balu. Balu rates their services very highly indeed, as they are the only airline to write into their Ground Handling Agreements that only a Lufthansa staff member can load or offload live animals.

The Hanseatic League was first documented in 1267. It grew from the need for a mutual protection system from the frequent invasion of Germany by the Vikings. The way it worked was that a Hansa city could call upon its League members for protection, and therefore had no need to pay taxes to the Holy Roman Emperor for this service.

The word *'Hansa'* actually draws origin from the old German *'Hanse'* – meaning 'convoy' – which in early days was a description not just of ships, but of bands of travelling merchants on land, as well.

A Hansa city was in charge of its own defence and trade and had its own legal system.

The League grew in prominence and influence, and at one time was the dominant manufacturer and supplier of global shipping. It dominated Baltic trade for three centuries and hanseatic power was hard to dislodge.

The Hamburg and Lübeck Hansa made trade agreements with Henry III of England.

They were soon joined by the Cologne Hansa, which had previously had trade agreements with Henry II.

King Edward IV renewed the agreements, but Elizabeth I revoked them in response to national pressures.

This decision was soon widely regretted, as it had a serious impact on the British shipping industry now divorced from the global power in shipping.

These echoes of the past resonate in present day affairs of the United Kingdom.

King James renewed the agreement but the Hanseatic League never regained the extent of power they had held when their walled trading centre in London was one of the most powerful trading areas in Europe.

This area was destroyed by the Great Fire of London in 1666.

The remaining vestiges are only to be found in Steelyard Passage close to Cannon Street Station.

This diversion into history was prompted by the coloured number plates of Cuba.

On the main highways of Cuba there were well-maintained fifties-era American trucks with number plate colours indicating their locality, their use, and official ownership of some kind; and hybrid varieties of those trucks with improvised mechanics and fittings – whose number plate colour indicated local private ownership.

Designations of colour follow this structure:

- **Yellow**: Private car.
- **Orange**: This has variations on a theme: If the second letter is a 'K' it indicates a foreign worker. If light orange, it denotes an Important Person (free fuel).
- **Red:** State owned, and must return to site after working hours. This designation is something that proved doubtful to me, as I saw many red plates ferrying families after dark. *As I said – how Cuba works is a mystery to many.*
- **Blue:** State owned, but allowed to not come home to base at night.
- **White:** Officials.
- **Green:** Army.
- **Light Green:** The Interior Ministry. This is the department in control of security and police. It has its own schools and teaching system, and oversees all Home Affairs. It is like the Home Office in the UK – but different!

Aside from number-plate-spotting, I was equally fascinated with chronicling the variety of vehicles on Cuba's roads.

There was the usual variety of trucks modified into camiones. These are seen daily throughout countryside Cuba.

There were mule wagons, donkey wagons, oxen carts, mounted horsemen and women, a lad on roller skates on a long-distance commute, several tourist cars like ours, a few motorised bicycles, and motor bikes with sidecars.

Away from the National Highway the same mix was apparent in different proportions. Here there were more animal-drawn vehicles and truck-buses.

There were horsemen both with, and without saddles and leather tack. In most cases the halters and girths were rope, bound at pressure points with fabric or cardboard to ease rubbing on the animal's flanks or belly.

The traffic we passed was occasionally punctuated by small mini-vans and by other rental cars filled with tourists.

Beside the road, we passed a semi-trailer laden with bales of tobacco wrapped in banana leaves.

Each region of Cuba produces a different type of tobacco, influenced in the same way as wine grapes are by *'terroire'* – the geography, climate topography, soil quality and characteristics, and overall growing conditions.

One family I met used a secret recipe of honey, vanilla, and rum added to the water as the tobacco is processed to give a unique flavour and style to their cigars.

Honey is generally used to glue the finished product together: factory cigars use maple syrup.

I had never seen banana leaves used to bale anything before, although I did recall them acting as large umbrellas in monsoon rains in *Viñales*, a top producer of quality cigar tobacco beautifully located in the mountains of the province of *Pinar del Río*.

Alongside the pathway to the Salo *de Caburní* waterfall I had seen a different use for banana leaves.

The trail is a one hour descent to the lovely falls and one and a half hour ascent. It is steep – as witness the different expectations of travel time whether climbing down or hauling yourself back up the trail.

The route is fringed with tree ferns and fragrant orchids. It takes you under striated rock formations that look as if marble cake mix has been mixed into whipped grey meringue and then frozen suddenly in mid-fold.

I made the trek in light leather shoes more suited to be dancing slippers than hiking shoes suitable to climb down a rugged track.

My pauses to gather breath on the route were put into perspective by my Tour Director telling the story of how he had helped a man carry his wife down this track in a wheelchair, so she also could enjoy the falls.

That certainly made my discomfort minor by comparison.

It seemed an oversight that I had come without hiking shows of any sort – but was it?

Those who know me would say it was intentional.

Once a great mountain and wilderness park hiker and canoe traveller, not averse to portage of my cedar strip canoe over impossible stretches, of later years my hiking has been limited.

I prefer to take wheels to my destination. That's why my Chow Chow Balu suits me so well. He is a short distance dog for walking with long distance tanks for travelling by vehicle, so roaming by car suits us both.

It was on this trek that I saw banana leaves tied between saplings to make organic rubbish collection hammocks into which the passing visitor may deposit wrappers and empty water bottles.

One of the jokes amongst my friends in Havana was how I kept scolding them from throwing litter to the ground.

I was asked by Nemo on an early trip how I was going to educate 2.1 million people in Havana to this goal.

My response was simple and short. I said: "I will start with you and work outwards".

Funnily enough, this was taken to heart and I found the circle of scolding increase as one friend scolded the next and then that person then took up the cudgel.

On our route by car departing Cienfuegos, we saw banks of banana leaves propped against the wire strand fence to dry. The ends had been cut into wide fringing to stop the leaves curling. I was to discover that before refrigeration banana leaves were used for packaging food because they contain natural antioxidants that give them medicinal value.

The country vistas along our route were magnificent – wide sweeping valleys fringed by verdant mountain ranges.

Roadside fences were punctuated by sturdy wooden posts at very wide intervals. The intervening wires were held up by saplings cut to make tall, regular interval stakes. These served to keep the wires apart, and to stop stock from wandering through.

There were many free-range mobs of cattle and flocks of goats that knew they had right of way, and acted accordingly, but frequently we travelled some distance without ever seeing another vehicle.

When we stopped at a lookout tower above Cienfuegos, I encountered a new experience in travel. I was staggered to discover that the road itself was trying to travel downhill.

On a steep 1:5 gradient of hairpin turns, the tarmac surface had succumbed to the heat and pressure of heavy vehicles on a road that had not been built as substantially as it could have been.

The result was that, rather than being a flat road surface of the sort to which we are all accustomed, it was more like a river consisting of a series of waves of slightly malleable tarmac.

As we drove, the road travelled with us. It was a most peculiar sensation and with a sheer drop off on the edges, rather disconcerting.

These waves would have made any novice surfer proud, for they were significant enough to qualify for the term 'wave', and yet not of dimensions that were likely to cause devastation – at least not as long as you negotiated them with appropriate caution and skill.

Looking at the photos now, I smile, for I had never seen a road in motion before, nor have I since.

No one seemed to remark upon the phenomenon. It was all considered a natural part of the trip. Perhaps to a Cuban it fell into the same category as what Marcus Aurelius described in Roman times:

A cucumber is bitter. Throw it away.
There are briars in the road.
Turn aside from them.

This is enough.

Do not add,
...and why were such things made in the world?"

Our modern version can be summed up as:

Get over it.

One night in Trinidad my Cuban friends decided we should go to *Club Ayala.*

If there is dancing, I am in, but I hadn't realised that this is a nightclub of a very special sort. It is more than 30 metres *(100ft)* underground.

We headed out to our usual throb of very loud music reverberating in the car, and in true Cuban fashion helpfully shared with the world by windows rolled down. Right on the fringe of town we were confronted by a track that seemed totally impassable.

The gradient was extremely steep, so it would require a bit of speed to get to the top – but the track itself was a series of humped undulations, from the top of the hill to the road beneath. This meant that you had to pick your way astutely, or rip out the sump.

As our driver paused to scan for the best route across the humps, a 50s Chevy crammed with locals passed us without pausing. It blasted up the hill ahead of us and as it swung into a flattened area at the top, I realised that there was a flat parking area above.

I have often observed that the more you look at something up close, the less you understand it – for you have no perspective – and so it was with the dauntingly steep gradient.

Having seen the progress of the previous vehicle, without further hesitation, my Tour Director dropped down a gear and we roared up the track as well, emerging with some shared sense of satisfaction onto the parking spot watched over by the usual guard.

Dollar notes changed hands and we set off.

For a disco in Cuba, it was remarkably quiet as we approached.

More shared music reverberated from every passing vehicle than from where they gestured to be the location of the night club.

After a short walk, we came to a small entrance and started down a long flight of stairs that then emerged into a long tunnel. Now you could hear the music at expected Cuban loudest volume.

Emerging from the tunnel, the dance floor suddenly opens up before you within a huge cave. Stalactites and stalactites are illuminated with brightly coloured lights. The bar is carved from the stone cave wall.

Club Ayala is an experience. I loved it.

Loud retro music throbbed within – mostly the Cuban favourites of the moment, so not to everyone's taste, especially that of some tourists who seem to think all Cuban music is salsa music.

There are huge plasma screens against the cave walls, showing music videos as popular here as anywhere else.

When we arrived, locals greeted my friends enthusiastically. As a result, I was hardly off the dance floor for the whole time we were in this subterranean disco.

There was a great live DJ-cum-compère on a metal bridge above the cavern dance floor. His personality and chit-chat made the evening livelier than it was on my second visit when he wasn't there, but both occasions were late dancing nights to remember.

When we departed, if I had thought getting UP the hill was an interesting challenge, getting DOWN it was even more so.

Thankfully our driver was not inebriated. This was questionable in the case of other vehicles of rowdy, laughing groups crammed into classic cars that peeled off the parking lot, undaunted.

We headed down with the same surety with which we had arrived – but a little more slowly. In both directions I was thankful that I had taken out the fullest car insurance: 'Just in case'.

I have a rule about insurance – either have the top level or nothing. If you have something less than the top, chances are the company will argue the toss and not pay anyway, or so my experience has proven over the years. Happily, we didn't need it.

In the course of our travels we were to take many tracks and short detours over barely discernible trails. Having been a rally driver myself, I have great respect for a good driver and I must say this was an unexpected bonus in my selected Tour Director.

There was only one time when I was pushed to make a suggestion about how to angle across a ridge in the road. Apart from that, we steered safely through some truly eye-opening tracks. In each case, when confronted by truly dreadful ways ahead, we managed to find something to laugh about as we considered the options.

Like most things in life, once you have committed yourself, on some of these roads there is no turning back, for there is quite simply no place to turn.

Reversing was exceptionally hazardous as there was minimal clearance each side of tracks carved into the side of sheer cliffs.

Sometimes, we agreed I had better walk ahead and point out hazards that may not be visible from the driving seat.

Sometimes, I paid the driver the respect of saying nothing. He needed no helpful advice.

It made me reflect over the many truly awful roads we had travelled as children on what were famously called the 'Lamacraft off-to-the-bush picnics'.

When I was very small my father was in what is now called the Australian Army Reserve. In the regular army he had held a high rank and so still had access to military maps and to non-public areas. His maps were extremely well-detailed.

In both military and civilian life, Papa's work meant that we moved a lot from one state of the country to another. Due to these regular 'off-the-main-track' experiences, in each location we were the family that knew more about the place than the locals.

We would set off with my mother's gourmet cooking keeping warm under layers of newspaper wrapping, or in a straw box where it continued to cook under the straw that lined the container.

Our route planning was minimal apart from a general direction and the Military Survey Maps to go with that area. As we travelled, someone would comment "I wonder where that road goes?" and off we would head.

As the road became a track, there was usually some sort of junction. Out would come the maps before Papa decided our route.

In this way, I probably saw more of Australia than most of my countrymen. We certainly saw parts of the country to which most people would never have access.

In the course of these picnics I certainly saw a master driver negotiate pretty dreadful trails in a plucky little car that didn't have very much clearance beneath.

On one such trip I recall the whole horizon filled with layers of native wildflowers: the cornflower blue of the *Leschenaultia* beneath, red and green of the *Kangaroo Paws* above them, and the waving grey of the *Smoke Bush* standing tall between these colours and a penetratingly royal blue sky.

Later, we emerged onto acres of crisp everlasting flowers splashing the whole vista with outrageously intense colours of yellow and pink.

These are happy memories – and proved good training for off-road travel in a month trip without a plan through Cuba.

It seemed that the two most important lessons of those childhood experience had ingrained themselves:

- Share the reconnaissance only after asking if is more helpful to do so, or to allow the driver to choose the route unaided.
- If the driver chooses not to have assistance, stay silent while the route is navigated unless there is something significant to point out.

An example of the second point learned in childhood was during one of our much enjoyed family off-road adventures. We were all crammed into said plucky little car along with Tom Watson Jr, the now very famous former executive VP of IBM who died in 1993 after a productive and fascinating life.

However, in this adventure Mr. Watson was not in the limousine of greatness, simply the family vehicle of his Western Australian Manager – later to become IBM South East Asia Sales Manager.

Now listed as one of the most influential one hundred people of the twentieth century, Tom Watson Jr. followed as company leader in the footsteps of his father who had founded IBM.

In retirement from that leadership role Tom Watson later served as a highly respected US Ambassador to the Soviet Union. Upon his death Cyrus Vance, Secretary of State under the Carter Administration and a former IBM Board Member, paid the following tribute:

"Tom Watson was one of the great business leaders of our time... and a marvelous man."

However, on this day, Mr. Watson was in the Australian bush enjoying a Lamacraft picnic with two young children and our dog Toby, the same one who shared the outdoor privy with two small children scared of the dark.

Before we went to bed my mother would tell Toby: "On your duty". He would get up with an air of resignation and escort us to the toilet and back. Perhaps he also wasn't that keen on the cramped quarters, or their circumstances.

On this day, my father was picking a route carefully over a bush track. On such trails it's difficult to see the cavernous potholes because they're often filled with what we called 'bull dust' – a sort of talcum-fine red-grey dust.

Everyone was quiet until my mother said briskly:

"Emu beside us".

A pacing emu can wreak more damage on a vehicle than that caused by hitting a kangaroo. Emus travel at speed, and if they panic after pacing beside a vehicle for a while they sometimes veer straight in front.

Toby was on the opposite side from the emu.

Mr. Watson sat by the open window on the same side as the emu.

We children were in the centre.

Dog saw emu and jumped across both children, making a grand leap for the open window.

Tom Watson had the presence of mind to grab Toby's collar when he was in mid-air and keep him inside the car, but this meant that the large dog now sat in his lap in that crowded space, quivering and whimpering in excitement at the pacing feathers outside.

A certain level of speed was vital to not losing the traction of forward motion critical to our progress. Until he found a spot where we could stop and despite the loud distractions from the back seat, my father held his course on the precarious track, keeping the emu's progress in his peripheral vision.

Finding a clearing, we drew to a halt. The emu paced on ahead into the bush.

This was the sort of moment when my mother's grace always rose to the occasion. She sweetly enquired if this was a good spot to have our picnic lunch.

It took a few moments to decant the dog from Mr. Watson's lap, the children who were wedged in the middle, and the picnic.

It was only then that the full comedy of the situation struck us. It made for some hearty laughter then, and always has done within our family.

I wonder if Tom Watson also enjoyed telling the tale when he returned home. Perhaps, as the National President of the Boy Scouts of America, he used it to illustrate their motto: *Be prepared.*

In the context of this childhood incident, I have often thought that it is over the rough terrain that you see the true nature of a person.

Although an icon of the US corporate world, Mr. Watson, as we respectfully addressed him, was a genuinely nice person. He was completely without any air of superiority and able to communicate with children as well as adults.

It says a lot about him that he was prepared to come on the trip. However, as an adult I realise that such an invitation would have been much more akin to his interests than the stuffy, more formal options offered by people whose invitation may have been more geared to self-advantage than interest in his pleasure.

My father's invitation must have held a welcome freshness of sincerity in wanting to show off the remote beauty of our country to a visitor more used to the cosmopolitan cities of the world.

I think the two men also shared a breadth of interest and the ability to converse on many subjects. Each came from a military background, had polymath tendencies that resulted in a repertoire of learning on a range of topics– and I believe each respected and liked the other.

I remember my mother's delight in recounting a story of their next meeting. Mother and Dad had alighted at Kai Take Airport in Hong Kong for the Hundred Percent Club meeting that was the reward of high performing IBM sales people of that era. They were headed across the tarmac when suddenly they were hailed by name by an enthusiastic Tom Watson who had just alighted from another aircraft.

It is another hallmark of leadership to know one's employees by name – but then our name was probably imprinted on his memory, just as the paws of Toby had been imprinted on his legs over the last few kilometres before we could stop on that bush track.

On our back roads in Cuba there was no risk of emus, but we passed several horse riders and a few ox wagons negotiating the terrain less comfortably than we. Here, the 'bull dust' seemed to have the same role in disguising pot holes as it did on our childhood bush tracks.

What I saw again as we travelled over the roughest terrain was the nature of the person. Even when we had a few bad moments of seemingly being unable to go safely forward or back, there was no posturing or sputtering in frustration.

Instead, inevitably and with an ever-ready flashing smile, I was told to R-E-L-A-X. We then surveyed the situation and came to a mutual decision before agreeing a way to proceed.

As the controversial American abolitionist Henry Ward Beecher said:

> *A person without a sense of humor*
> *is like a wagon without springs*
> *...jolted by every pebble on the road.*

What did the Cuban Approach accomplish?

During our travels, the negotiation of the best way forward was done objectively and carefully – whether creeping through Havana on tyres that were determined to deflate, travelling on the generally fine surfaces of the Cuban National Highway System, or picking a way over tracks that had diminished into barely passable thoroughfares.

The trip was punctuated by smiles and the frequent admonition to R-E-L-A-X, despite requiring solid concentration on the best way forward.

Letting people get on with it is a much better method than making a commentary on the road system in general, or wishing things to be other than they are.

A perfect illustration of applying this philosophy was the response to the undulating downhill progress of the road itself above Cienfuegos.

This was seen as just another factor to be considered to bring me safely through my journey.

I come from a country where the definition of a road is somewhat broader than most, being merely that it is an area set aside for the 'present or future use of the travelling public'.

In Australia, this includes stock routes or what are known collectively as 'The Long Paddock' – a 'paddock' being the equivalent of an English field, though usually not as lush or small. Paddocks in Australia can be measured in square kilometres *(or square miles)*.

Because of the challenges that Australian weather brings in its extremes, and has done since recorded history, citizens have a national legal right to graze their stock along these routes.

The only legal obligation is that to prevent overgrazing, when your stock feed on The Long Paddock you must move along 10km *(6 miles)* a day.

Often, on long night drives back home after meetings in halls in the middle of the bush I would be puzzled by a sea of eyes reflecting my headlight. The animals to which they belonged materialised as I got closer.

When I saw those night eye reflections I knew that we were sharing our grass with people who would otherwise see their stock suffering from drought. They had been brought there to benefit from better weather in our area that had resulted in nutritious green roadside grasses, while their burnt-out, or parched local area recovered

In such instances, I was reminded of the great problem Australia has with water in the form of precipitation. It has either not enough or too much. Recent TV footage of sudden and devastating floods in Australia was used by the then Prime Minister as an example of global warming, but they were no more dramatic than those I experienced in the same region as a child.

In Cuba, we saw a lot of stock along the roadside. Although I wasn't sure of the grazing rights, I did find out the alarming realities of beef production.

It is absolutely forbidden for Cubans to possess beef for consumption.

Although all cattle belong to the state, most Cubans don't have the chance to enjoy the meat.

Farmers suffer extensive penalties by Inspectors in the case of the loss of a cow or calf – even if it is stolen. In the case of theft, the penalty is for not looking after it properly.

Once a country where cattle outnumbered people, since the Revolution a combination of land degradation and poor farming practice has reversed the situation. According to an article in the Cuba Times in 2016, the Cuban ration instead provides soy mincemeat fattened with cow ears and tripe: not that tasty but with some nutritional value.

Horses are also at a premium. They are also often stolen but seldom eaten as they are more valuable alive. They still form an important role in transportation.

I don't know the official designation of what a road in Cuba is, or whether there are such things as stock routes, but I do know that what we passed along in many cases probably weren't officially roads at all - just local tracks. They reminded me of many I had travelled in my home country.

It seemed that all the Cuban drivers I saw were quite calm about the frustrations of road conditions encountered. It wasn't just an acceptance of the reality, it was the very pragmatic 'It is what it is' approach: there is no point in getting excited about things like this, as there are far more vital things in life.

The alternative transportation by rail has its own challenges. In a country that proudly had the first steam railway in Latin America – even before Spain had any rail travel – the rail infrastructure of Cuba has deteriorated to such a degree that the few remaining trains are on what we sometimes call 'milk runs': short-hop lines.

There is a two tiered fare system for foreigners and locals – the same on ferries.

The reliability of train schedules can best be described as 'variable' and in many cases are the sources of national parody.

For example, trains 11 and 19 en route to *Santiago de Cuba* are notoriously slow, and fraught with delays of all sorts.

The reasons given for the delays certainly equalled those that were a common source of parody in Britain.

The reasons for delay of the old British Rail included: 'slugs on the line', 'heat buckling the rails', 'sheep on the line', 'ice on the wires', or 'person under train'.

In Cuba, there was often no explanation – and no train.

In 2007, the Venezuelan Investment Bank announced massive investment in the restoration of Cuban rail infrastructure through fibre-optic-based computerisation of the transmission system.

To a visitor's eye progress is invisible, but in May 2010 Cuba announced her intention to focus on rebuilding the rail infrastructure – including a new training centre for railway workers.

The answer to whether the plan for refreshing the rail infrastructure ever materialised or not, is best judged by the current state of train travel in Cuba.

According to *www.seat61.com,* the fantastic website I always check for international train travel:

- In 2014 trains 1, 2, 3, & 4 were cancelled to have their carriages refurbished. They seem to have never reappeared.
- The former *Tren Francès* (French Train) carriages from Train 1 & 2 are now used on 11 & 12.
- In November 2016, the trains 11 & 12, 13, 14, 15 & 16 went from running every three days to every four days: this despite a fleet of new Chinese locomotives.

By contrast, 'Tren Francès' crosses the island in relative comfort from Havana *to Santiago de Cuba* in 12 hours.

'Tern Frances' stops at *Santa Clara* and *Camagüey* and boasts working air-conditioning and a cafeteria car. Your ticket is sold with a promise of a full refund if it arrives more than one hour late at its destination.

We had made a conscious decision NOT to take the train to Trinidad – especially after my friends had recounted stories of the length of time it took by rail compared with bus.

It was in this context, that when we were travelling back from *Sancti Spiritus* one late afternoon I heard a low mournful braying sound.

It sounded like a donkey in pain.

I was so used to seeing rusty rail lines indicating long disuse that I was surprised when those beside our road gleamed silver in the sunlight. They suddenly came to life with a little cigar box of an electric coach.

This was the creature uttering its mournful 'Hee Haw'.

I never did find out from whence it came or where it was headed: just one faded and mottled blue tube of a coach with a red stripe down its side and a mournful call.

It reminded me of the dry irony of Margaret Thatcher, who observed:

> *You and I come by road or rail*
> *but economists travel on infrastructure.*

Step 8 of the Cuban Approach: Unmade roads: The rougher the terrain, the more you value good humour.

Adjusting your sails: I have had more experience of driving off-road than most. Some of that was in rally driving, where speed constantly needs to be balanced against risk.

Against this background, I had a valuable lesson to learn as we traversed our unmade roads.

Quite simply, that lesson was to let go and let the driver drive. We women of the English speaking world often find this difficult.

Zipping the lip and letting the person in control, be in control, is somewhat contrary to some women's view of the world and their place in it. Happily it is something that I have learned – or should I say, relearned.

My mother was the consummate diplomat at this – but I had to re-learn it after being a rather headlong 'take-command' and somewhat definite, younger person.

Family tales tell that as a toddler I pushed away willing helpers with a determined "I'll do it mine self".

In my defence, when it suited me I was also recorded as being adept to employ other tactics, like when my trike got stuck by calling out to my brother and his mates: "Boys! Boys!" Of course they came running to help. This latter skill I kept.

I am still able to 'Do it mine self' when I really have to, but as can be demonstrated by the following story; I save that for when my back is to the wall. As an adult I know when to graciously accept generosity of aid when it is offered.

This example is from when I was driving back from a big conference with a female colleague.

We had taken with us a giant lobster in a wicker lobster pot that usually lived on the wall of a local restaurant.

This was part of a display we had made to support my successful bid to host a regional conference in our local territory.

I had been told on the quiet, that if we proposed holding the conference in Port Campbell on the Great Ocean Road, we would probably win the bid. For anyone who has been there, you will understand the logic.

The Great Ocean Road runs along a truly spectacular piece of coastline, and is one of the most visited national icons of tourism.

It is usually said that most tourists to Australia come to see the three Rs:

The Rock,
    The Road and
        The Reef.

Port Campbell is a jewel on The Road.

Naturally, I responded affirmatively to the hint to bid to hold the conference in Port Campbell despite remonstrations from my colleagues. They were visibly distressed and told me there was nowhere to hold such a conference in that part of my region.

I replied that there definitely was.

They thought my relative newness to a place where they had lived for many years meant I just didn't understand.

It wasn't so. I just thought differently.

Remember my mother's advice to *Make every fault a fashion?*

Port Campbell is within a National Park. We needed no physical structure. I knew there was none suitable, but we could make our lack of conferencing facilities a feature.

This we would do by holding a conference under canvas, with gourmet bush cooking for catering, and the ability to toast your breakfast bread over campfires.

Sufficient accommodation was available in local hotels small enough not to have the type of conferencing facilities normally required, but with great views and hospitality.

To provision the conference there were few funds available, so we employed other tactics. I talked the cliff-rescue squad into doing a practice session and lowering barbeques into Loch Ard Gorge so we could host a dawn breakfast.

I managed to get approval for the award winning Victoria Police Pipe Band to attend at no cost to us.

On the first day of the Conference and after a spectacular under-canvas opening dinner the previous night, I had buses collect sleepy conference participants just before dawn.

At that moment, I could see that my popularity was exceedingly low as they were offloaded at the cliff top.

Just as a huge sun rose on the ocean horizon to blaze across deeply emerald waters in stunning crimson, they were piped down the steps into the gorge by the State Police Scottish Pipe Band.

It was spectacular.

My thinking at the presentation had been to make a feature of the lack of something by replacing it with something quite different and special.

I believed that our approach of having a 'Conference under Canvas' would make it memorable.

If we did it well, then the very fact of NOT having a suitable facility would do our marketing without advertising: everyone attending would speak about the experience and the magic of the place.

They did
                    and still do.

But on the day of this story it was after my successful presentation where we had just won the bid, and we now had a flat tyre on a country back road.

On the way home we had detoured to Wolf Blass vineyards to buy wine boxes of our favourite wines, two each: in my case two large cases of Yellow Label Cabernet Sauvignon. All four boxes were stowed in the trunk/boot of the car.

This meant that before we could change a tyre, or even get to the jack, out had to come:

- the giant lobster in his wicker lobster pot
- several glass fishing buoys in macramé rope encasements
- an old sepia toned framed photo of the clipper the Loch Ard whose wreck in 1878 is still famous and gave the gorge its name
- four cases of wine
- boxes of printed flyers we had used for our promotional display

- a long colour photo of the famous Twelve Apostles in an elegant redwood frame– the Apostles being a series of limestone sea stacks formed over centuries by erosion from lashing coastal waters of the stormy Southern Ocean. There are now only seven apostles. Erosion has sent the others to a watery grave – often unexpectedly and on one memorable occasion stranding tourists taking photos on the point of one when its stone bridge to the mainland collapsed. They were lifted off by helicopter.

The wine boxes were last out. Just as they were stacked on the dusty road, a local farmer on a quad bike arrived on the other side of the roadside barbed-wire fence. In the character of Australian stockmen, he was wearing a Drizabone oilskin coat and flanked by two sheepdogs who rode on specially designed platforms, fore and aft.

They all three now peered at us in curiosity.

Once he assessed our predicament, from under the well-personalised, battered brim of the stockman's Akubra felt hat came a languid drawl:

"You girls need some help?"

My colleague Marg shouted in reply, "No thanks, we're fine".

Before he could respond I called out quickly:

"Thank you. I could use some help getting the lug nuts off".

I actually hadn't tried this time, but the last time when I did change a tyre myself it was a real battle to loosen the wheel nuts that had been tightened with a pneumatic tool.

As he dismounted and climbed through the fence, my friend Marg muttered to me that she knew how to change a tyre. I responded quickly that so did I, but had never seen the point of doing so when someone offered to do it for me.

Life has a way of sorting you out, and rough terrain is often a good place to learn.

Reading the winds: Before I accepted the welcome offer of my Tour Director, I had observed his driving and recognised his competence.

However, it was not until we were traversing the rough terrain along our No Plan route that I saw his real value – the pleasant calmness that he brought to dealing with all of the complications of life.

Many of the cousins I met told me my Tour Director was 'Loco' – crazy.

He was. He is.

He is crazy enough to believe things can change, and determined enough to travel through the roughest terrain to get to the next base, because he has a view of what his future could be.

He is now well on that path.

Like our trip, the terrain is rough and there are lessons to learn along the way, but a street-wise and charming nature usually overcome the hazards. The trick is to hold to the dream.

Certainly, it is a good idea to choose your route carefully, viewing the whole and then breaking the journey into smaller sections on which you give total concentration.

This applies whether negotiating unmade tracks, undulating surfaces of roads that seem bent on beating you to the bottom of the hill, or the potholes of the city.

It also helps when you find yourself in a real pickle the nature of which is unfolding in increasing misery day upon day.

We have all had such times.

In my case after my partner died I ended up with:

- No job: having resigned to spend together whatever time he had left after diagnosis.
- No car: my car went with my job and his vehicles were off limits to me by his family.

- No home: I had sold mine to move to be closer to him as he ran an architectural practice and couldn't move.
- Owning a fraudulent franchise: that had been purchased from someone who specialised in such transactions with people facing death, but was very convincing to the still living.

I had tried to keep the business going and had been told by savvy business people that it was designed to fail. By making sure it didn't, and fixing problems as they arose, I was ruining the business model.

This I denied, being sure that 'this couldn't happen to me'.

We've all been in circumstances the true reality of which we denied, because if we were to accept that reality it would challenge every coping mechanism in our repertoire.

When a supplier who had been ready to work with me declined to provide services, I asked why and was told in confidence what they had found in the process of Due Diligence: There was no money in the main company – just a string of shell companies that filled pages.

The purchase had been made by my partner in his desire to make sure I was well looked after following his death, proved to be a classic case of selling an empty box to someone who wanted – in fact needed – to see it full.

Being on borrowed time forces decisions, and some are made that shouldn't be made under such circumstances. But that is what the con men know.

There is a bitter lesson there.

I had read that you should never make a life decision – an important decision – for two years after the death of a loved one.

It seems that you are in such a mental state that any decision made in this period can be subject to a lack of your usual judgement.

After his death I did follow this advice, although I thought I was coping remarkably well, given all the circumstances outlined above –

but we are all prone to self deception. I think this is never more so than when we are wrong in our judgement.

It is only from the distance of years that I can see how valid such a recommendation is.

I was good at window dressing. From the outside it looked as if I was coping, but inside I was falling apart.

Although we have this good advice about *after* death, there is the same that should be applied when *facing* death.

At any time when we are facing life and death situations we should be aware that despite the fact we think we are doing fine, we are actually incapable of processing the immense weight of emotion that such situations bring.

However, it is what it is.

In my case, in addition to the circumstances described, I now found myself a possible accomplice to fraud. Fortunately, I had enough experience of business to have not banked the franchisee cheques that I held from my enthusiastic franchisees.

I hadn't banked them because although my own account was empty – and I mean totally empty – I was unsure of the ability to actually start the business without the agreement of supply.

No supply chain – no business.

Had I cashed them before checking the company out, I also would have been guilty of fraud.

Instead, I returned them to the disappointed potential franchisees and we started a case with the Fraud Squad – a vastly over-burdened police department. Our case wasn't 'big enough' to warrant their diversion from major cases.

Not to be deterred, I asked whether they would prosecute the case if I gave them a folder with everything tabulated according to their needs.

I did, and they did, and eventually in the High Court we won.

There was just enough to pay off my key business partners and the legal fees they had provided.

All this was set in the context of:

- My parents both being sequentially hospitalised.
- Me having an anaphylactic shock attack following dental work.
- My Dad having a heart attack in the back of the car as I drove us to a beach-side holiday apartment for some respite.
- Discovering that my parents had been relieved of their $320,000 retirement savings through false dealing of a 'professional' while my Dad was busy being carer for my mother.
- Arranging with my brother for them to receive a particular relief program provided against assets under a protected arrangement offered by the military to ex-service people.

It was at this time that a friend I had known from when I was 16 years old resurfaced.

Who says there are no angels?

I got to know Chris when he was at the Royal Military College. My brother had wanted to join the Army, but it proved that he had flat feet and was rejected. This came as a terrible disappointment, but some of his friends went to the College and as a result I became almost the class mascot.

There are several ceremonial balls and events during their four years at the college and whenever a cadet in that year had no one to take to any of these, or to the end of year Graduation Ball, they would invite me. I was sort of the ready reserve, for I knew them all as friends and none was my boyfriend.

During this process I became Chris's Regimental Godmother when I went to a Grad Ball with his Regimental Godfather. The tradition at the Australian Royal Military College is that the person ten

Regimental Numbers above you is your father, ten below the son. Further lineage only came into play when the father left, leaving a gap. These would be filled by grandfathers or in some exceptional circumstances great grandfathers. In the way of companionable groups that make up such things for their own entertainment, new adoption processes allowed for godsons when all other parents and grandparents were no longer there.

Chris's Regimental Godfather was my first military angel. When I returned to Australia and was working in Economic Development I had accidentally met Steve at a meeting in Canberra after so many years of not being in touch. Now, after the death of my partner, I received a call that would provide me with much needed consulting work.

Steve had been a well-paid logistics consultant, working from his Quartermaster experience in Vietnam.

Now he had moved to Indonesia and set up an online services company and we agreed that indeed, as he suggested, the company could benefit from my own experience.

I was duly engaged to take on a small contract.

Steve said he would arrange for his travel agent to be in touch. I pointed out that this is what the internet was about. It could save money by remote work. Sensibly, Steve thought it best to work in person.

I was thinking: 'Djakarta. Riots' when I asked where in Indonesia he had located the company.

He answered: Bali.

Mentally thanking God, I then asked where in Bali.

He answered: Ubud.

Thank you extra God.

In the course of some work that was a pleasure, I had my soul soothed by the beauty and grace that is Balinese.

I inhaled daily the exquisite perfume of frangipani flowers, my very favourite flower, had the cook outdo himself each day with the artistic arrangement of food into fantastic culinary pictures representing animals and scenes, and had a truly life-changing massage.

The masseuse rested her hands above my body but before touching me, walked around to my head and bent down to look me in the eye: "You have to let this grief out", she said.

How did she know?

I answered that this I knew, but didn't know how.

She mixed a new combination of massage oils, and when she finished her massage I started to cry.

I sobbed for nearly two hours.

I did need to let it out, and she had released something within me to enable it.

My Regimental Godson was my next military angel.

When I made that memorable trip to my school reunion when not well enough to do so, with old school mates we drove past the barracks that housed the Australian SAS. I commented that I was a Regimental Godmother of an SAS officer. It turned out that my old school friend's husband was also in the Army and a good friend of the same officer.

When I asked where Chris was at that time, she replied that she thought he was in Canberra and told me that he was now one of the most senior soldiers in the country. My later roles saw me often in the Federal Capital and one day remembering this conversation, I tried to find him.

I thought the first starting point should be the SAS Ward Room. It was a correct starting place, but they told me that he was no longer in Canberra but based in Darwin. It turned out that he was indeed one of the most senior soldiers of the land. He was now a Brigadier heading all defences for the country's northern coastline – civil and military.

They gave me the telephone number and a very smartly spoken aide at Larrakeyah Barracks answered the phone.

When I asked to speak to the Brigadier, I was told that he had a really busy schedule at the moment and it was doubtful he could be disturbed, but could I please say what was the nature of my call was.

I just said: "Tell him it's his Regimental Godmother".

There was a startled silence before, "Yes Ma'am".

Moments later Chris was on the line: "Paquita, where are you?"

That had been some years earlier.

Our separate visits to Canberra had never coincided, so our thoughts that we could meet up while both there to swap stories of the years between had never materialised.

Remember what I said about not believing in coincidence because it is God's way of making things happen?

Now, when totally bereft of everything of importance, I suddenly had a phone call. Chris had flown to nearby Townsville to farewell his troops as they departed to Timor. He thought he would just 'pop by' to see me.

When he did and found my current situation he said: "I had no idea what a mess you are in". He then sat me down on the floor of my resort beachside apartment and on a big piece of paper, together we mapped out my options to regroup and stabilise.

Chris taught me something really valuable then.

I pass it on.

There may come a time when it will guide you out of your confusion, as did me from mine.

He said that with the SAS behind enemy lines in Vietnam they never tried to take the whole hill. Instead they went from tree to tree until they had gained the whole hill.

Chris helped me get from tree to tree out of the disaster.

It would be slow to progress but – with a little help from my friends, I made it.

The point he made then, was now just as valuable as we faced awful tracks along our route.

Once you establish your situation reference point, over-analyzing doesn't help, and momentum is vital.

Sometimes it is best to admit defeat. This doesn't mean giving up the destination – just re-thinking your route. In Cuba there were times when we did.

I have few photos of these tracks. I might have not been exactly 'back-seat driving' but I was concentrating hard on the route ahead as well. There was no time for photography.

Although we had no incoming emus, the focus of the driver was solely on the path ahead.

Mine was on the general route and its wider implications – like the time when I quietly mentioned that, on my side, the drop off was very close and extremely steep – about 200 metres *(about 650 ft)* straight down.

This was a useful piece of information about which side of the track to use – and was something I had perspective on, but the driver didn't.

Rough terrain
is always best negotiated in partnership.

CHAPTER NINE

The view from on high

Climbing upwards despite your fears

From Trinidad, we made a day excursion to the valley of the sugar mills, reached from the road to *Sancti Spiritus*.

Here, in the *Valle de los Ingenios* just 12 kilometres *(7.7 miles)* from Trinidad, you get a fascinating insight into the days of the great sugar barons, their plantations, and the slavery upon which it was built.

The Spaniards had introduced sugar to Cuba in the early 1500s. By the 18th and 18th century it was a dominant sugar producing and exporting nation.

Between 1790 and 1846 there were over 50 mills in this valley and more than 11,000 slaves making up the work force.

Originally these were local natives but with European diseases depleting their numbers, slaves were imported from Africa.

In 1820 this practice became illegal.

The American emancipation of slaves by President Lincoln in 1863 helped a bit, but under Spanish influence it would take longer for this to also end in Cuba. By that time, land degradation and water shortages had led to increasingly lower quality of product.

In addition, other markets had developed and what was once a primary export from Cuba lost its international dominance.

Now most of the mills and houses lie quietly in ruin. However, the heritage has not been totally lost to the world. In 1988, the three interconnected rural valleys of *San Luis, Santa Rosa* and *Meyer* that make up the 225 km *(close to 140 miles)* of the *Valle de los Ingeneros*, together with the city of Trinidad became a single UNESCO World Heritage Site.

Now, there is just one relatively intact mill site that stands witness to a bygone era of the cane barons of Cuban history. Of this original Iznaga plantation, just the tower, the plantation house and some slave quarters remain, along with some sugar milling equipment that sits by the river bank, rusting with its memories.

At one time the Iznaga Tower was the tallest structure in Cuba and was a visible statement of the power and stature of the cane plantation owner, *Alejo Maria Iznaga y Borrell*.

Cuban scholars have found records from 1795 when *Pedro José Iznaga* teamed with *Pérez de Vargas Machuca* to buy the site of the future plantation for 24,000 pesos. *Don Pedro's* son *Don Alejo* inherited the property in 1831 after managing it for many years. He died in 1845.

Much has been written about *Don Pedro*, but who was *Pérez de Vargas Machuca?*

Despite many references noting the illustrious background of the name, it's harder to trace what happened to him. I certainly had no success. But whatever became of him, his heritage is a proud one.

Diego Perez de Vargas was a 12th century knight who is widely recorded as having broken or lost his sword in battle and stripped a branch from a tree to bash his enemies to death – henceforth having the additional descriptor '*Machuca*' attached to his name and to that of his descendants.

'*Machucar*' means to crush.

Don Diego is even mentioned by *Cervantes* in the famous story of Don Quixote. This is the story of a knight called *Alonso Quixano* who has read one too many historical romances and lost his grasp on reality.

Don Quixote's adventures are well-summarised on the website 'Goodreads' this way:

'In the company of his faithful squire, Sancho Panza, his exploits blossom in all sorts of wonderful ways. While Quixote's fancy often leads him astray – he tilts at windmills, imagining them to be giants – Sancho acquires cunning and certain sagacity.

Sane madman and wise fool, they roam the world together, and together they have haunted readers' imaginations for nearly four hundred years.

With its experimental form and literary playfulness, Don Quixote generally has been recognized as the first modern novel.

The book has had enormous influence on a host of writers, from Fielding and Sterne to Flaubert, Dickens, Melville, and Faulkner, who reread it once a year'.

My trip to the *Manaca Iznaga Tower* that was once part owned by a descendent of this famous warrior, was on a hot dry day.

The entry was unprepossessing.

We swung into the homestead complex through dusty tracks beside which sat small houses with their complement of chickens strolling knowledgeably away from the car, seemingly aware that we didn't want to run them over.

Hand-worked tablecloths for sale fluttered from clotheslines in a soft breeze, and to a background hum of cicadas.

There was just one stall selling the tablecloths, although I have since seen photos of banks of stalls in high tourist season. In those photos these handcrafted linens create a series of fluttering curtains that frame the walk to the tower.

In the stillness of the day I was there, a voice could be heard across several acres.

The place seemed at rest with its memories and the quietness was interrupted by only one tourist: me. My two Cuban escorts who climbed the 184 steps to the top of the tower with me had been there before.

The tower itself is as artistic as it was once utilitarian. In the past it housed a bell tower calling everyone to prayer three times a day. It also announced the start and end of the back-breaking daily work day.

At 43.5 metres high *(almost 143 feet)* and made of hard packed clay, wood and metal, it now leans slightly, but that seems to be the only effect of years.

It still stands as a sentinel over the once busy valley.

The tower was robustly built. It has withstood cyclonic winds, tornadoes, lashings of rain, and I read that it has also survived 'the effects of telluric currents' during the intervening centuries.

'Telluric' are the electrical currents that flow under the earth's surface – often thought to follow ley lines, and frequently associated with earthquake activity.

We may best know them as the subject of fiction where they feature fairly frequently.

Some of the most famous references include Umberto Eco's 'Foucault's Pendulum' where protagonists hunt for the centre of the earth. Here, they hope to be able to achieve control of earth energy. Telluric currents also feature in 'Dr. Who' in the 'Missing Adventures' novel.

New Age literature suggests that telluric currents generate sexual promiscuity, but there certainly was no trace of such a legacy in the tranquillity of the Manaca Iznaga Tower when we visited. I felt much more the sadness of the slave heritage: so many individuals whose lives were valued only for their labour.

The lookout ovals on each of the seven levels of the tower give stunning and far reaching views of the surrounding countryside. They make for the creation of spectacularly framed photographic cameos of the lush valley surrounds.

It seems that fame and fortune require structures to honour the prominence of their owner. Around the world this mania, best described as: 'My tower is bigger than your tower', persists to this day.

Although certainly such a statement was part of the reason for building the Manaca Iznaga Tower, it was a common custom of plantation management to have a watch tower.

This one enabled guards to check for pirates off the coast, attempted slave escapes and plantation fires.

It was a sort of insurance policy. Fire in the cane is an imminent risk on plantations, and the slaves were valuable property whose escape was carefully guarded against.

So, while this tower reveals an appreciation for good design, within the context of place and time it is unremarkable in its purpose.

As the famous architect I.M.Pei wrote:

Architecture is the very mirror of life.

*You only have to cast your eyes on buildings
to feel the presence of the past, the spirit of a place;
they are the reflection of society.*

The Manaca Iznaga Tower design brings to the plantation itself traces of the grandeur of the luxurious city residences in Trinidad and Havana that its labour made possible.

The sugar barons built grandly in the days of their dominance of a world-wide commodity. However, local legend says that the tower had another, and perhaps a primary objective.

It is said that the brothers *Alejo* and *Pedro* fell in love with the same woman. Instead of a duel, they competed to create the best construction: *Pedro* with a 28 meter well *(147 feet)* and *Alejo* with his tower.

The well has long since been lost, if it were ever constructed as per the local tale, but the tower was certainly built to impress. They say Alejo still watches everything in the Valley from its viewpoints.

Built in 1860, the seven levels of the Manaca Iznaga Tower change in geometric shapes from the square to the octagon. The wide arches within the internal staircase give easy air circulation and this cools you, making the rise to the top seem less arduous in the heat of the day.

It was only as we drove over the plains back to Trinidad that I reflected on how calm I felt in my tower climb.

Due to a depth perception problem, I have a long history of falling both down *and up* stairs. The tower stairs are very slender and steep. The fact that on climbing them I felt no fear suggested some other influence than being enfolded within the clay walls.

In seeking the cause of my calm, I thought back to a course I had arranged some years before. It was a team building exercise to bring seven defensively individual offices together to realise that they were all part of the same company. The objective was to break down some barriers of mistrust.

The whole event was intended to demonstrate the benefits of collaborative working. I had hoped to show rather than tell that through collaboration each person would actually achieve more. Fortunately it did work. It proved much more powerful than quoting to them the maxim of Aristotle that the whole is more than the sum of its parts.

During this event, one exercise was to ride a 'Flying Fox' or 'Zip Line' as it is more recently called. We were all quite safely harnessed and with well-reputed trainers, so being 60 metres up *(almost 197 feet)* before we stepped off the platform, was an exercise in 'mind over matter', not one of daring. It certainly posed minimal risk.

Having spent much of my childhood up trees with my brother and his friends, I was quite undaunted and eager to try something that had captured my imagination for years. But when it came to my turn I was holding onto the trunk of the tree around which the platform was built. When the trainer turned to me and said: "You next," I still had my arms around the tree trunk and asked could I take the tree with me.

I was inexplicably absolutely terrified.

I did step off,
     but it took everything in me to do so.

I thought the second time would be better,
     but it was worse.

The next day was the ultimate self-challenge.

It was totally optional to undertake this part of the course. Our trainer emphasised that the people on the ground are as important as the ones climbing, for their support is invaluable. So it proved to be.

The task was to ascend an 80 metre caving ladder *(about 262 feet)*, then climb from it onto the branch of the tree to which it was secured, leap off the branch, and hit a bell hung slightly distant before being lowered by your harness to the ground.

Following the briefing, I was the second person to get up and don a harness. Before me was a young lass who had actually passed out from fear on the Zip Line the day before.

Our colleagues asked us why we – the two who had been most scared on the Zip Line - were going to put ourselves through this.

The young girl had her own reasons about proving something to herself.

To the cheers of her colleagues below, she climbed doggedly upwards and flew off the branch to ring the bell loudly on her descent. Satisfaction was written all over her face as she was congratulated by us all.

Her self confidence had noticeably grown. At the close of the two day event she told us that she had learned so much from the response of everyone to her passing out. People ran immediately to her aid and she awoke to a circle of people holding her in their arms and encouraging her not to feel anything but pride in having tried.

She had learned to trust
        and that led her to trust herself.

My reason was different.

I wanted to overcome a fear that was new to me.

Overnight I had pondered where this new fear came from, and I thought I knew.

About two years previously a very dear friend who was a tree surgeon suffered equipment failure while doing a favour for friends, and fell out of a tree to become paraplegic.

I had regularly visited him in hospital over the terrible first three months of his recovery.

This experience of seeing a strapping and charismatic outdoorsman so incapacitated seemed to have left an inerasable mark on my memory. It must have imprinted an unconscious level of caution that was previously absent from my judgment about heights.

Once he recovered, my friend used his experience to build a business based around a very pointed safety message.

This is that:

> *Safety is not just the responsibility*
> *of the company for whom you work:*
> *it's yours*
> *– and you ignore this at your peril.*

Before the accident I had helped him develop his public speaking skills. He was then starting his journey to become a national speaker in his field of work as a tree surgeon and as trainer of others in that same profession. After his accident I helped him develop this different message. It has proven a very powerful one.

So, when the day came to face this new challenge of climbing the caving ladder I told the group that I didn't intend to climb to the top. I just wanted to prove to myself that I could overcome this new fear, so I would climb as far as I felt comfortable. I thought that to be about one quarter of the way up.

However, when I reached that point, my colleagues on the ground shouted their encouragement and I took one step more, and then another. So I progressed, slowly inching my way upwards.

There were times when I had to stop and speak sternly to myself for I was still quite terrified.

A caving ladder has lightweight, round rungs. These are strung of high strength wire cable. Because it swings, you climb this ladder with your legs wrapped around the outside wires, placing a foot at a time onto one thin rung after another.

I was so scared that I gripped the ladder exceptionally tightly and for six weeks thereafter my inner thighs were black and blue with bruises. But I did climb higher, until finally I touched the branch.

This was the new goal I had set myself when halfway up.

On achieving this I called out that I was jumping back and did so to reach the ground and burst into tears of relief.

My colleagues surrounded me with a giant group hug. When I recovered my composure I was proud to have forced myself to overcome a fear that had never been there before.

Since then I have never felt that awful terror again. More importantly it proved to me that I was capable of doing the thing I was sure I couldn't do.

Later in my life when faced with seemingly insurmountable challenges I remembered having overcome this fear.

The memory of this achievement gave me courage to go ahead and try, one step at a time, climbing upwards towards my goals.

As Henry Ford said:

> *One of the greatest discoveries*
> *a man makes,*
> *one of his great surprises,*
> *is to find he can do*
> *what he was afraid he couldn't do.*

Leaving the area around Trinidad behind, we arrived in *Sancti Spiritus* just as there was major construction underway to set up a government sponsored music performance that was to take place the night after we arrived.

The narrow inner-city streets were jammed with vehicles held up by the manoevering of an enormous semi-trailer load of scaffolding and materials to build a huge stage with back-projection screen.

Eventually we pulled into a back alley, parked the car, and walked around the block to the *Parque Serafín Sánchez,* the central square of Sancti Spiritus.

This was before the 'beautification' that removed the grassed areas for paving (later apparently to be marble-faced) in time for the hosting of President Raul Castro at the 65th anniversary celebrations of the successful revolutionary barracks attacks at *Moncado* and *Santiago*.

As with all the other Cuban cities I visited, the central park is a gathering place for all ages. Along its edges used to be the site of the home of one of the most prominent doctors, politicians and land-owners of the area, and it was to his former residence that we were headed.

When the good doctor and his wife and family left, like all those who left Cuba in those fraught times just before the doors of exit closed for decades, they were only allowed to leave with what they wore.

Descendants of the Doctor still live there and they eke out a meagre supplement to their living with a coffee and refreshment hatch that used to face onto the square.

It was once a grand house, although not opulent. There are still expensive Limoges statues and lamps, crystal chandeliers, fine furniture, and blackening silver that revealed a life much richer than that of the current residents.

The rooftop terrace was beautifully tiled and must be a refreshing place to sit on a sultry evening. Small ceramic plaques with little quotations about the benefits of wine and friendship, or of invoking the blessings of the saints, are embedded in the terrace walls.

The family was very gracious and insisted on me coming to a formal dinner which was carefully presented a few nights later. Once again, I was to be humbled by the hospitality of people who had so little yet made what was served delicious and exquisitely arranged on each platter.

We managed to have a conversation despite my appalling Spanish, and this was made easier by the fact that the young man of the family was busy trying to teach himself German.

It is handy to have a mutual extra language even of a rudimentary variety: on his part in German in which by then I was fluent, and on my part Spanish, which for me was at its most stumbling, 'still-translating-as-I-speak' stage.

We talked about how beautiful Germany is, and they recounted tales of their ancestors who had travelled the world. There was a bit of scuffling about in drawers and out came a 1920s postcard package, about the size of a sardine tin (although obviously not as thick).

It was of the very section of the Rhine where I then lived. This section is punctuated by castles either side and with one tiny one in the middle. It is known as 'The Romantic Rhine' to distinguish it from the more industrial nature of most of the busy river.

They insisted I take it as a keepsake and it now sits with other precious mementos in a special chest of memories.

The contents of this box of magic are varied: the poems written about me as gifts when I departed from a location where for a brief period I shared the lives and experiences of some wonderful people; the letters and cards of thanks that show that in some small way I made the world better for someone.

It is to this box I return when the world hangs heaviest on my heart.

As I look at these marks of a life full of ups and downs, each sparks the memory of a past moment in time.

They remind me in dark times just how wonderfully colourful my life has been, and that I have accomplished some things that are really worthwhile – mostly for others – and these are the most important, for they gave someone else a nudge upwards in *their* darkest times.

This delightful family were thrilled to be donated a package of Dallmayr coffee.

It is sad to 'take coals to Newcastle', for that is the equivalent of giving German produced coffee to people whose country used to be a known supplier of some of the best coffee in the world.

The courtyards had been neglected for decades and the library of books showed an eclectic taste. I was told all the other volumes where in boxes and was sad to hear this, as those on display were all leather bound and I suspect the others to be the same.

Loving books as I do, I hate to see beautiful volumes stored away, and especially when that storage is by people who have no interest in the books or what they contain, and therefore may not have stored them well.

The uncle of the family was very talkative and my Tour Director said he loved to dance and had heard that I did too. We headed off to a small local bar and danced the night away, lubricated by many Buccaneros and a few Cuba Libres.

On our return, his son, the German language student, asked me to join them the next day at the big concert for which we had seen the early preparations.

He shyly told me that he had dreams of a different future. He is now overseas and pursuing those dreams. I don't know how and I would never ask.

The next day I went on one of my lone wanderings about the town.

In front of the sheet glass windows of one of the banks a temporary stage had been set up.

The footpath there had two wide steps of about 8 metres *(or about 26')* wide. On the upper step that had a depth of about a metre *(or a bit over 3')* the stage backdrops stood. These comprised three individual panels of wood.

To the frame of the two on the outside, heavy material striped in three shades of green had been attached.

On the outside corners were bunches of three balloons and in front of each was a microphone stand with portable mikes.

On the centre panel, a clown's face graced the white sheet covering beneath. A festoon of balloons along the top bounced in the light breeze giving the effect of an outlandish hairdo.

The lower step had its own similar microphone stand.

Three lovely young ladies with long flowing hair and wearing harem girl outfits were entertaining a fascinated crowd that had exceeded the seating laid out and now spilled into a wide band of standing audience.

Off to the side of this crowd were small sales tables behind which sat the artisan creators of things knitted, wood turned, or painted.

I stood on the edge of the audience.

In front of me were some more little harem girls and a group of girls and boys wearing cleverly created animal masks:

- A piggy with a wonderful round snout.
- A tan coloured dog with floppy ears and pasted on whiskers of thinly cut paper.
- A white rabbit whose ears stood straight up with tufts of shredded paper pasted both between them and crossways beneath the eyes and nose. Below this moustache effect, pipe cleaner-type whiskers stood rigidly out on either side.
- There was also what could have been a rooster. It was hard to tell with the blue face and deep, round goggle-type eyes – but I came to this conclusion based upon the yellow beak, below which dangled a red crop of felt.

Immediately in front of me was a creatively outfitted flamenco dancer. Her skirt and cropped bodice had ruffles sewn into loops of decreasing width, so that they bunched at the centre back. These were edged in shiny gold ribbon and it was only by looking carefully that I saw that the white fabric was sheeting. Her headdress was artistically crumpled gold foil wrapping paper.

The compère may have been their teacher. She was dressed as a clown with a jaunty red and white striped cap and her face freckled with big black spots and a round red dot on the end of her nose. With genuine enthusiasm she introduced the story that was then enacted by the children with total aplomb.

It struck me how comfortable the children were with performing in front of an audience.

Knowing a little about the school system I knew that they would have had plenty of previous practice, so it may have even seemed quite natural. None of them looked the slightest bit nervous before their performance.

I couldn't help but think how fortunate they were to have such composure. Self confidence is a great gift to a young person as their personality is formed. That is one of the real gifts of a Cuban education.

Leaving the street performance, I heard music coming from the local church. It was not traditional church music but was an interesting guitar-based mixture.

I walked quietly into the church and tried to get photos without being intrusive. Although I was unsuccessful in doing so, I really wanted a video of them rehearsing.

Their Stage Manager was a stickler for attention to detail and would break the flow with an explanation about what needed changing. This made several shortened attempts of recording resulting in my battery running down and as my spare was back at the apartment, I just sat and listened.

The music was really terrific and the main guitarist was extremely talented, and even in practice, charismatic.

Not being able to be close enough for my liking, I moved down several rows of pews to get a better viewpoint, taking still photos instead of the planned video.

I thought I was being relatively quiet and not overly touristy. It was a delight to sit in the cool of the church and listen to such a talented group of amateur musicians. Eventually, I left and further up the street found a street market.

On one stall there was relatively new scuba equipment for sale: wetsuits, tanks and regulators, but no flippers.

On the adjacent stall there was a safety helmet that looked like that of a fireman. The associated uniform with its reflective banding, plus steel toed boots, a mattock and long handled metal cutters, and a fire hose together with brand new water valve attachments all sat beside a small portable generator. All were in as-new condition.

What did I say about not understanding how Cuba worked?

At the other extreme, just a few tables further along were brilliantly coloured ornaments made from *papier-mâché* and coconut shells.

A few steps later I almost bumped right into a young musician with guitar in a case over his shoulder. He had been stopped by another young man and was taking down an address in his notebook – perhaps a booking for a fiesta.

A little further along I stopped before a table full of tiny and exquisitely detailed miniature oil paintings. Each was framed carefully in painted bamboo frames, the bamboo having been split into slivers small enough not to dwarf the pictures that were about the size of the box that encases a new Android phone. Each tiny masterpiece illustrated how, with limited access to oil paints or suitable paper, an artist had adjusted his painting style to allow expression of the evocative scenery of the region.

One of these little gems now graces my wall in the dining room.

The big music event was held later that same night. When we finally worked our way through the streets towards the stage it seemed as if the world and his wife were with us in the streets.

Given the size of the Cuban Flag and the revolutionary placards around the stage, it seemed to have been organised by the Communist party.

To my taste, the music was unremarkable, but what truly amazed me was the stage back-projection. The songs were all about the glory of revolution and about the wickedness of other nations.

I have no argument on the subject of wickedness, for it seems our fate as humans to commit one atrocity after another, either by direct action or by a decision not to act, either way in the name of things benevolent.

What I found repugnant was the blood and gore in the images shown to accompany the singing. They were incredibly graphic and searing. I had thought this to be a momentary thing as a backdrop to just one song, but was wrong. As the concert continued, the polemic increased and the images were even more viciously graphic.

The contrast between the unsponsored performances I had enjoyed earlier in the day and the expensively staged one was vivid. In my mind there was no comparison: passion and engagement cannot be bought. The earlier performances had these aplenty and I had no doubt that they would prove more memorable.

I was just about to turn away to go back to my apartment when, from within the dense crowd of the big event a young man edged his way towards me and greeted me as if I should know him.

I was puzzled and it must have shown. He was visibly disappointed and asked if I didn't remember him.

I had to confess not. He grinned and explained that he was the guitarist I had wanted to film in the church.

If I could be recognised in that crowd, obviously I had not been as unobtrusive as I had thought. I was delighted that he had made the effort to greet me and chat and we stood talking and ignoring the exceptionally loud music. It turned out that he was a member of a band that was about to go on tour, and he confessed that he had every intention of staying outside Cuba and building his musical career in another land. I later heard from him that he has succeeded.

244

I left and made my own way back to the charming apartment a few streets away. It looked onto a busy little workshop which made for interesting viewing from above, and gave some insight into the daily workings of the place.

It was closed now, so from the roof I just stood and gazed across the rooftops and wondered at the future of a country where so many of its children wanted to leave for better pastures – or at least new ones.

One of them ended up in Haiti, so I really don't know that this was a step up in economic opportunity, but perhaps so. We each have our own priorities about what makes life important.

What did the Cuban Approach Accomplish?

The experience I had of supporting my friend after he became paraplegic had deeper impacts than I had recognised.

It was strange that it took a month with no plan in Cuba so many years later to identify just how much it had done so.

It made me reflect again on the power of trust, just as the later performances in Sancti Spiritus made me focus on the power of passion, and how it always engages an audience at a level incomparable to that well staged but without it.

The Cuban Approach allowed me the time to wander Sancti Spiritus and be part of the ordinary performances of the local school.

I remember so many of the wonderful costumes my mother made for me.

Later, having been roped into making a cougar for the school play of one of my 'sons', the son of my friend Linda, I appreciated just how much effort goes into these costumes and props.

They are true labours of love.

Such efforts abounded in the school performance and I felt that the young children would also look back in time in appreciation of the efforts of their mothers.

After several young men confiding their dreams of a life outside their homeland I had felt saddened for the country for losing so much talent.

But on later reflection perhaps it is not uncommon.

I did the same.

I felt that my future lay outside my country and so it has proven.

I have come to the conclusion that we all have to find our own place in this world. For some it is where we were planted. For others, there are infinite possibilities.

I think the confidence to make that choice is the great gift that can be given to a child.

There is no point, however, if parents develop that 'stand-alone' capacity and at the same time use emotional blackmail in keeping their brood close for their own purposes of emotional dependency.

My parents were amazingly supportive of my choices. While I see the world as my back garden, they loved their Australian life and preferred to just enjoy regular trips north of the equator – a total of twenty-seven it proved when they totted them up before their death.

I have been told that there are two types of people in life: those who make their own paths and those that just let life happen to them.

I believe that everyone has the capacity to make his or her own pathway. The key is confidence.

In that context, I ask you to build confidence at every opportunity.

Most of us know our own faults. Many of us feel them in the extreme and let them overshadow our abilities. We don't need constant reminders of them.

We need to accept that having faults is part of being human.

We also tend to feel we shouldn't say we are good at something, in case we are thought to be big-headed.

Recognising our gifts is not being big-headed: it is allowing us to shine so we can help others shine.

Please try to do so, and help everyone you care about – and perhaps even those about whom you are quite lukewarm – to shine as well.

The world needs more of this sort of shine instead of out and out bling and bravado!

Step 9 of the Cuban Approach: The View From on High: Ensure your safety and then keep on climbing towards your goal.

Adjusting your sails: To visit parts of Cuba the way I did on my No Plan adventure, is to gain a tiny glimpse into the layers of life upon which the modern Cuba is built.

From an ever troubled past of foreign occupation and subjugation, to an independence that offers little individual independence, has been, and continues to be, a troubled journey.

There is no doubt that much has been accomplished over the recent years to try to bolster the economic position of the populace. Whether those efforts have had the success they may have been thought to provide is a mute point.

When an island is blockaded by a super power, it means that the leadership has untold complications in providing the basic civil provisions of life. This is something we should always consider in our criticisms.

However, I was always taught in business that you never design a system based upon your belief in the goodwill of mankind.

You design a system that can work no matter who runs it and no matter what unexpected events arise.

Accountability lines have to be clear, or you generate the risk of blaming an upright person for a calamity that was the fault of an imperfect system.

The one thing that brings colour and delight to me in Cuba is not just the beautiful land that caused Christopher Columbus to proclaim it as the best he had ever seen, but the spirit of the people, and the way that is expressed in so many creative ways.

My No Plan taught me a lot about life, about myself, and a little bit about Cuba.

It taught me how the power of trust can transform even the bleakest situation.

It taught me that a smile and a generous spirit are parts of a universally-understood language.

It taught me that if you approach life gently sometimes, and passionately and with authenticity other times – and know which goes with what circumstance – then whatever we do, it will be memorable.

In doing so, we have the chance to leave a legacy in our wake.

The Cuban Approach No Plan also had me sitting in front of a wonderful small selection of what is apparently a much larger library of equally fine volumes and wondering how those in boxes could be preserved.

I value books highly. They are part of our history. Award winning Scottish writer Sara Sheridan expressed well my feelings on why they are important:

"Our archives are treasure troves – a testament to many lives lived and the complexity of the way we move forward.
They contain clues to the real concerns of day-to-day life that bring the past alive".

I was taught that books are our friends.

They have so proven to be in my life, and I hope this book will be a friend to give you courage and help you follow your dreams.

CHAPTER TEN

The Hourglass

Telling the time

Time is a curious man-made concept.

It is something that we measure, meter, and try to mould to our own purposes.

We want to control it,
invest in it,
save it –
and set our lives by it.

I couldn't have travelled to Cuba from a more contrasting cultural ethos about how to handle time.

In Germany, punctuality is one of the great social essentials.

There is a joke that all German brains are wired at one end to a watch and at the other to the Atomic Clock.

Being late in Germany is quite simply not acceptable.

In Latin countries time generally indicates what the English call the 'ish' – a slang term that denotes that you mean somewhere vaguely about that time, as in "I'll see you at 12-ish".

Cuba takes this concept to perfection.

Because through necessity and not desire, waiting is a national pastime, people in Cuba tend to be very relaxed about the non-punctual arrival of the person expected.

However, even for Cubans, my Tour Director took this to extremes. The world more or less ran around his schedule, which was influenced by doing this, that, and the other, and doing things for so many people that it took waiting to its infinite extremes.

I had the option to choose someone else with whom to travel, someone who would be more within the general Latino concept of time-keeping – not one like his that made you question if you even had the right day.

But the reality was that my Tour Director has what my brother calls the 'It Factor'.

The 'It Factor' is something almost impossible to define but it marks one person out from the pack.

The 'It Factor' is one of those curious things
that is so hard to describe
that instead of doing so,
you work backwards to a definition
by knowing it when you don't see it.

The 'It Factor' in this case included charm, style, and self-confidence without being boastful.

My Tour Director had these elements to a degree that made me confident that I could trust him and that we would have an entertaining trip together.

In all this I was not wrong.

The downside was that I knew that any estimation about time he made would be way off any concept of the same that I might apply.

This proved to be so.

I would get a call to say he would be there in twenty minutes. An hour and half later he would arrive with a big smile as if he was punctual to the planned minute.

Whether he had a different clock or had thrown his clock away, I don't know. But it did cause me to contemplate the whole concept of time and what it means when you are travelling.

Obviously, even he could be on time for a train or plane. There are times when, whether you are there or not, the event doesn't wait.

I learned that as a Flight Attendant.

One day in my first few months of airline employment I was three minutes late signing on, only to find that the Dispatch Officer had already replaced me with a Reserve.

I had committed one of the great sins of airline culture.

When I remonstrated that I was 'only' three minutes late, I was told I could have just as easily been three minutes early: a deadline is just that – a deadline.

I was never late again – even allowing for severe snow storms, or for the time black-ice on the road caused me to slide off at speed and rejoin the road after some cross-country experience.

That was a time when I was glad to have had some off-road driving training – to know not to brake but to speed up as I hit the embankment at a severe angle likely to roll the car had I not accelerated.

That statement 'A deadline is a deadline' – and the lesson it taught me –have been mainstays to my work life.

Since then I have seldom missed a deadline, have tried always to deliver the required material before its due time, and, unlike some of my friends over the years, have not seen it as a mutable point in time, but one at which whatever was promised should be delivered.

In the event of something catastrophic or unable to be expected happening to makes this impossible, the simple rule of telling the bad news early – together with my proposed remediation – has stood by me.

Many holidays have a need for some level of daily time keeping so you don't miss the hotel breakfast or the local dinner hour, the bus tour, or the last train. But I was on a month with no plan trip through more remote parts of Cuba.

It has been years since I wore a watch, having long ago given up that level of focus on time. These days I can always consult my mobile phone, but in the past I just asked someone if I wanted to know the time.

Think about the folly of what we say about time.

We try to save time.

We spend time and we waste time.

We think time is a definable commodity.

We teach courses on the management of time, but not on how to throw away the clock and measure our moments only by the delights they bring us.

In our modern expectation that we can control the world we live in, we seem to think that time is something tangible and not the abstract construct it really is.

Back on the Bay of Pigs, watching the brightly coloured fish in a lagoon that reflected the surrounding tropical vegetation, it was as if there was no such thing as time, above or below.

In Cuba I have found that time takes on a different quality. When there, for me there is no past and no future – just the moment.

I reckon that is what makes Cuba so special to me, for we of other countries have mostly forgotten how to immerse ourselves totally in a moment.

I have often commented that it is a symptom of modern life that no one is where they are any more. They are either plugged in to earphones, checking or sending text messages, or talking on the phone.

The moment, with its scents, sounds and curiosities, is not being absorbed.

The only thing that seems to remain for most people is a fogged recollection of place, of people, and of their interactions.

To those trying to connect in person with them, they give a superficial pretence of 'being there' when in fact their focus is on the abstract other world of electronic contact.

Those of us who travel to seek the soul of a place
Understand that the time spent waiting is not lost.

The time we thought was to be spent doing one thing can be well invested elsewhere:

- in watching,
- thinking, or
- just sitting with eyes closed, listening to the ocean and smelling the fresh saltiness of the air.

I have sat this way on the Malecón for hours, not speaking to anyone, not thinking about anything, just being there.

Since we were travelling on a time schedule regulated by our interest along the way and not by having to be anywhere at a particular time, we could spend time to do what W.H. Auden recommended in his much quoted verse:

> *What is life, if full of care*
> *we have no time to stand and stare.*

It seems a fundamental reality of most of our non-Cuban lives that we don't have – or think we don't have – time to stand and stare.

That can best be translated as: we don't *take the time* to stand and stare.

Did my time staring at the fish accomplish anything? No. Unless you consider that it started a deeper thinking process.

Is that important?

My answer is that it is important. It slows you down.

It stops the worrisome habits we develop about thinking of many things at once – that usually translate into trying to juggle soot.

Are all the things which fill our minds really as vital as we think them to be?

Must we do most of what we do: feel pressure to do?

In my one month with no plan in Cuba I had plenty of spare time. I had nothing particular to do, and all day to do it.

Each day we would agree on a general focus, which is a bit different from making a plan for it.

As I am writing, I have the benefit of just one such day to remind me. There is a small red flower that rests on my keyboard. It was one of the treasures I brought with me from my trip.

My Tour Director was off on a mission of his own in Cienfuegos and we had agreed to meet in the José Martí Park. It is a lovely place and I had strolled to it from Cienfeugos Boulevard, the longest tree-lined avenue in Cuba.

The road is flanked by neo-classical architecture, and I ambled along taking photos as I went.

Knowing I would have a long wait ahead of me, I sat in the shade, 'people-watching' as the daily activities of the square took place around me.

There was a group of little girls just outside the *Teatro Terry*. This theatre of some magnificence reminded me of the often quoted saying that behind every great fortune is a great crime.

Tomas Terry made his fortune from the illegal importation of thousands of slaves after slavery had been abolished. They were imported to work on the plantations that provided the wealth to create this great theatre in which years later, Caruso sang and Pavlova danced.

Terry even reputedly had a program of slave breeding. He selected the best candidates from his latest imports to expand his holdings – despite the fact that children born of slaves and those over sixty were supposed to be free.

It is ironical that from this tragic history there is now benefit to the young of today, many of them perhaps descendants of this cruelty.

These little girls were obviously waiting for a dancing class. Their clothing formed a rainbow of colours – leotards under bright dresses or small dancing skirts over colourful trousers.

It was lovely to just sit and watch their antics.

Suddenly they rose as one. It was like watching a flock of reeling, multi-coloured birds. They had spotted their teacher and swirled around her as she approached, kissing each in turn.

I was smiling to myself in pleasure at this scene when a little toddler appeared before me bearing a tiny red blossom. She was in the care of what appeared to be her grandparents, who were sitting on a nearby bench under the arching hibiscus.

This little girl had been watching me. We had exchanged waves and a smile when I first sat down. Now, she offered me this tiny floral memoire with all the dignity of someone presenting a bouquet to the Queen.

I hope I accepted with such grace as would Her Majesty.

I brought the flower home with me, carefully pressed and intact inside my Passport.

It reminds me how pleasurable it is to sit, to have no plan, and just to enjoy the everyday sights of a place, and 'feel' its character.

As I watched these little girls, I realised how much I still felt the loss of the seven children I might have had if fate had not deemed it impossible through one miscarriage after another.

The things that sear our hearts the deepest
never truly heal.

You get used to the hurt
but it remains somewhere in your soul.

My wish to have a family of my own wasn't to be – but fatefully I decided that if I had no children of my own, I would cherish those of my friends and of all children who came into my life, for however long.

It is as if this conscious decision transmitted itself to the universe.

This little Cuban princess was one of many unexpected encounters I have cherished over my travels.

I remember walking the mountain trails in Oregon with friends from South Africa.

A crowd of young hikers approached us and two of them eagerly tugged at my sleeve to show their finds, with all the wonder that hikers of no more than seven years bring to an adventure.

My companions were stunned as they left.

"Fancy meeting children you know out here," they said. "How do you know them?"

I replied that I had never met them in my life – but that all children can see the word 'KID' on my forehead from fifty paces.

Perhaps they can on yours as well.

This happens regularly to me.

On a Rhine Cruise at age twenty-one I was reading on deck, when a little lady of about five tugged my sleeve with the eager question: "Would you like to play with my dolly?"

Friends with painfully shy children who don't interact with strangers have worried me with their shocked looks when they return to a room to find us playing and laughing together. However, I find that the shock only reflects surprise that I have the key to the magical kingdom of fantasy, where children create one of the best things in life: wonder.

Apparently, to children I don't appear to be an adult.

Many of my friends can relate to thinking the same!

Luckily I am graced with friends who have generously shared their children with me.

One cherished memory is of my two American children Dee and Amy hugging me when Dee got married.

In the group hug of the three of us, Amy said:

"Don't ever forget, we're your children too".

When I was living in America, I received a message from another friend, who three times had announced she was off with her husband to make a baby and did so – just as I was losing one of my own.

She and I had worked together at Gatwick Airport in England. Many years later and long before I ever encountered the country, they were living in Cuba where my friend's husband had a diplomatic role. At that time their children were diagnosed with a rare genetic disorder that would mean the eventual death of all three.

When I got the news of this, they had moved to be close to the facilities of a major American hospital. Fatefully, I was then living in Texas. It seemed powerful to me that, had I my own children, I could not have dropped everything to help her in this dreadful time of anguish.

I learned a lot from the experience and felt honoured to have shared it. The attitude of the parents was a lesson to us all:

> *Don't think of the time you won't have*
> *– think of the time you do have*
> *and make it joyous.*

They did.

Several times I flew up on midnight 'Red Eye' flights to spend time with them and the children.

I had arranged for the 'Make a Wish' people to visit. Knowing they had been there, I called to find out how it went.

My friend said they were very nice, but were thinking in terms of baseball caps for the kids. She had been thinking in terms of a family Caribbean cruise. We laughed about differences in expectation.

When I arrived on my next visit I carried a huge Mexican sombrero on the side of which were glued plastic champagne glasses with their stems crossed, streamers, dice and paper blow-out whistles.

As usual my friend was there to meet me. I passed the hat to her, saying that I couldn't spring for a cruise in the Caribbean and asked would this do as a substitute.

257

This resulted in her arranging a dinner party when I was there – with us all dressed to the hilt: ladies in evening dress (mine borrowed) and gentlemen in tuxedos – while she enjoyed her one night's cruise in the Caribbean, without leaving home.

With such pressures of looking after the needs of the children, the couple didn't go out to socialise, so on another occasion we held the Bridesmaids' Ball.

The favourite hospital nurses and friends arrived wearing the most hated bridesmaid dress they had been forced to wear. Someone donated one for me as she couldn't decide which in her collection was the worst - and these two vied for first place for being so labelled.

One lass arrived wearing football socks under a frothy wedding cake of a dress full of frills – most unsuited to her own preferences.

My friend and her husband kindly reached out to many less financially secure people whose children had also drawn the same fateful gene. They ended up being the strength for them, and for many of the extended family and friends who are affected by such tragedy.

They also experienced something I had painfully learned after my many miscarriages.

People sometimes respond very cruelly – I am sure without meaning to.

Because they don't know what to say, people cross the road rather than speak to you.

They compound your sorrow and distress by isolating you from chances to talk – even about normal everyday things, not necessarily about the hurtful reality you are suffering.

Please don't ever do this.

There is nothing you *can* say that will help except to say that you don't know what to say, but that you care.

That is the dearest and most cherished of treasures, knowing that you aren't alone in this agony of loss, or worse – somehow held responsible for distressing other people to such an extent that they cross the road rather than meet you face to face. When people do so, or ignore you by electronic means, they add guilt to grief, as if it is somehow your fault for giving them such discomfort.

At the time, I remember my friend saying that she and her husband were amongst the happiest of the couples they knew. She felt it was because they had learned to take their happiness in five-minute increments. We can all learn from that.

When my partner was dying in a foreign hospital I had no family or friends nearby to support my vigil.

I was then comforted by the wisdom I had experienced with this family whose three lovely children faced the same outcome.

The memory of the laughter of those three children lifted my soul.

Similarly, it was Adam *(then 13)* and Alex *(then 10)*, who are the children of my friends in Sussex, who rescued me when I returned to England with the ashes of my partner.

They had their bicycles ready, and one for me.

Before we set out, I was solemnly told that we were going to the bluebell woods and the badgers hide and the sledding hill with its woodland tower – but in the woods we would stop by a small bridge.

Alex told me that on that little bridge you could hear nothing but the whispering of the wind above and the busy burble of water over pebbles below.

I remember as if today being told:

"It's a magical place that makes you feel far away from the world – and hopefully it will be the happiest day of your life".

So I do have children after all.

My reveries on all these children were triggered by the gift of a flower in José Martí Park in Cienfuegos.

This little girl left a little piece of herself in my heart and left me smiling. Her gift of a flower brought to my mind memories of all the children whose infectious laughter and spontaneous affection has been mine to share.

Perhaps I treasure these more because I only have them 'in five minute intervals'.

In the shade, I smiled to myself, recalling so many gifts that have warmed my heart in the same way: gifts of the sort that only a child can give.

Does it have to be *my* child who does so?

Of course not, but to appreciate each small gift and each precious moment takes being open to the gifts that each new day brings.

That allows the power of each small gift to do some housekeeping of the soul in the process.

In times of great sadness when I have felt so alone, I played a game I made up for myself. It is called: *'What Five Good Things Happened Today?'*

Sometimes, it has only been the beauty of the V of geese flying against an autumn sunset on their southward journey that counted as one of the five.

But I could always find five.

I had a journal book with me when we were in that Mexican Hospital.

On one side the cover was a drawing of a ginger cat stretched happily in the sunshine. When turned over, the other side of the book had a cover with a drawing of the same cat with hair standing on end, arched in response to thunder and lightning.

The sides were labelled respectively: Good Days. Bad Days.

In all that period I never had a totally bad day – even the day he died.

On that day all these things were part of my Good Things:

- The kindness of the ward crew who came and took me to their little under stairs coffee hideaway and comforted me with their genuine care, despite us not sharing the same language.
- The nestling to my side of the big Old English Sheepdog who used to visit the terrace restaurant.
- The sound of rain on a corrugated iron roof, seeming to connect that moment to sounds of my childhood – as if to show that in life, everything is a continuum.
- The best good thing was that I know he died surrounded by love.

My No Plan Cuban adventure allowed me lots of time and space, free of interruption from the everyday activities of my regular life. On this spur line where I had managed to shunt myself as a pause in my forward life journey, I seemed to be letting the valuable things of my life be sorted and placed into meaningful but peaceful storage. In the process these were also dusted with a more positive hue.

The negatives of the situation seemed to dim as the positives wrote themselves indelibly into my memory. It made a precious accumulation of lessons learned from both good and bad experiences.

On another day on my No Plan travels, we took a mountain trail that passed over a small brook. Beside the bridge was an old sugar cane press, a remnant from a slave past. There was a small open air café close by so we stopped for a refreshing Cristal and Bucanero, drinking it in companionable silence in the shade.

The sugar cane grinder was in our line of vision and it made me think of what time does to our perspective.

We think that our own time – this precious period we are given to enjoy and form our lives – holds some relevance in the greater scheme of things.

We do so because we naturally think we are important to the world – which we are – but not *that* important.

We do so because we measure our lives in this strange construct called time.

That is also quite valid, but also, when considered in the broader view, not that relevant.

Does it really matter:

- how old we are,
- what year we were where, or
- with whom?

Surely it is more important that even the slaves at this sugar-press loved, had friends, sang and danced, and did the best they could to make the most of each positive moment – however few these may have been.

In reflecting on the concept of time, of our place in the continuum of life and the role of those we love who have died but yet live on, I agree with lawyer Bonnie Freedman who is quoted in the New York Times as saying:

An unhurried sense of time is in itself
a form of wealth.

Without an unhurried sense of time, our subconscious cannot sort the increasing load of emotions, experiences, lessons, and delights of the past, so they can inform a better life in the future.

Step 10 of the Cuban Approach: The Hourglass: Time is a variable construct: on vacation it should elongate to savour the small moments that make the big memories.

What did the Cuban Approach accomplish?

I had made a clear choice at the outset.

My Tour Director chose to not live by any sense of timeliness. His time-keeping was something so removed from normality that even his Cuban relatives and friends shook their heads – and they were holding to a flexible Cuban version of being on time, something to some considerable extent more elastic than mine.

That was my trade-off. I knew I would have to live with it.

There were times along the way when he was off with his relatives or friends, a visit to whom our route made possible. This left me hours to fend for myself.

Should I go exploring by myself, I had no way to communicate with him to say where I was off to and when I would be back. This meant that I often stayed put because he knew where I was and I figured he would turn up. Eventually he did.

Perhaps I could have seen more had I wandered off alone. But this trade-off was a known aggravation factor. I figured it was the speck in my eye from the wind of opportunity.

I also wondered if the Universe was sending me a lesson.

I am someone who is tremendously organised at work and there my time-keeping is usually good.

In my personal life however, I am not at the opposite end of the same continuum that marked out the time-keeping of my Tour Director.

- Twice, I told my parents the wrong day of my arrival back in Australia.
- I have muddled the birthdays of friends and family too often, and
- I have been known to be a day, an hour, or a week early for an appointment. I am not sure why.

Perhaps my Tour Director was there to let me see how aggravating it is for me to be like this – and to value even more the forbearance of friends and loved ones who have tolerated this failing of mine for years.

On the plus side, all this waiting enabled me to refine my ability to be alone, and just be.

This is not always easy to do, let alone in a foreign city where you are dependent on the good offices of another.

The trick is not to let aggravation spoil the times when you do have company, even if it's that same company that caused the aggravation in the first place.

Because I had the time to sit and wait in Cienfuegos under the shade of a mimosa tree in José Martí Park, I realised how many children there are in my life. I recalled how many have passed through it, leaving imprints on my heart.

Because I had time to sit, I received a tiny red blossom that accompanies me yet.

Because I had time to sit, I saw all the details of how the little girls and their dancing teacher interacted.

The nature of being relaxed and accepting of delays works from this principle:

> *The way things are*
> *is the way things are.*

This is the gift such an attitude can bring.

When my partner was dying in that Mexican hospital, I wrote that quote in big letters and stuck it on the bathroom door of our hospital room.

It reminded me that thinking about why and how this could be happening was useless.

It was worse than useless, for such questioning about something that was merely a fact of life would bring negativity into a room which needed as much love and positive thinking as it could hold.

To focus my mind, instead I sketched the big English sheep-dog with the very non-Mexican name of Toby who used to visit us in the garden each day.

This sketch I gave as a parting gift to a lovely couple from New Mexico who were there with their Dad.

My time at this hospital was one of learning.

It was a time to learn about the value of life rather than of death.

It was a time of learning Spanish and of also learning about how things work in a city like Tijuana.

It was a time to learn about bakeries and bookshops (I wanted to buy a book on architecture in English as a birthday present for my partner – not the easiest thing in a Mexican city, but I did find it), about markets, about how to return something to shop with pigeon Spanish, and about public transport.

Each evening I caught a taxi in and out of Tijuana – a local adventure of shared transportation that took some courage and halting Spanish to negotiate.

I had found that there was a language school beside the hospital. The few words I learned on the course were all to do with pain medication and hospital terminology, so hardly useful for polite social engagement outside that environment.

It was on my training ride with my Spanish teacher that I learned that you never sit in the taxi seat behind the driver in the station-wagon.

That seat is for four bottoms, and if one or two said bottoms are of generous proportions, your fate is to be squashed between them.

Having clambered into the back of the station-wagon (or estate car as it is otherwise called) or into the boot for we English, the trunk to those using American English, I was unsure about the expected number of people the protocol allowed for this flat area. On each occasion it was well packed, but I am unsure if it was at capacity.

My only way of entry was to hoist my skirt indecorously high and climb in. Once seated, I noticed that there was no handle on the inside, and realised you have to lean over the back – another indecorous move if the skirt is even knee length – to open from the outside handle.

From this position, I was unsure how you managed to pay. When I asked how to pay the driver from the rear of the taxi, I could see an easy fix. I suggested that you must just throw your fare over the head of the other passengers toward the driver.

My lovely Spanish teacher Bonnie took pains to explain the system to me. She laughingly told me not. Once out of the taxi you walk to the driver's window to pay.

Wondering how to recognise my taxi route for the return trip, I was told to look out for a sign across the front windscreen showing the street address.

I stared at passing taxis and could see no such sign.

"There goes one", called Bonnie, pointing.

I shook my head in puzzlement.

"It said ..." and she quoted the street on which we stood.

Again I shook my head, saying, "No. It clearly said 'Looney Tunes' on that windscreen".

She laughed helplessly.

The sun visor of that vehicle certainly had said 'Looney Tunes' but I eventually learned to pick out the unfamiliar street name on ill-placed placards inside the windscreens of passing vehicles. This meant that I could travel to the city and home to the hospital safely on my own.

Once in the city, I would make a quick tour of the bakeries and local markets and bring back things to entertain us all in our long vigils – things to taste and things to play with, for we all needed distraction and laughter.

Bakeries are different the world over – yet the same.

I just pointed and brought back selections of things that we then tasted with all the delight of naughty children breaking boarding house rules.

I am still in contact with my friends from New Mexico and also with their two sons, who very wonderfully regard me as family though we have not yet met.

Their ranch is on my list of places to go soon.

I will never forget Bonnie Delgado, my wonderful Spanish teacher. Her support and help was so heartfelt in that awful period in a foreign land where the formalities of death took on even greater complexity. It was beyond any level of her actual responsibility as a language teacher.

My partner's daughter had asked me to please make sure that there was a minister at her father's cremation service.

At the time of that request, she and I both believed that her father had no known spiritual belief or faith - perhaps something approaching Buddhism – but not the familiar faith of the Anglican or Roman Catholic Churches.

This was later disproved when, a few days before he died he asked me to climb onto the bed with him.

We talked about where he wanted his ashes interred – about how much he loved his daughters and how he ached not to be able to see them live out the delights of their life and their accomplishments. He then amazed me by saying that he now knew that there is a spiritual force greater than us, and that it was with us always.

It was a great comfort to me – and when I later told his daughters, I believe also to them.

However, true to the promise about getting a Minister of the cloth to attend, I employed the lovely Bonnie to find an Anglican priest in the very Roma Catholic Mexican city of Tijuana.

To my amazement she did.

We made arrangements to meet him the following day before the cremation which was to take place at noon. The timing was important as it meant I could catch a flight later that day to Santa Ana in California to the support of my lovely friend Linda.

I had been asked by my partner to do whatever was the tradition wherever he died and Bonnie helped me do so.

We had a fabulously colourful wreath.

The cemetery people had explained all the processes to Bonnie who, at about 23 years old, was graciously acting as my interpreter at this harrowing time.

Then we waited for the minister to arrive.
And we waited.
And we waited.

Finally, the officials came and explained that they could only wait a short time longer due to the logistics involved.

Bonnie called the minister's wife. He had definitely left and he was definitely going to the correct cemetery of the four in the city.

He never arrived, and when at last we realised that he wasn't going to be there, I chuckled.

Bonnie looked at me in a puzzled way.

I explained that it was my partner having the final say!

I was sure that somehow from beyond this life he had arranged the delay, since a more informal ceremony would have been his preference.

Faced with the absence of a priest, I said it was now up to us. We found a few scraps of paper and I wrote out a little service.

As we went to his side to read it, Bonnie quietly asked if I would mind if she read something she had written. I was deeply touched.

Here it is, in part:

For life has always been.
God has always been.
So now you will be purely spirit.

...

You will be in all of life.
As your soul rests, your spirit is set free to be.

It was heartbreakingly eloquent.

I hope that one day Bonnie will find me, for I have lost track of her.

Of course Mexico also runs on Latin time, so who knows what happened to the minister.

My learning of the Cuban Approach probably began there.

It was in Tijuana that I learned that by using time carefully I could compress it to achieve what I wanted in the very short time away from the hospital

I also learned that the long hours of waiting beside the bed of someone you cared for so deeply could be an exercise in self-control and of banning any sense of negativity. I told myself: "You are the last link to life. It *must* be positive".

Time therefore took on different meanings for the same elapsed period. If we are honest, time is like that. It can seem to creep along or race, depending upon our emotions and environment.

In that hospital, I learned:

- About the importance of creating a positive environment to surround someone who is dying with laughter.
- The delights of baked goods smuggled into a hospital with a focus on the healthy.
- The challenge of trying to learn Mexican children's games and compete with your fellow patients to learn faster.
- Instead of being what many people are in hospital – nothing more than their illness – to make a point of having conversation about everything else *other than* the illness and its treatment.

For a competitive man such as he was, my partner drew enormous satisfaction from being the first of the patients to perfect a Mexican children's game. It was a simple toy I had brought from the city market for the entertainment of the patients. They used to have alternating tries at it in the hallways – and it caused a lot of laughter.

He was truly delighted to be triumphant.

He died a few days later.

To be normal is so essential in such an atmosphere, for death is normal.

It is just that, with our strange view of time and our Western societal avoidance of reality of death and dying, we don't know how to deal with it.

We selfishly think we need to keep our loved one with us for as long as possible.

But, like the native peoples of the world, I believe we each have our path.

The end is possibly not the end.

What is important
is that you live while you live,
and you feel all
that is good and positive before you die.

That is my belief.

In that respect it is the ultimate test of what is time.

Since our loved ones still live
within us and our memories,
did their lives end?

Now that I look back on that hospital time from a distant perspective, I realise that it was waiting without hope, yet it never felt that way.

Strangely, it was an intimate and peaceful time and in turn it offered me a lifetime gift: that of knowing someone I loved very dearly had died well.

It is not a small thing.

Our time together was not long, but how do you measure the value of what is special? It has no time measurement.

It just is.

We want to manage our time.

I guess we are taught that early in life. This, then colours our response to delays that take the ability to manage time out of our hands.

It seems that we organise our lives around the set of constructs that come from the sum of our cultural experience, and perhaps one of the strongest of these is this one about 'time'.

Non-Latino Latin Dancing students learn at an early stage to deal with the contrast of their expectations with those of others.

Any Latin Dance event that is supposed to start at a certain hour will not actually start until possibly two hours later than that. However you should be there 'just in case'.

You learn that the concept of 'Latin time' is not the same as yours, but because you love the final result of dance, music, and that passionate enthusiasm that makes an event an *event*, you adapt.

Some people don't adapt. They 'put up with it'.

In other words they develop a level of aggravation that is incremental in proportion to the amount of elapsed time from the expected original hour.

This may or may not be concealed but it always has the same effect: fretting and fuming. Even done inwardly, this loses what the period has to offer.

So often we find that the delay that upset our plans and caused us aggravation turned out to be a gift, for it brought other possibilities, experiences – even life-saving ones.

I learned this after an experience of a life-saving delay when living in Canada.

At the end of the Easter break we were driving at night from Vancouver towards home in Edmonton. The route took us through the Rocky Mountains.

I was suffering from a violent reaction against what we later deduced to have been a drug in my drink at a party the night before.

My brother had always told me that if I ever felt a drink tasted odd to spit it out and get out of the place immediately.

I had done so, gathering up my young colleague after taking her drink from her hand.

The next day we stopped at a roadside diner before crossing the Rockies.

I felt really ill but had not managed to be sick and get rid of the offending substance.

As a result, while the rest of my friends ate heartily I just tried to concentrate on not throwing up in public.

They got up to leave but by then I had to excuse myself.

At last my stomach had cooperated with my wish to get rid of this awful feeling. It took some time to rearrange myself after being really, really sick. I emerged embarrassed and apologetic.

We continued.

About fifteen minutes later we arrived at a catastrophic scene around a bend in a mountain pass.

There had been an avalanche minutes before.

The cars whose lights we were following could be seen no more. They were somewhere underneath thousands of tons of snow that had crashed down on them.

That would have been our car had I not been violently ill and delayed our departure.

This, and other life events, has taught me that a delay may be a gift, so I try to exhaust the intervening moments of their potential.

Adjusting your sails: Whenever those governed by the clock travel to where time is treated more as a guide than a guard, they have the choice:

- of frustration
- of adaptation, or even
- of turning the period into a building block of thought from which can come better things.

Frustration is self-defeating on many levels.

Adaptation to the flexibility of concepts of time is challenging, but opens so many opportunities – not the least of which is to re-examine yourself.

The thoughts that arrive through having no need to think anything in particular, are when great discoveries have been made.

At such times great insights have illuminated previously unclear thought, and unlikely solutions have been arrived at.

Such times allow the jumble of overlapping thoughts and pressures of a busy and overtaxed mind to be sorted and stored into more useful categories in the great library of the mind.

Once the mind is uncluttered and calm, it is open to absorb things that may otherwise go unnoticed.

It begs the question of why we should expect that our interpretation of the importance of the clock, a schedule, a strictly- held traditional convention of time-keeping ought to be universally applicable?

Reading the winds: These winds of time were variable.

Just when I thought I had set my sails to capture the best opportunities, the winds changed direction. I therefore needed to be continually adjusting the lines that tethered me to the sails of a modern western expectation of how time should be handled.

Whenever modern-day western society meets the rest of the world there is a fraying at the edges of the fabric of daily life.

The challenge to the traveller encountering a new social concept about time is perhaps one of the hardest to read.

Is a lack of focus on an appointed meeting time universally rude or thoughtless?

In Cuba, it was obvious that there was considerable flexibility about the whole concept of time. This is not uncommon in a Latin culture.

So, how we think about time is perhaps changed by context. When the future is unclear, a focus on the moment is natural.

If you are truly in that moment – with the people, the scenery, the whole atmosphere that colour that moment – why break it for something arbitrary such as a self-imposed fixed point in time?

I knew from experience that such cultures can differentiate between immutable time like aircraft departures, and self-imposed schedules such as arrangements to meet.

Their attitude to time is not irresponsible or capricious, although it may be flexible to the point of some frustration.

It was clear to me that even though I had previously learned to read the winds of time, I still had much to relinquish before I could adjust my sails to capture all that they held for me.

CHAPTER ELEVEN

Incommunicado

Electronic dependency

My mobile phone decided I should be incommunicado.

For reasons neither the Cuban telephone company *ETECSA* nor I could fathom, my mobile carrier had blocked it. Perhaps while examining my phone's few functions, one of my Cuban friends had inadvertently pressed a wrong command.

Whatever the cause, it refused to speak to me or allow me to speak to anyone else until I got to Madrid on the return trip. Then, it obligingly responded to every command without the code it had previously demanded.

Perhaps it was because I did have forbidden GPS localisation on the phone as part of my telecoms package.

This phone was really a precursor to a 'Smart' phone, which I had deliberately taken with me instead of my newer one.

By contrast to today's technology it was a 'One day I could be Smart and in the meantime I can get you to MapQuest' phone. I couldn't disable these direction finding capabilities, rudimentary though they were.

Whatever the cause of my inability to make or receive calls or messages in Cuba, I took it as an omen.

I am a fan of omens.

At the command of the Universe, I was obviously being immersed in a sort of congenial Cuban time warp.

Who was I to upend the plans of something as grand as the whole Universe?

I knew from experience that it worked the other way around.

The Universe always had plans that won out over my own, no matter how carefully they had been constructed, so this time I went quietly, accepting my fate as a truly lone traveller.

However, I did send a text message from the phone of my Tour Director to let key people know this was a number on which I could be reached.

Then, I rather relished the whole idea that the rest of the world was doing its own thing but leaving me untouched by all the things that would normally come my way in a usual day.

Having realised I couldn't fix the situation, I found it rather freeing.

The thought of complete electronic isolation could be unnerving.

It is probably more so for people who have to communicate their every life moment and thought in excruciating detail on Facebook or by Twitter; or who always leave their mobile phone on the restaurant table in case they miss a call or text message.

These not being my habits, I wasn't so anxious, but had thought I could access my email. This proved a false expectation based on past experience.

Times change – and so do internet connections.

Having paid for the expensive time at the Internet café in Havana, I could see messages, but not read them.

It seemed that in the intervening years since my last visit, time had moved in a zigzag of contradiction familiar in Cuba.

On the one hand, now locals could have an email account.

On the other, where once visitors eventually had access to accounts despite torturously slow connections, now, with no better connection time, your messages couldn't be read or sent.

You could see they were there, so you were tantalised by the subject line, but barred from any further access.

Once I got over the frustration of going backwards in time in this regard when visiting this Cuba as distinct from the last Cuba, it occurred to me that this confirmed that despite our expectations to the contrary, one really has very little *need* to communicate with the outside world.

How would any of us have coped in the era of the great adventurers, where letters would arrive in bundles that revealed months and months of diligent correspondence? Then, each letter had been composed while never knowing if the person had yet received the last one.

So how does one maintain relationships with no phone calls, no text messages, and no email?

For me the answer was easy.
I didn't.
I didn't need to.

Most of the people I care about knew I was away for a month. Therefore, when I reminded myself of this context it was not as unsettling as it first seemed when the full extent of my electronic isolation revealed itself.

My best girlfriend, Linda, whom I previously mentioned, moved to California from Houston about the same time I left Houston. A West Texan beauty *(inside and out),* she was once my boss. When she moved, she said apologetically that she didn't do letters or emails and hated talking on the phone.

I replied that I knew that. I also knew she loved me whether I heard from her or not.

Facebook seems to have become Linda's medium but since by choice it is not mine, we still revert to old ways.

Every now and then I get a card. Inside is written simply:

'Love ya – Linda'.

When I flew in to Santa Ana airport from Mexico after my partner died, none of our bags were fated to arrive with me. They were delivered to the house the next day after a side flight to some other destination.

On arrival, the absence of luggage was not immediately apparent. As I approached the baggage carousel I was clutching the metal box with the ashes of my partner, and I believe I was still in shock.

There was Linda, with outstretched arms and tears running down her face. There was no elapsed time in our friendship.

Luggage wasn't important: heart and soul caring was.

This, and other lessons along the way, has taught me that while electronic contact is important, it is not critical to maintain that invisible thread that binds you to those you care about. That is stronger than fibre optics.

So in Cuba, despite being as incommunicado as I was, off we went into the countryside.

With no phone to interrupt my reveries and no method of contacting those remote from me to organise things, fill in time, or change the arrangements, I just had to stick with the agreement of where to be, by when, in order to continue on our trip.

Those of us old enough to have grown up without a mobile phone remember how that works.

Of course we were in contact with Cuban friends and relatives through the phone of my Tour Director. Even this was a different experience.

When the phone rang, it lit up like an old jukebox with dancing coloured lights. This was such a delight to my Cuban friends that everyone used to sit and watch it as it rang. It was only answered when the tune was exhausted of its magic illuminations.

I was often tempted to beg for the call to be answered, especially when it was ringing late at night and I thought others would be disturbed. However, that proved to be just another cultural difference between us.

Anyone who has ever tried sleeping in Havana outside the tourist zone knows that it is a challenge:

Noise is ever-present.
  Loud noise.
    Constant noise.
      Varied noise.

The uninitiated traveller is confronted by a night punctuated by the sound of heavy trucks, often tractors, people calling to each other, and loud music emanating from every passing vehicle. It seems a badge of honour to share your music, no matter what the hour.

Add the sound of neighbours coming and going in various stages of inebriation, and even as a champion sleeper able to fall asleep almost on demand, I found this challenging. Goodness knows how light sleepers get on.

I guess in that context, if you are a local and have been sleeping to this background since infancy, the sound of someone's ringtone is relatively insignificant.

This phone was an early version of the Smartphone and we all used to sit around it to watch the Novella – that long-running, highly romanticised and not very close-to-life, but much loved serial that has been running every evening for as long as I have been visiting Cuba.

Like most soap operas, it was relatively easy to catch up despite the many years of not having seen it.

I would hardly call use of this mobile phone a dependency. Status symbol, definitely – especially with its built-in light and sound show at every call.

Back in England and less frequently in Germany, having watched groups of friends sitting at a restaurant table, every one of them spending more time sending messages from their mobile phone than speaking with the people who are there in real life, I now reflected on the dominance of electronics in our life.

It is so easy to 'Google it' – even if that means you use Firefox.

People born to these technologies consider the following normal - using applications that:

- Give you torchlight.
- Help you find your way to your destination.
- Tell you where the nearest bank is located, or which star is ahead of you in the night sky.
- Make a family virtual shopping list.
- Find the name of a tune.
- Call a taxi.

I also appreciate these apps, but a month with no electronic contact to the outside world created what a layout artist or an author would call a great deal of 'white space'.

White space is the unoccupied space left to isolate the text or image within it so that its meaning stands uncluttered for consideration by the reader.

So it was in my mind. There was lots of white space between my thoughts. This allowed them to be contemplated in isolation from the usual jumble of thinking with which they would normally have to compete.

At the beginning of the following year I would be eager to reconnect with my friends through sending my traditional reflection of the year past.

Each year I send a short piece that distils the soul of the year just departing. I do this in a way that frames a special welcome to the coming year and all its promise.

The New Year was weeks away. In the meantime, a month without direct contact with them had not diminished the presence of my friends in my life.

In contrast to the digital natives of today, my own introduction to the computer age was with selling the first IBM PCs. This was when all components were sold separately and stacked high in their own boxes.

For $1,565, the new computer came with VisiCalc *(a spreadsheet)* and EasyWriter *(a word processor)*, and boasted 16KB of RAM.

That is about eight pages of text – give or take a bit.

Consider this in contrast to the fact that a good-sized book is usually about 500 pages – or equivalent to 1 Megabyte.

An expanded model of that era came with 256KB of RAM and two floppy disk drives. This was considered beyond a reasonable expectation of what could be needed by an individual.

The new PC was a revolution not just in the technology of the finished product, but also in how its components were sourced, and how it was sold.

At the time, conservative suit-wearing classic 50s style management of IBM informed much of universal management practice.

However, IBM retained one hallmark of its founding ethos and this was characterised by its marvellous magazine called THINK, published in the early era of Watsons, father and son.

Despite the oft quoted misjudgement of Watson senior that there was probably a world market for maybe five computers, 'Think' is just what IBM management of that same era did.

From this *THINK* they set in place the development of the home computer. It is hard to imagine what a revolution they created.

Conservative managers are widely quoted as having wondered why they should invest in a personal computer for the home. Computing was an office-based task, one which IBM dominated.

At that time, home working meant a briefcase full of papers and possibly also one of the new advanced calculators that were just being perfected.

I remember that my Dad had witnessed the mainframe revolution and the famous competition between an IBM Mainframe and a champion fast user of a Chinese abacus.

Famously even the electronic calculator had previously faced the abacus test.

> In 1946, an American soldier and Japanese postal worker faced off in Tokyo, with weapons of choice. Each was a champion at operating his device.
>
> Private Thomas Wood had an electric calculator.
>
> Kiyoshi Matsuzaki held a *soroban*, a Japanese abacus.
>
> In 4 out of 5 competitive rounds, the abacus won.

How times change!

The briefcase full of papers and all encompassing dedication to the job of manager were things I knew about first hand.

My Dad brought home such briefcases. In fact, when he didn't, because all the tools of his work were based at his office, my Mother brought us and our homework to join him there after hours.

This was the only way we were able to keep some elements of family time in his busy schedule.

It was when my Dad stayed at the office to work late that I taught myself to type on an IBM Selectric.

The Selectric typewriter had completely disrupted the typewriter market with its revolutionary golf ball typeface. This ball containing the required keyboard characters rotated, so that the page stayed in one place and the golf ball moved across it.

It was a new way of thinking about type, and meant the page didn't have to move to accommodate the key positions of a traditional typewriter.

The Selectric was an example of how cross-over technologies can create whole new perspectives on problem solving.

A thing called variously a 'whiffletree', or a 'wippletree', was the key to enabling the golf ball typeface to make digital-to-analog conversions to 'select' the right key, hence the name.

Wippletrees had long been used to equalise different load forces between a draught animal and its load. You are probably more familiar with them through your windscreen wiper blades. They are also adapted for use in telescopes, naval gunnery and in early analog computers.

My Dad was a touch typist. As a teenager he took the class solely because it meant that he could walk my mother home afterwards. He loved his Selectric and kept it even after he got his first computer – the first Mac.

His typewriter was great fun for a child to use. Ever after, I have been unable to unlearn my rapid fire 'hunt and peck' typing method developed on it. At the time I was teaching myself I had smashed a finger between two rocks and it was in a splint.

We had been preparing for a game of bush cricket on one of our many weekend family picnics. A second rock had arrived in a solid pitch from my brother, who was gathering them and throwing them to me to stack as a temporary wicket.

Unfortunately, I hadn't yet moved my fingers away from stacking the first he had thrown, and the impact of the next to arrive broke my finger. That is why it was in a splint when I taught myself to type. As a consequence, even now when I type, one finger remains unused, poised in the air above the flying movements of the others.

This is something I was quite unaware of until a few years ago when someone asked me what I had against the first finger on my left hand, because I never use it.

The typewriter heritage lives on. At the moment, computers still need a keyboard but with the swipe and tap of a Smartphone, and developing technologies that recognise hand movements without their actual touch, perhaps even that will soon be obsolete.

IBM is still out there prepared to THINK. They now don't make hard disks, computers, disk drives or any of the equipment of the past. Instead they are in the business of creating solutions to the knotty problems that make life difficult.

It is an interesting thing to learn from. Even a successful giant can rethink direction and try to make a difference by pursuing something worthwhile.

It has always been a regret that I didn't learn to touch type, and never more so than when using an expensive state-run internet café in Havana.

Here, every minute counted and you could swear the online connection was being made by an arthritic tortoise laboriously travelling between your computer and the outside world.

During this period I came to the conclusion that Andy Rooney was right *(as he so often was with his observations)*:

> *Computers make it easier to do a lot of things,*
> *but most of the things they make it easier to do*
> *don't need to be done*

In Cienfuegos I made a half-hearted attempt at using an internet café. The results were no better.

Now they have rolled out WiFi hotpots in parks and along the Prado. After the first rush of delight at such access, locals have almost stopped using these.

The problem is that all their telephone credit disappeared in Facebook posts or other access that made no visible impact on their lives, other than to empty their valuable phone account.

Anyway, if you are in Cienfuegos there is so much to see. The city is located on a beautiful bay, with lovely colonial architecture reminding visitors of its once powerful role in the economics of the country.

It was a wealthy city whose contribution to the world of that era helped make Cienfuegos to become known as the 'Pearl of the South'.

Now, on one side of the bay are a fertiliser factory and the mothballed oil refinery that closed with the collapse of the Soviet Union and its support of the Cuban economy.

A small fishing fleet is moored there.

The reduced numbers of fishing boats are a reminder of the demise of the Cuban fishing grounds as a result of pollution and over fishing.

There is a long promontory that juts out on one end of the harbour. Along its banks sit the now slowly decaying mansions of wealthy plantation owners and industrialists, set grandly within wide gardens.

Only a few have been restored, but the ambiance of affluence still lingers.

It makes a lovely harbour-side drive. You pass the still magnificent Yacht Club used by visiting international yachties to the most opulent of them all, the *Palacio de Valle*, built by local businessman *Acisclo del Valle Blanco*.

At seventeen, Blanco had emigrated to Cuba together with two of his brothers from his native Asturias in Spain.

Smart, hard-working, and with an engaging personality, *Acisclo* rose to become an executive of powerful companies, Vice President of the local Rotary Club, and eventually a much-respected and liked Mayor of Cienfuegos.

It is said that the inspiration for his fanciful villa came when visiting his family home in Spain. While there he saw a fantastic structure built as a wedding present by a wealthy Asturian industrialist for his daughter.

Perhaps he had always been interested in architecture. According to German researchers, Blanco had gathered photographs and lithographs of styles that fascinated him from architectural journals of North America and Europe.

This 'Cuban Alhambra' is thought to have been designed by *Pablo Donatello Carbonell*, the same Cienfuegos architect who designed the *Palacio de Ferrer* that flanks the José Martí Square where the little girl had given me the flower.

For this romantic mix of Gothic, Baroque, Neo-classical and Moorish style, materials were sourced from afar:

- Carrare Marble and alabaster from Italy
- Chinese porcelain
- European crystal
- Ceramics from Venice and Granada, and
- Mosaic materials from Toledo in Spain.

This mixing of styles is heady stuff.

The garden seating is surrounded by crenulated walls and a cast-iron railing securing baroque balustrades.

There is a neo-Gothic portico with a neo-Moorish kiosk and magnificent mosaic floor with jousting knights.

The rear has a Spanish-Moorish effect with Venetian influence, and one of the towers looks like a dome-shaped Indian *Chhatris* (literally 'umbrella' or 'parasol').

Cuban stained glass in primary colours filters light into the quadrangle with its horseshoe arcades reminiscent of the Alcázar Palace in Seville.

Inside, the styles run from French Baroque to the contrasting more restrained lines of the Louis XIVth era.

Confusion?
Yes, but grand confusion.

Palacio de Valle is now a restaurant with tables set uncomfortably close together to give the dining room a very cramped appearance – even empty, as it was when we visited.

Extortionately expensive cocktails are served on the rooftop terrace.

You are obviously paying more for the experience and the view across a beautiful bay at the edge of which nestles a UNESCO World Heritage city than for the quality of the drink.

I found the place to be a disconcerting exclamation point on a peninsular of stately grandeur.

Christopher Wren[6] memorably wrote:

> *The secret of architectural excellence*
> *is to translate the proportions of a dachshund*
> *into bricks, mortar, and marble.*

In those terms, Blanco seems to have started not with a dachshund but a crossbred afghan-poodle-husky.

I have always felt that a building retains some of the character of its owners, or of those who have lived or worked within it, but in *Palacia de Valle* I gained no sense of family, although eight children were born here.

They proved an international family.

Perhaps enticed to travel by the architecture of their home, they roamed far: one son to Mexico, one to the USA, and two daughters to Spain.

Perhaps they took with them so much of the impact the place had on their formative years that there is nothing left to impart to those who follow.

The disinterested attitude of tourist guides may also have contributed to my impression of total effacement of any personality from earlier years when *Palacia de Valle* was a family home.

In Cienfuegos we had found a wonderful place to stay in a *Casa Particular*. An apartment had been built alongside the family home. This was off the road alongside the seawall. Here, tourists could stay, eating their home-cooked meals on the terrace overlooking the harbour.

As I sat eating dinner one night, there was a terrific clattering of hooves outside on the street that hugged the sea wall. I dashed to the edge of the garden to see a wonderfully silly race between two horse-drawn taxis – one rising to the challenge of the other.

---

[6] *Christopher Wren was the architect of St Paul's Cathedral in London*

It was the equivalent to those great street drag challenges that feature in old American movies of the 50s and 60s.

This spontaneous challenge was obviously hugely enjoyed by horses, passengers, and drivers. We bystanders relished the exhilaration of the participants.

I could just imagine a couple of taxis having a drag race in our society and the repercussions it would cause – let alone with horse-drawn vehicles.

The contrast between our attitudes and their context and those now demonstrated here within a Cuban context brought to mind the quotation that I had seen in the centre of Cienfuegos. It was painted on the bumper bar of a bus and seemed a good summary of the problem with how our society has evolved.

Translated it said:

Live your own life: not mine

The terrace where we dined gave a wonderful view of the returning fishing fleet, industrial ships, and of the two single rowing sculls that skimmed past daily.

The rowing skulls fascinated me.

I had discovered that unless given express approval by the authorities, Cubans are not permitted to board a boat, let alone to own one.

There is a real paradox in the loosening of regulations for Cubans to travel and to stay in hotels and that somehow seems to preclude boarding a sea-going vessel – let alone having one.

An example of this anomaly is that on the north coast of Pinar del Rio Province, Cubans are permitted to stay in the hotel on *Cayo Levisa* - but they just can't board the boat to get there.

Were these diligent scullers in Cienfuegos Harbour members of the Cuban rowing team? Or perhaps they were headed for the lightweight sculls in the Rio Summer Olympics.

It was while watching the horse taxi race in Cienfuegos that I discovered that my Tour Guide was wearing sneakers that were in a competition with the little red car for losing their tread. He was walking more on the road than in his shoes, so I volunteered the funds to get new ones.

Mindful of the impact shoe shopping would have on our No Plan explorations, this task he delegated to our hostess.

Obviously, he did have some sort of plan about the day or it wouldn't have mattered to spend time shoe shopping.

It turned out that wanted to show me a tower in the mountains that gave a fantastic view of the city. This was where the road travelled downhill with us rather than under us.

While we were off exploring, our hostess set off with the advance payment I made in the interests of warding off lameness in the person key to my No Plan travel adventures. Upon our return there was a boxed pair of new sneakers to greet us – perfect fit.

The pleasure this gave to the recipient was well worth the investment.

Step 11 of The Cuban Approach: Incommunicado: The ties of friendship are stronger than fibre optics.

What did the Cuban Approach accomplish? Because I stayed at a *Casa Particular*, a family home, instead of a hotel:

- I had front row seats at a spontaneous horse taxi race
- ate some amazing home cooked food
- learned a little bit about the development hassles in setting up a *Casa Particular* with the challenges being not just the funds to do so, but also the ability to navigate the paperwork necessary
- witnessed firsthand the kindness of one person to another when the landlady went shopping for new sneakers for my tour guide.

Cinderella's glass slipper had nothing on the impact of those sneakers. It made me realise how many *things* we have, and therefore how few are really treasured.

Inured to constant noise from the Reggaeton inside our rental car and its punctuation by the magical juke-box-styled mobile phone ringtone, I easily slept through the cacophony of the back streets of Havana old town.

Thinking back over my father's extremely over-developed work ethic, I had time and space to think about what that had meant to my mother, and how lonely it made her life.

A funny, witty, artistic and resilient woman, my mother had never been daunted by the odds against her:

- At sixteen she accidentally pulled a pan of boiling water over her bare leg, resulting in a scalding burn that went to the bone. It had to be bathed daily with boiling water to prevent infection. One can only imagine the pain involved. I was always taught to make sure saucepan handles were turned away from the edge to prevent a recurrence.
- When I was a baby, she had polio and was temporarily paralysed down her left side and lost the power of speech. Remarkably polio left no residual damage.
- She succumbed to the first world epidemic of Asian flu. I remember as tiny tot outside her door hearing her struggling for breath and asking my father was she going to die. How I knew about death at that age I have no idea. Perhaps I had overheard someone.
- She had undiagnosed asthma for at least twenty years of her life, and so daily struggled to find breath until the relief of asthma inhalation remediated the situation.
- When I was thirteen she was operated on for uterine cancer. It was so extensive that the surgery took most of the day and the prognosis was uncertain. The doctor said he had done all he could. He said it was now up to her.

Before having the operation my mother had told him to be as extensive as he possibly could because she had the will to live and would do the rest.

My mother was barely hanging on to life so my father came to get me from school to see her – and possibly to say goodbye.

Our parents had not gone into detail with my brother or me about why she was going to hospital, so I had no idea that she was really that ill, but as soon as I saw her I knew she was about to die.

She just refused to. She was madly in love with my Dad – and he with her. That bond gave her the courage to fight against such tremendous odds.

In those days there was no counselling for cancer survivors, and she had no moral support. Her friends were all living hundreds of miles away, as were her sisters and brothers. She often said that it was the dog – that same Labrador-cross who escorted us to our childhood last stop before bedtime – who kept her going.

My Dad was busy being Mr. IBM and rising to the top. In later years when he was she was very ill and unable to cook, she looked at an exquisitely presented meal he had prepared and said to me:

"Look at that. It looks as if it came from the pages of Gourmet Magazine".

It probably did!

She was a gourmet cook herself and my father, who to our certain knowledge could boil an egg but not much more, went to no end of trouble to hold her standard. She quietly added: "I think he is trying to make up for all those years, don't you?"

I replied that no, I didn't *think so*, I *knew so.*

With renewed respect I smiled at what a role model she remains although no longer physically here.

I still hear her laughter.

I was later to recount these thoughts to my good friend Carmen, in England. In doing so I added that I loved and admired my mother but didn't understand her.

Once I said this to my Dad, and he responded: "Guess what?"

I grinned and gave voice to his next intended sentence: "She doesn't understand me either?"

He nodded.

My friend gently suggested that perhaps we hadn't bonded when I was a baby.

Of course I hadn't. When my mother was fighting for her life with polio, I was a new-born baby in the care of a neighbour.

Perhaps that is where my independent streak comes from.

The realisation of this came to me long after mother had gone off to remodel heaven and take out a wall here and put a window over there to its general aesthetic improvement.

What a shame the realisation hadn't come sooner so we could discuss it.

But it is what it is.

It may have come late, but this realisation has helped me put so much into perspective.

Reading the winds: In my No Plan travels these thoughts had their space. My life experiences were presenting themselves to be reviewed and filed away in more secure places in my memory than they were before.

Adjusting your sails: If I had prepared for it and done some research, I could have seen more of Cienfuegos, but such was not the style of this trip: I was letting things take me rather than making them fit into a plan.

My choice of No Plan travel meant that each day I was unsure about the destination of the next. However, for this very reason each new place was met with a sense of wonder and anticipation.

For me there is nothing more delightful when I travel than to wander.

When I wander I find so many things that show me the real character of a place – things like the horse taxi race.

Years ago in Havana following a deluge, I watched *(and captured on film)* boys street surfing on rain-flooded roads by hanging onto the bumper bar of a local bus.

Unlike my companions who were non-Cubans still constrained by their home rules and regulations, I didn't mutter anything about Health and Safety rules that could apply to such risky fun.

Instead I laughed at the sheer joy of it all.

The lads weren't going to fall under the bus. The worst that would happen would be a nasty graze if they hit dry ground without anticipating it.

My travels in Cuba had always involved a day-to-day adjustment of the expectations common to my upbringing, so that they sat better with those of a different culture.

In Cienfuegos I was learning again to slow down, to allow the day to unfold, to let the place tell me its stories in its own way.

This it did, untainted by guidebooks or anticipation of the iconic 'Must see. Must do' activities that guide many others in their travels.

Reading the winds: By the time we reached Cienfuegos I was happy to risk missing a 'must see' sight just to experience those that presented themselves unannounced.

In all my travels, this letting go of expectation always triumphed with insights into my own life as I experienced the reality of how other people live and experience the world.

The American poet *e. e. cummings* wrote something that has stuck with me since I discovered his work while at University.

> *To be nobody-but-yourself*
> *in a world which is doing its best,*
> *night and day,*
> *to make you everybody else —*
>
> *means to fight the hardest battle*
> *which any human being can fight;*
> *and never stop fighting.*

In Cuba, I found people everywhere steadfastly being themselves – and succeeding against the challenges that living in a dictatorship brings. As I saw it, they were having more success than many who lived in freer countries.

We tend to willingly – or at least without thought on the matter – embrace the ties that restrain us from being the best of ourselves – or even of remembering who we really are.

Our challenges are the daily assault of email, of social media, of the expectation that there are certain fashions work or peer group expectations that demand our attention

These challenges we think we are unable to override, but when we loosen those ties, we are better able to read the winds.

Then, we can take advantage of every opportunity to ride them to safe harbours or to exciting new destinations.

CHAPTER TWELVE

Oopsa: Improvisation

Finding alternatives is an art. Such alternatives are the source of much of the creative improvisation we encounter in life. One purchase made en route is a typical example.

En route one day we stopped to get fuel at one of the credit-card-enabled fuel stations.

I was waiting for the connection to be made between the card machine in the dusty forecourt and the server in Havana to enable the transaction – something that often took several tries.

My unease about the system was such that I always had the cash handy just in case it was unable to connect – but this safety reserve was only needed once.

As we waited, my Tour Director spotted a roadside vendor strategically placed on the corner of the adjacent crossing of main roads. He was selling Tiffany lamps.

Fuel paid for, we swung across to the intersection and stopped.

There were three lamps available and following a series of negotiations, one was selected.

Handing it carefully to us, the seller warned us to be careful to keep it still and fasten it securely in the car as it was still wet.

I stared at it in curiosity as it didn't seem wet at all.

Like their more famous counterparts from the New York Tiffany studios, these Cuban designs are original, handmade, and held together along similar principals.

The original Tiffany was made of Venetian glass cut to a cardboard pattern, carefully finished to shape, its edges bonded with copper foil, and then the pieces soldered together with the copper foil as the bonding element.

While for hundreds of years the finest Tiffany lamps were thought to be the sole works of *Louis Comfort Tiffany*, it was only recently discovered that the loveliest of these actually were the design and work of one *Clara Driscoll*.

I guess this reassignment of creative authorship shouldn't come as so much of a surprise. This was at a time when the inheritance of a daughter transferred in its entirety to her husband upon marriage, and female talent of all sorts had to masquerade as masculine to find its place.

This Cuban Tiffany lamp was created along the same manufacturing model as the original, but with some accommodations to the limitations of life in Cuba at the time.

The glass had been gathered from various different sources: from breakages, or perhaps demolitions.

These unrelated pieces had been well-matched for shade, pattern, and colour.

The bonding element in this case was black and not copper, but the lamp was a masterpiece worthy of Mr. Tiffany, if not of Clara.

I rescued this newly purchased Cuban Tiffany Lamp from being placed in the trunk / boot where it would have been vulnerable to shifts of the rest of our luggage and instead secured it on the back seat with the seat belt.

The lamp had an innovative carrying mechanism that involved two pieces of cardboard through which ran some string. One piece of cardboard was within, and the other outside the bowl of the lamp itself.

I linked the seat belt through the supporting string and off we set to our usual loud beat of Cuban music, stopping frequently for photo opportunities and chatting happily together.

It was a particularly picturesque route and we frequently stopped so I could take photos. Each time I could smell what seemed like fuel – or worse – oil.

When I raised the issue, my Tour Director responded that he was so used to the little red car that reeked of gasoline that he thought this rental car smelled quite normal.

The smell increased and I thought we were finally going to pay the price of travelling over interesting but less-than-perfect roads.

I feared that we had somehow put a hole in the sump and that oil was now leaking out. I paled to think about the cost of repair – and where to get such a repair in the hinterland – and wondered if insurance would cover it.

We stopped outside a small roadside café and each got down on our hands and knees to peer under the car. There was no visible sign of oil or of gasoline leakage. I was puzzled, as the smell was getting more, rather than less intense.

However, while we were on our knees another cousin appeared. He had been driving an ancient truck along the highway and recognised my Tour Director. His attention had been drawn to us as he passed, for we were the source of amused viewing by all the waiting bus passengers and others who had stopped for refreshments at the café.

Someone different in a remote village is always to be found a subject of interest, and here we were with noses down and tails up.

With delighted greetings, the newfound cousin invited us home. It would have been rude to say no, so we made a quick stop for coffee and for the family to greet each other and catch up on events.

While this happy chatter took place I wandered about, looking at a pig in its wire enclosure close to the house and wondering at the number of varieties of magnificent roosters and their ladies who strolled importantly around the house.

Eventually, we set off again and finally pulled onto the track to the carpenter's house and parked on a hilly ridge.

This was our mid-point en route to *Sancti Spiritus* and proved to be an important part of my Tour Director's route planning.

I may have had no plan, but he did – and indeed I relied upon him to have one, despite the knowledge that it would be sketchy at best.

The fact that his plan reflected self-interest didn't bother me for I was losing nothing in the transaction, and in fact got to experience more of the Cuban way of life as a result.

I was now really concerned about the high level of oily or gasoline-laden fumes that filled the car. Again I got down on my hands and knees, but could see nothing.

With a shrug I said that after we had stopped for a while any leakage would announce itself with deposits on the grass under the car.

Some hours later we emerged and after the car was pulled forward a car length the grass was inspected. No trace of oil. It was very puzzling.

We travelled on to Trinidad where I was found a lovely apartment of my own. My Tour Director secured his spot on the couch of yet another cousin although there was plenty of room for him in the two-bedroom apartment.

When cousin and Tour Director left me to my own devices I sat down to write.

It was then that I realised why we had been smelling oil all afternoon.

When we unloaded the luggage, the Tiffany Lamp had been carefully placed on the spare bed that lay at the end of the dining room.

Sitting at the table close to the spare bed to write, I realised that the smell came from the lamp.

Where an original Tiffany Lamp has its glass pieces bonded by an edging of copper that is carefully soldered together, not having the same materials available, this Cuban version was yet another example of good Cuban improvisation.

Instead of the copper-edge binding, each piece of glass was held in place by a thin line of the sort of bitumen that comes in a tube from the hardware store – a sort of black caulking material, probably meant for marine use.

THAT was why the seller had admonished to be careful as it 'wasn't dry yet'.

Riddle of the oil smell solved, the lamp went onto the veranda, but then rain threatened so it came back in again. It travelled thus in and out during the three days there, until later, when it was left at the carpenter's house for safe-keeping, and to 'dry'.

Examples of improvisation aren't hard to find in Cuba. It is what people do when what is really needed isn't available. I saw many examples of it.

The ability to improvise in costuming was everywhere evident as young children performed at local events:

- Animal masks made from carefully stylised animal faces of paper :
- some with paper whiskers,
- some with floppy paper ears,
- some with curled over smaller ears or straight up pointed ears
- some with bills or beaks
- other noses glued on to be almost three dimensional.
- Caps and shawls made special by the creative addition of small pieces of braid or netting or ribbon.
- Headdresses of golden coloured wrapping paper carefully cut into long pointed fronds gathered into a frothy topknot.

En route I saw:

- Old metal chairs with fabric seats, now held up by piles of stones after the metal has corroded away.
- Windscreen wiper rubber strips reattached to wooden slats to form floor tile cleaners.
- Bare heating elements wired directly to the wall socket to be plunged into containers of water to make a kettle.

- Hot plates wired the same way.
- A car parked over a concrete culvert to form a servicing bay by using the now dry channel for water as the alternative to hoisting the car upward.
- Instead, here, the service man lay underneath by going into the rectangular ditch over which the car had been parked.
- Banana leaves used as strapping ties holding a fence line in place by strapping three lengths of sapling into a tripod corner post.
- Banana leaves wrapped to make a tube encasement for rather weather-worn steel cables that supported a suspension footbridge.
- Wooden pallets and flat box bases of every size, with wheels attached to form wagons on which all sorts of goods were transported (from beds to produce, spare wheels to refrigerators).
- These were propelled by the use of sometimes a rope handle, and other times by wooden or metal attachments.
- Cleverly modified bike frames, with tandem rear wheels attached to various models of stylized lengthened cross bars. This enabled the attachment of all sorts of boxes to the rear or forward of the driver to make a mobile vegetable and fruit stall.
- Cleverly adapted street advertising signs originally used for symposia and conferences that had been 'adopted', and the metal cut to shape to make rooftops for pedalos.
- Carefully constructed shacks on the back of half ton trucks, so workers can shelter en route to the work site.
- Workers resting on a bed of lemons and limes in the tray of a truck transporting produce to market.
- A clever wasp trap with the neck of a bottle cut out and reinserted into the opening in reverse, knowing that insects try to climb out and won't fly out of the open centre.

In Cienfuegos in the artisans shop in a small museum there were a variety of clever and rather beautifully crafted items.

- Stylised cameras made from pop and beer cans, all neatly lined up for sale.
- Brightly painted cups made from coconut halves and hung on an equally colourfully painted 'tree' rising from a painted coconut husk base – all laid out for sale on a stall.
- Papier-mâché biplanes of all hybrid sorts hanging in the archway so you could select your make.

In the main art market on the wharves in Havana, quite apart from the beautiful carvings and paintings in all media, there were:
- Peaked caps made of pop and beer can metal that had been flatted and reshaped.
- Tropical fish crafted from the same material, but artistically and colourfully painted.

In old glass cases in a several shops that had no produce to sell, they opted instead to provide a sort of flea market in which the goods on offer ranged:
- dainty girl's shoes
- torsion wrenches
- brass hinges
- a fold up baby pushchair of pink nylon
- wigs of long hair
- a pair of wire strippers
- a bullet-bobbin sewing machine
- a single fancy metal café chair with swirling patterns in its back support.

In one such shop called *El Ilusion* in Remedios, you could buy at one end of the counter:

- a roll of barbed wire
- nails by weight as measured in a rather fine old cast iron set of kitchen scales
- horse shoes
- polypropylene pipe, or
- a milk churn

– and at the other end:

- paint brushes and scrubbing brushes
- a children's doctor's kit in bubble pack with its own stethoscope
- next year's wall hanging paper calendar with pictures of flowers native to Europe
- a vase but only in one size, or
- a carefully carved ornament that comprised a palm tree under which sat a water barrel on an ox cart.

Games are often open to improvisation, and games of chance always so.

Where there is a fair, there is usually also a fun fare, and that on the streets of Remedios before the grand pre-Christmas fiesta was no exception. The only difference was that this fun fair was one of itinerant entertainers.

It seemed to be a gathering of opportunistic flimflam men, each with his own little gamble to offer the eager crowds.

There were flat boards with painted games that depended upon throwing the right combination on a pair of dice.

There were cardboard boxes, weary at heavy use and taped together at the corners with masking tape, all stuffed with toys on sticks – odd looking colourful dogs with plastic ears, whirly Catherine Wheel wind toys, small trumpets, those fun whistles that come rolled up and unroll as you blow, and balloons in bright primary colours– the real thing, not condoms .

There was even a great little family of furry street entertainers.

These were guinea pigs upon which you bet, guessing into which hole they would run. The options were a form of archways under a square of demountable 'arcades' of wood ply.

Each arcade hole had a number on a card and a prize above it.

Between acts, the guinea pigs rested in a clever cage made from two aluminium grills held apart by chicken wire at the corners.

There was obviously not enough chicken wire available to the owner when making this crate, so the rest of the sides were woven into a replica of the chicken wire pattern using all sorts of bits of string and twine of varying colours. As a result, it looked a bit like a not very well made quilt.

The performer of the moment sat on his owner's shoulder to receive an adoring public of small people eager to see where he would run.

But the improvisation that most captured my imagination on the whole trip was that which created two fantastic rafts. These were made up of pallets lashed over buoys of white fertiliser bags filled with empty litre water bottles. The oars were lengths of bamboo with flat shaped paddles made out of wide wooden slats and wired to the bamboo.

The two fellows who were aboard the raft were laughing heartily together and shouting in triumph as they hurled their catch to their friend on the shore.

Fishing with their large white seine on this backwater lagoon, they seemed to be quite successful.

I stood at a distance and took photos as the fish flew to the banks and the two fishermen cast the seine again.

What did the Cuban Approach accomplish? Charles Caleb Cotton's much quoted comment applies to the Cuban Tiffany Lamp:

Imitation is the sincerest flattery

Without the money or materials to create a metal-edged glass creation soldered together in intricate art-deco fashion, the local artisans gathered pieces of coloured glass that went together harmoniously, and then used a sort of black caulking asphalt to weld the lamp together. It really shouldn't have gone to market (that is to say the junction of two main roads) until dry, for this would have ensured that it remained round and didn't risk becoming distorted during transportation.

But, like any market economy the rule 'Buyer Beware' applied.

The vendor had been clear about the state of the lamp.

It would be our fault if it distorted.

We were careful to keep its shape because it sat in pride of place on the back seat, which for a change was remarkably empty of extra cousins.

The lamp had an adventurous trip from street corner to Trinidad apartment, to woodworker's hamlet, to Havana. It is now hanging in my tour guide's apartment and is the object of much admiration.

Given the roads over which we had travelled, it seemed possible that the oily smell indicated a leaking sump.

Until I found the origin of the smell, the lamp had caused me an increasing level of concern. However, this was the only down-side of its attractiveness.

Beauty is in the eye of the beholder
and sometimes the character of the imitation
is greater than that of the original.

The lamp's value benefited greatly from the story of its adventures and its impact on my No Plan travel. Many people chuckle when this lamp is mentioned, for now it is more than a lamp – it is a part of an adventure which the wider family could share in the telling.

When we left it behind and were destined to take another route back to Havana which would mean it would be impossible to retrieve on this trip, it seemed only appropriate that after such care, we should make every effort to retrieve it. In view of the previous eager anticipation of the delight by my Tour Director's partner when it graced their living room, the formerly planned route via Santa Clara could wait until the next trip!

Improvisation is to be found everywhere in life, but in our current western societies with our focus on the immediate and the disposable we are often too spoiled for choice to bother thinking of alternatives.

Necessity truly does seem to be the 'Mother of Invention'. In Cuba, it is a skill that thrives and one which in future better times should be the hiring criteria.

It doesn't matter what the education or paper certificate says, someone who has the ability to thrive, no matter what the social impediments in which they find themselves, is the person who will be your best investment.

A Cuban employee may challenge your thinking and even test your patience as they learn the workplace of your design – but for a most effective way of getting something done – Cubans are often experts.

Step 12 of the Cuban Approach: Oopsa: Improvisation. Imitation and improvisation together can create an original whose value is doubled by its story.

Adjusting your sails: They say that all those who are successful in life, are masters of that great skill called 'Plan B'.

Reading the winds: Because I had a no plan, we were able to

- Stop to buy an imitation Tiffany lamp.
- Wander the streets of Remedios and Cienfuegos just people watching.
- Drink a leisurely Buccanero or two at a bar, restaurant and sweet shop called El Louvre that has continuously served Remedios residents and visitors of all ages since 19th October 1866.

Much of the Cuban improvisation I saw fell into two categories:

- Things to entertain – especially things to entertain children, and
- Things that made the everyday easier to cope with.

Neither had practical relevance for me, but I certainly appreciated the effort and creativity that went into both types.

It made me thankful that my mother had expended the same type of 'make something special out of bits of leftovers' that had characterised my childhood.

I remember when I had to go to hospital to have my tonsils out at age six. I didn't have a dressing gown, and we were on military pay and had few luxuries, so my mother took a grey army blanket and made one for me. It was embellished with pockets on which she embroidered a bunny face and whiskers.

The bunny had appliquéd long ears of pieces of red, wide-wale corduroy. The same material formed a very luxurious looking collar. The belt was a lovely red, thickly twisted cord, with long tassels on each end.

My mother's improvisation and creativity thus transformed what would otherwise have been a drab coat for a little girl into something so quirky and whimsical that drew comments everywhere I went in the hospital.

In the era of poodle skirts, my mother made a miniature one for her little daughter – but true to her sense of humour, instead of an appliquéd poodle, mine was a red gingham cat – with embroidered eyelashes that were in 3D.

The cat had a very superior expression.

On a pine green imitation-suede skirt it looked wonderful. I had a little waistcoat and beret of the same green material and hated the fact that people kept looking at me.

Despite that, I still have the cat that I cut off the skirt.

I just couldn't part with it, for I knew the effort my mother had gone to in creating such a magical piece of appliqué. It lives now in a scrap book of my happy home memories.

Both my parents were very creative and their creativity often went to the quirky. I recall driving home from a far away beach holiday with a huge branch of driftwood tree laced to the roof of the car so that it could be installed on the interior open brick wall of the modern home my Dad had designed for us in Perth.

My father used to make up wonderful birthday party games and I recall one used my brother's Dinky Toy cars as tokens to progress along a chalked out F1 track on the huge boarded veranda of our rambling house. All of us were interested in classic cars and in motor racing, and the local children who may or may not have been, nevertheless really enjoyed the improvised game – every one of us providing the sound effects appropriate to the movement of our vehicle.

Seeing similar innovations in Cuba I was reminded that beauty and fun are everywhere to be found, or to be created.

A love of both is a great legacy for a child, and Cuban children receive this legacy in abundance.

CHAPTER THIRTEEN

Keepsakes

A Saint in your wallet

Another adventure benefited from the telling in quite a different way. It shows that human beings the world over seem to have a need for a belief system. When theirs is banned, it is supplemented with a hybridisation of the one to which they have been directed/instructed to follow with that they originally held – thus enhancing and/or cloaking their former beliefs.

So it is with *Santería* in Cuba, with its melding of Christian Saints and *Santería* gods.

The background for my reflections on the nature of belief in the supernatural was my day trip from Havana to the *Parque Almendares*.

This park flanks both sides of the Almendares River which was traditionally a valuable water supply for Havana. The water here has flowed from the ranges about 45 kilometres away *(about 28 miles)*.

Sometimes called the *Bosque de la Habana*, or Havana's Forest, this is a man-made urban forest that was part of an insightful effort in urban planning and beatification designed by the French landscape architect and city planner, *Jean-Claude Nicolas Forestier* along with Cuban architects – or was it the other way around?

Cienfuegos native *Pedro Martínez Inclán* had developed a master plan for Havana, with wide boulevards and tree lined streets. His designs were laid out in the publication *La Habana Actual* (Current Havana) in 1925. He, and the Minister for Public Works *Carlos Miguel de Céspedes*, then invited Forestier to Cuba to set out the urban structure for the new post-colonial Havana.

Forestier visited Havana regularly between 1925 and 1930.

He shared the ideals of his Cuban colleagues in the reasons for undertaking beautification plan, with well-designed urban space and a park area to be the lung and lifeblood for a vibrant cultural city.

Although Forestier was the principal designer of *Bosque de la Habana,* the new plans used much of the early work of his Cuban colleague *Inclán.*

Forestier is better known for his design of the gardens Champs-de-Mars of the Eiffel Tower. He also redesigned the *Malecó,* giving it the small parterres with leafy trees that punctuate its fringe.

Forestier was also responsible for introducing the palm trees that still remain all over central Havana, and also for contributing to the design for urban décor, including the benches and lampposts that mark the city character to this day.

The Parque Almendares was a success, but only in part. None of the associated planning was realised.

The result is that now Havana sits in isolation from its original planned network of breathing spaces that were to be the lungs of the growing city.

From its outset, however, the introduction of the urban Havana Forest has attracted Santería practitioners. They treat the area as a sacred site and leave all sorts of offerings there.

It is quite surreal to walk beneath the feathery growth of overhanging vines and dense foliage of the huge trees and find circles of candles, and plastic bags that emit stenches relating to sacrificed animals or now fetid food offerings.

There are sometimes fabric bands tied around sacred trees as offerings to particular gods.

Recent efforts to try to address the resulting pollution and the stench on the hottest of days has led to certain trees being designated as offering trees, with signs attached accordingly.

We wandered in this lush rainforest along beautiful little trails and across rotting great tree trunks that had been felled by hurricanes years ago. These now formed insect condominiums decorated by strange shapes of fungus.

The overhanging vines and lushness of the Almadares Park quite dominate it. Lush green vines drape over every tree.

It wasn't until recently that I have discovered that the culprit of this stage drape is a plant mistakenly called *Kudzu* when translated incorrectly for the Japanese from where it originates and is known as *Kuzu*.

The way that this Galloping Gertie has overtaken the landscape of many southern states of the USA is a classic example of an introduced species run riot.

Now covering some 1011 square kilometres, *(a quarter of a million acres)* of Alabama and 28,327 sq km *(7 million acres)* across the whole southern states, this was a plant widely promoted to save the drought-parched earth during the Great Depression.

Over 85 million seedlings were distributed to landowners for fixing the soil.

Fix it does. It travels some 10 to 30 metres in one growing season, blocking out the native growth with its dense foliage.

One single root crown can produce 30 vines and in America is widely known as 'The Vine that Ate the South.' There, it is now officially a noxious weed.

The spread of Kudzu reminds me how foolish we are to intervene with 'better fixes' than nature provides. No matter to what you attribute the creation of our beautiful world, nature seems to have it all fairly well worked out.

From decorative but invasive vines valued for their pretty flowers in Cuba and America, to rabbits in Australia, what was introduced as ornamental, soon can dominate the natural.

It reminds me of how one culture gets dominated with another – and always has – whether by force or by common adoption.

Sometimes adoption of a culture simply creates a niche that enriches the wider culture. Take jazz and its followers, worldwide. But other aspects of our cultural invasion are not so appealing.

Authenticity is a wonderful characteristic and one I found in abundance on my travels in Cuba. It endorses to me the importance of having the courage to be who you are, and to respond in a manner that is genuine.

When living my happy seven years in Germany, I became truly impressed by the quality of acting demonstrated in TV shows. Here, the characters look true to life. They are devoid of universally even and unnaturally white teeth, hair that was just recently made perfect and immaculately coordinated attire.

By a contrast of these I could easily pick an American show as I channel surfed.

It seemed that the audiences of Europe and the United States required different versions of reality: one more authentic than the other.

The Novella of Cuba *(which I believe to be actually Venezuelan)* seemed in contrast to both, to be a beautifully costumed but highly implausible period drama. Authentic it is not – but yet captivating in the way of any good melodrama. Perhaps as in North America, some audiences prefer total fantasy.

At any rate, I digress.

The cousin of *kudzu* in Cuba is *marabú* which is just as pesky a plant but with a lovely ornamental pink and bushy flower with a hanging yellow stamen that looks like a tail. It was described in an article in The Economist in 2017 as "a cross between a Chinese Lantern and a Muppet".

Why was The Economist writing about a galloping plant in Cuba? Because the so called 'artisanal charcoal' made from it is one of the first legal imports to the US from Cuba in more than fifty years.

The same article reports that since 2009 Cuba had global exports up to 80 thousand tonnes *(88,184 US tons)* of marabú charcoal.

Its uses? Amongst others, firing hookah ovens in the Middle East, and pizza ovens in Italy.

But on the day of my first close up introduction to the hanging vines shrouding the Almendares Park, they formed a canopy for the small group ahead of us who soon found a clearing and stopped.

There were two men and two women, plus two younger women and a lad who seemed to be part of a family. With serious faces, all were following the instructions of an older man who probably was a spiritual healer or *espiritistas.*

In plastic bags on the side of the clearing where they had gathered were various offerings and two unfortunate birds – a chicken and a duck that had been sacrificed to the pleasure of the gods.

One of the young girls wore a colourful skirt made in panels of green, red, yellow and two shades of blue, each panel edged in white lace that ended in points towards the earth.

I was fascinated to find myself witness to parts of a *Santería Santiguo,* or healing ceremony, and watched for a short while before we moved off. It felt like an intrusion to stay.

Above their clearing and a little way off at the head of the old stone stairway the group's taxi driver patiently waited, standing beside his large Desoto station wagon.

Apparently taxis are often hired for such excursions to and from central Havana and the forest. The healing spirits here must be thought to have strong powers.

Further along a 1953 Ford Prefect dressed in its umpteenth layer of paint, this one blue, was parked on its own under the almost eerie vines. As I was taking a photo of it, a man pulled up a bit further along the road, leaped out of his car and loped to the edge of the undergrowth before hurling a half filled plastic bag into the valley below.

The car engine was still running. Having dispatched his sacrifice the man jumped back in and drove off.

My Tour Director explained that this was common. People made their sacrifices at home and brought them here – or sent them with someone who had a car – to be deposited in this holy place.

The result of such devotions can be smelled on a hot day. The efforts to clean up the area seem to be an uphill battle. It must be a struggle, given the volume of sacrificed foodstuffs and dead animals.

It seemed natural then, to constantly see vultures gathered together on scavenger hunts in the undergrowth. It must seem like a Vulture's Deli, constantly being kindly re-supplied.

The things that are sacrificed right into the river join with heavy chemical pollutants from factories along the shores higher up.

The government has since closed the two breweries, the Tropical and the Polar. In addition they have reportedly improved the technologies of the Coppelia Ice Cream factory and the gas plant. But there is a solid waste landfill and also several pharmaceutical plants that also discharge into the river.

In 2017, it was reported that the former closure of an upstream rubber plant had been revisited due to 'political considerations.'

In the *El Fanguito* district of Havana that edges the mouth of the Almendares River they still recall the days when they could fish and swim in crystalline waters. But as was quoted in one recent article that locals there suggest that now, all you can catch is infection. They might be right.

In 2005, the river was reported to be in critical hygienic situation by CITMA, the Ministry of Science, Technology and the Environment. The report listed 70 sources of contaminants, including heavy metals.

In addition, the free flowing of the main river has been restricted by about 17 dams and reservoirs in its tributaries, the *Marinero, Santoyo, Orengo* and *Mordazo.*

The report stated that at that time 200 litres of sewage flowed into the Almendares every second.

Examination of the sewage of Cuba has been an international area of interest in the debate about antibiotic resistance.

This is the one country where trade embargoes have limited chemical imports. Despite the resulting very limited use of antibiotics in medical treatment, or in agriculture, antibiotic resistance is relatively high in Cuba. A possible source of this resistance is thought to be ingestion of high levels of pollutants in potable water.

The Almadares River is struggling.

Clumps of plastic bags and bottles can be seen as the river reaches its mouth and I was told that sometimes the river lights up from the high level of hydrocarbons it carries.

This is quite some clean-up job that is being tackled.

Recent samples from four measurement locations in the Almendares Park reveal a 50% reduction in pollutants. However, a CITMA representative reported in a 2017 article that despite reductions, there were still 50 pollutants recorded. Another article in 2017 was pleased to report a 5% oxygenation level as an improvement.

The gods to which the sacrifices of Santería followers are made have their work cut out. It seems that there is an unspoken need to not just respond to the prayers that go with the sacrifice, but to give some assistance from their holy power to help the environment as well.

My accidental proximity to the healing ceremony of the Santería believers led me to review my own manner of merging my beliefs with traditional religion to heal my own soul.

I have discovered that by changing my perspective to focus on something good – anything good – like a child giggling – had the capacity to lift my spirits from dark places of emptiness.

I grew up attending church with my family and attending a church school. Even as a child I recognised that neither place exemplified by their actions anything I could recognise as real Christian kindness.

Perhaps I was unfortunate in this respect but it never dented my faith.

I have always had a strong faith, but was often asked to stand outside in the corridor during Scripture classes in school because I asked too many inconvenient questions.

I think the last straw for the minister taking one course was when he was giving a stern lecture on why people should be in church on Sunday morning and not down at the beach on their surf boards.

I challenged him on this pronouncement, because it seemed to me that it was quite possible that the surfers out there on the blue Pacific waters in the beauty of post-dawn colour may in their own way be giving thanks to God for such a beautiful world.

This was roundly scoffed at.

Apparently according to his version of religion this could not be so.

This defied all that I lived. I made the mistake of saying so and found myself in the corridor again.

This conflict between religion and faith gave me the determination to just follow a few guidelines:

- Be kind.
- Ease other's burdens when you can.
- Send smiles and hugs to replace sadness.
- Scatter courage to those who need it most, even when your own is a bit fragile.

Religion in Cuba has been a legacy of conquest and adaptation, but no matter what the official religious direction, the saints are ever present.

The miracles of Cuban history often revolve around their saints, and as statues of the Blessed Virgin seemed to survive shipwrecks better than their crewman in early voyages, these are often at the hub of the folklore.

One of these is another of the Cuban Virgin Mary legends, and this one is the basis of why Remedios is the only town in Cuba to have two churches at its centre.

Remedios is about an hour and a quarter drive from *Sancti Spiritus* in the centre of the island and is only about 3 km *(almost 2 miles)* from the coast.

The reason it has two churches at its centre is all down to the wandering spirit of the *Virgen del Buenviaje*.

Rescued statues of the Virgin Mary seem to take up a restless spirit when relocated to Cuban soil and that in Remedios was no exception.

Two fishermen off the coast found a box of about 1 metre *(3')* floating towards them. Inside, and quite dry *(as are they all)* lay an image of the Holy Mother, holding the baby Jesus in her arms. The fishermen named her the *Virgen del Buenviaje*, seeing her to be the Virgin patron of Good Voyages for the good fortune they felt at having found her – and of hers in having come safely to land.

Back on shore they loaded the box onto a mule to bring to the local priest for blessing.

Stories vary about what actually happened thereafter.

Some versions state that the mule was overburdened and collapsed.

Others say the load just shifted causing the box to fall.

Whatever the circumstances of her fall to the ground outside the hermitage where a paralyzed slave lived, she was left in his care.

The next day he was supposed to advise the parish priest of her arrival.

316

He didn't, but she was discovered by some locals and they built a small alter before her on which were placed offerings of flowers and candles before they prayed to her.

When the fishermen returned and found her not registered with the priest as promised, they came to fetch her, and in a grand parade she was brought to the parish church of St. John the Baptist, the *Iglesia Parroquial Mayor San Juan Bautista* where she was reverently installed.

The next morning our virgin had returned to the hermitage.

She was restored to the church but again retuned to be with the hermit.

Perhaps it was the simple and heartfelt homage she found there when she arrived that beguiled her, for this boomerang arrangement continued several times until finally the local people interceded on her behalf.

Since the Virgen del Buenviaje didn't care for the existing church, they built her a new one by the hermitage. She was to see out her days here, for in 1862 on Good Friday, the candles of the *Iglesia Buenviaje* caused an altar fire that rapidly spread to destroy the church.

It had earlier been established that this statue of the Holy Mother had been carved in Barcelona, so a new one was quickly commissioned.

Not having travelled here of her own choosing, and therefore not having any attachment to the old location, the new statue of Our Lady was duly installed in the much more elaborately decorated church of St. John the Baptist.

Not knowing any different, she seems to be happy there. Unlike her namesake, she hasn't wandered.

The *Iglesia Major of San Juan Bautista* had been built in 1692 in a neo-classical style atop the remains of an earlier stone church. When it was first established is unclear, but it had been recorded by Bishop *Juan del Castillo* in 1570.

It has been declared one of the most sumptuously decorated on the island.

Inside this ornate place of worship are thirteen golden altars and they formed what any insurance company would call 'an attractive nuisance' - or something that begs disobedience - to pirates who frequently sent raiding parties inland. Many marauders came to Remedios but by far the most infamous was one who actually came from the *Vendée* region of south-west France.

As a boy, *Jean-David Nau* had suffered a period of bloody indentured service which was not very different from slavery. He went on to perpetuate and perfect that bloodiness in his future career becoming later known – and deeply feared – as the buccaneer *François l'Olonnais*.

I was to learn that although he may act in a manner that to us would proclaim him as such, a buccaneer is not a pirate. A buccaneer is in the service of a government, and is given his ship. In this case, François l'Olonnais received his ship from the French so he would attack the Spanish.

In my definition then, a buccaneer seemed to be a sort of contract pirate with a less pejorative name. Whatever the name, the actions of each bear semblance to the other, as can be seen by a short summary of some exploits.

We know that François l'Olonnais attacked a town called *'de Los Cayos'* in 1658.Since Remedios had many names in its early days - *Santa Cruz de la Sabana, Santa Cruz de Vasco Porcallo, Santa Cruz de la Sabana del Cayo*, and finally *San Juan de los Remedios de la Sabana del Cayo* - this could have been the site of the attack.

Records variously attribute the following incident as being either in Remedios or on the Island of Tortuga:

François l'Olonnais was known to be particularly vicious. Rape, and torture of bizarre forms were his specialty, so when faced with his approach, the terrified townspeople of Remedios sent an urgent message to ask the Governor in Havana for help.

Discovering this, the buccaneer lay in wait for the rescue ship which arrived carrying its own gallows and hangman to deal out immediate justice. After a vicious battle, all of the rescuers but one were decapitated. The sole survivor was returned to Havana with the message that this buccaneer would never give quarter to any Spaniard and that 'he had retaliated the kindness you designed on me and my companions'.

This vicious buccaneer was a pirate by any name. When he dominated Maracaibo in Venezuela, it was called hell on earth.

However, it was to prove that just as in the biblical reference in the Gospel of Matthew: 'Those who live by the sword die by the sword'.

After years of wreaking havoc on many cities including Gibraltar, François l'Olonnais found his ship barricaded by sea by the Spanish. He escaped on a raft, travelling up the coast. While on foot foraging for food, this vicious buccaneer was captured by the Kuna *(or Guna)*.

They reputedly sliced him slowly into very small pieces.

The Guna originate from Central America and are variously thought to have emigrated due to ethnic battles with other tribes, or to escape the Spanish. If the latter, they could well have mistaken this Frenchman for a Spaniard upon whom to take out some vengeance.

The Guna are one of the few native peoples to have survived independently, and it thought that it is their emphasis on being productive traders that has been the core of that success.

At any rate, when he attacked Remedios, this buccaneer stayed a very short time, plundering the treasures of *Iglesia Parroquial Mayor San Juan Bautista* - but not the altars. Perhaps that is because before his arrival they had taken on their white disguise.

From whenever this disguise first was applied, it seems that from around the 1600s to 1944 the altars remained cloaked under white paint.

The gold beneath was only discovered when Cuban multi-millionaire *Eutimio Falla Bonet* funded the restoration of the church he had discovered to be the baptismal church of his ancestors.

At that time, the false ceiling was also removed to reveal a magnificent *Mudéjar*-style roof. This style is a remnant of Moorish rule and can be seen in Spain in many local buildings – especially in Aragon and Castile.

Under such a roof in Remedios, the ceiling has a fascinating optical illusion.

Look in one direction and there appears to be a line of lilies.

Look in the opposite direction along the same line, and this image takes on the resemblance to the way the face of Jesus is popularly drawn by European artists.

Falla Bonet was of pure Spanish heritage but was born in Cienfuegos and was fascinated with the history of the Cuban people, creating a well-documented genealogical heritage record for the island. He had discovered that his ancestors were founding fathers of Remedios, although they later moved to Santa Clara.

Moving to Remedios himself, he reputedly invested over a million dollars for what would prove to be a ten year restoration project. In the course of this he returned the church to be more in character with the other architecture of the town.

By the time he started this project the building was in decay, much of which was probably accelerated by the earthquake hiccup of 1939. This was measured on the *Medvedev–Sponheuer–Karnik Scale* which for obvious reasons was generally abbreviated to MSK.

For many years since it was developed on 1964, the MSK was widely used in Europe and the USSR. Many of its principles were the founding basis for the later developed European Macroseismic Scale.

The 1939 earthquake in Remedios was measured at MSK VII (7). The maximum MSK is twelve, so there must have been considerable damage.

It was fortunate that this philanthropist and lover of architectural heritage took it upon himself to undertake the restoration.

To bring magnificence to the restoration, Falla Bonet is reputed to have sent architect *Aquiles Masa* to both Mexico and Peru to make copied of famous altar pieces.

Then over a period of two years, a well-respected Cuban craftsman called *Rogelio Ata* carved the altar we now see. It was then covered in 22 carat gold leaf.

I have neither been unable to trace the relationship of today's altar to that of the original, nor to discover how much of the white paint took with it the gold beneath, when removed.

Falla Bonet must have been a dancer – or at least appreciated dancing. He had a statue of a pregnant Virgin Mother dancing flamenco installed within the church. She dances still.

In a world of stilted impressions of an idealised Virgin Mary, to me it is refreshing to see that Falla Bonet wanted us to see a young woman displaying a passion for life as she dances with delight, just as do the people of Cuba.

Perhaps, like me, Eutimio Fallo Bonet agreed with Friedrich Nietzsche's declaration:

> *I would believe only in a God*
> *who knows how to dance.*

Like all churches, the saints within are thought to have miraculous – or at least powerful – attributes.

Local girls are reputed to believe that if they approach the statue of Saint Anthony inside the church and tie a knot in his robe, their wish for a boyfriend will be granted.

I tied no knot.

But it is not just for its churches and its saint that Remedios is known. It is the site of one of the most well-known and oldest parties of the island.

This festival is called the *Parrandas*.

This massive pre-Christmas celebration of light, fireworks, floats and dancing makes up the great battle between the two city barrios of San Salvador with its symbol of a rooster and colour of blue, and El Carmen with its sparrow hawk and the less striking colour of brown.

The festivities begin with the tolling of the church bell at 9pm on Christmas Eve, and then the competing rumba dances begin.

The 'battle' is waged: dance team against dance team, fireworks against fireworks, and a decorated float of one neighbourhood against decorated float of the other – the winner being the one as judged by the citizens of the town.

We arrived in Remedios as the construction of the supporting infrastructure was well underway.

Electricity cables were strewn across the square. One of the flatbed trailers had stopped midway across an intersection. Several people were attempting a tyre change on one of the sets of dual wheels.

A tractor pulling workers from the Salvador barrio was leaving the central square. The flatbed tray had nine workers riding it – the three oldest with legs over the 'v'-shaped tow bar and the rest sitting cross-legged or leaning their arms across their knees as they watched the activities around them as they travelled.

On the radiator at the front of the tractor was a cardboard sign: 'Via Libre' (free way).

I had heard many ironic references to 'Via Libre' and to the popular drink of rum and coke known as a 'Cuba Libre'.

Each of these had its own clever parody in the play on words, and that is what is so powerful.

It is just possible it might have mean 'Freeway', just as it may have truly meant 'free way'.

Other more colourful tags attached made me grin at the clever innuendos and satire that were displayed by good word play.

The *Parrandas* are reputed to stem from the desire of a new local priest to get the adults to attend midnight mass on Christmas Eve.

According to urban legend, this priest organised the local children to use whatever they could to make as much noise as possible as they roamed the streets.

The principle was that, quipped with stones in tins, saucepan lids and fireworks, the children would make so much noise that their parents couldn't sleep, and would come instead to mass.

It's another 'It's like life really' lesson.

As is often the way, a story takes on a life of its own and Chinese Whispers has nothing on how a story like this can be transformed by the sequential embellishments by each teller.

When I researched it a bit more, I discovered that the priest in question was one *Francisco Vigil de Quiñones*, who was from Asturias in Spain.

In Asturias it is a tradition to take to the streets after the Christmas dinner which is there, as in the rest of continental Europe, eaten on Christmas Eve, for that is when Christmas is celebrated.

The closer to midnight it gets, the crowds swell and the streets are filled with the sounds of singing, clapping and loud drum beats.

Perhaps the good Father was just re-creating the familiar traditions of his origins.

Nevertheless, it seems that all this good fun of noise, fireworks, and general craziness was far too good to only have children enjoy it, and so in 1820 the *Parrandas* were born to expand the concept into all out battle between two city barrios.

To celebrate, *el Louvre,* the restaurant that boasts being the oldest in Cuba to serve as bar, restaurant and ice cream parlour cum sweet shop, created a special drink.

Known as a 'Parish Punch', this drink of milk, rum or sugar cane brandy, aromatic herbs (usually including crushed orange leaves) and cinnamon, is still served today.

The Parisian style 'El Louvre' probably hasn't changed that much since it opened in October 1866. Its grand interior gives us a quick glimpse into late seventeenth century architecture. The only real change seems to have been the installation of energy saving light bulbs in the chandeliers and the addition of a fantastic Italian Rancilio coffee machine.

From its beginnings in 1927, Rancilio was one of the proud champions of Italian coffee culture. Their machines were an esteemed hallmark of any establishment.

Founded in 1927, the company grew organically, before in recent years being bought by investors. This can go either way. Given their proud history, I hope it is in a way that retains the ethics and attention to detail of the founder.

Open from 7:30 in the morning until midnight *(1am on Saturday)*, 'El Louvre' has been the watering hole of choice for many famous personalities visiting Remedios, as also for its famous sons and daughters. It sits on the main square sits on *Plaza Martí* which started out life in 1852 as Plaza Isabel II, being redesigned in 1960.

El Louvre is the colourful gathering spot for the city, especially at night. Sitting in the café you can see the world pass by.

When you look at the aging framed photos of the square on the walls of the restaurant you can see t'was ever thus.

Remedios, like all Cuban cities, is a place where baseball is the top sport – and two Remedios sons have played in the American Major leagues: Jorge Toca with the NY Mets, and *Dayán Viciedo Pérez* for the Chicago White Sox.

I am sure they, too sat on the terraces of *El Louvre* and watched the world pass by, as probably did the famous Cuban born musician *Alejandro Garcia Caturla*.

Although of purely Spanish descent, Caturla devoted his life to Cuban music and to the practice of law. Growing up in and returning after his student days to Remedios, Caturla's combination of the symphonic and Creole music won him many prizes, and has left an inspiring legacy.

Caturla and his teacher *Amadeo Roldán y Gardes* are regarded as the founders of modern Cuban symphonic music. Sadly, while acting as a judge in Remedios, he was stabbed to death at the age of 34 by a young gambler whom he was to sentence within hours.

Death is our only certainty in life, and yet in our English speaking world we are not well able to cope with it or with its inevitability or its normality.

We don't even say that someone died. Instead they 'passed', 'are gone', or even more bizarre, are 'lost'.

I always am tempted to tell people to look behind the sofa when that is said, but one cannot be flippant about someone's grief.

I guess that expression comes from the loss to the life of the speaker, the loss of the constant of having the living person present.

Perhaps it is because we know death to be our ultimate destiny we think that it will not take place until after a long journey through life.

As we see every day from events around us and in the wider world, this may not be the case.

One never knows what happenstance may cause an earlier than planned departure from this earth.

It continually amazes me that people don't relate this possibility to the need to make every day count – and to make our approach to others one that is friendlier.

I am sure that it is our inability to deal with death that generates our universal and historical need for belief in some future incarnation. Perhaps it is our attachment to this life and the awfulness of thinking there is nothing more.

Although not Catholic, I subscribe to the philosophy of my friend Reinhold who declared his religion as BuddCa – a Buddhist Catholic. I think he is far more Buddhist, but really what he is proclaiming is a seeking of an expression of faith that fits one's intuitive beliefs, and not that prescribed by a traditional church.

I am nominally Anglican, but as mentioned, like many I find no solace in organised religion. I also find the hypocrisy I see in it difficult to deal with – but that is probably unfair as there is hypocrisy everywhere to be found. Nevertheless, I go around thanking God a lot.

They say that people who have near death experiences generally become quite self-possessed in their faith. This absence of a need for religion to interpret that relationship is not uncommon to those who have had that experience. I have had such a one.

I remember being on the ceiling looking down on the doctor who was trying to revive me after a great deal of blood loss.

She said to the nurse: "Take that bag off there" – indicating with her head to the saline drip that presumably also held other life-giving medication.

She then went on "Hold it straight up in the air. When I locate a vein that hasn't collapsed and get this in *(holding the needle as she searched)*, I want that thing going like gangbusters".

It was a very calm thing to be there watching.

I felt that I had the choice to leave the body below forever, but she then said "...and get her husband in here. We need all the help we can get".

That meant I wouldn't leave because I really loved him - so instead, very serenely, I returned.

I don't recall ever being afraid of death but since then I certainly am not. I see it as a very peaceful thing.

That has helped me as I have watched those I love approach death.

It has also eased my anguish afterwards, helping me to understand that this heartbreak is at my loss, not their opportunity to be released to travel onwards.

What did the Cuban Approach accomplish?

The experience of other people's faith is always something that gives you pause.

It generates reflection about your own beliefs.

Briefly, I was witness to what appeared to be a Santería healing ceremony under the heavy vines forming screens of green beside the Almadares River.

It led me to contemplate our relationship with the realities of this life and the inexplicable. The most inexplicable of all is that despite race, colour or geography, we all seem to bear the capacity of having faith.

It led me to ponder the circumstances of my life and of where fear and faith intersect each other.

It led me to reaffirm my own rules of life.

It led me to me reiterate my own beliefs.

It led me to imprint again in my mind the value of each day.

It led me to commit to give back in some way in thanks for all the good fortune I have in my own life, and especially for the amazing friends whose generosity and support has humbled me.

It reminded me that though we worship in different ways, belief in the intermediaries of our choosing gives us strength to pass through the most challenging of times.

For that reason we should value the beliefs of others and accept that there are zealots in every religion, even our own.

In the name of their beliefs, such zealots have wreaked a fair amount of despair over history, and others will no doubt do so in the future. It has always been so and probably also will be, but that is out of our own control.

What is in our control is the maintenance of our own values and the way we interact with others.

To me it seems that it is our job to stay our own course.

The saints of Cuba, like the saints of all lands, may guide us in that quest, but some angels have very real physical incarnations, as many know who have had someone materialise to provide the needed support at a critical moment.

Some of those angels never even know just how they helped.

I remember when I was told by the surgeon who came early from the Sydney hospital operating theatre to tell me that they wouldn't continue the surgery.

My darling partner's cancer had spread irretrievably and the surgeon had the unenviable job of telling me that he had perhaps eight weeks to live. It proved that he actually only had six.

Devastated, I went into the corridor by the lifts to call my parents. They didn't answer.

I called a close friend. She didn't answer.

I called another close friend. He didn't answer.

I have never felt so achingly alone.

Although both of us knew that there was an option that this could be the outcome, somehow neither of us ever believed it would be.

It is a human reaction. We believe we can overcome even death by love and by intent.

Sometimes we can. Sometimes, as he later wrote to me, life is like a river. You try to guide its course but eventually we have to go with the flow.

On that day after receiving this news, I was truly heartbroken. Sitting on a ledge by the windows of the foyer of that floor in the hospital, I sobbed uncontrollably.

A man was waiting for the lift. Of course it was impossible not to witness my distress.

Instead of taking the lift that had arrived, he so kindly came over and asked was there anything he could do.

I thanked him and shook my head.

What he will never know is that he already had.

That kindness in coming over and having empathy for the heartbreak I was showing, was a real gift.

He was my angel who reminded me that I wasn't alone.

There is a whole world of people who share your humanity and want to help you through the troubled parts of life: many you don't even know.

Perhaps someone will tell a man who came home to tell his side of this story, just how important was that simple act of kindness.

Perhaps this story will encourage you to reach out to other strangers in a similar kind way.

I have found in my life that when I am absolutely at my limit of what I can cope with, I have said: God, I know you know this, but I really can't take any more. Please help.

The pressures have immediately been removed to a manageable level until I could regroup and muster enough courage to keep moving forward.

I am sure that many other people in many other cultures have also called on their God in a similar way.

I would never deprive someone of that belief, for in times that tear your heart apart, we need all the support we can muster.

Those of you who have lived through similar experiences of supporting a dying loved one will know that there are practicalities that need to be dealt with.

These practicalities need to be handled in a compression of time that is cruelly urgent.

It is the same time during which you want to create the last magical memories of togetherness.

My partner had built a very successful architectural practice and wanted to be sure he provided well for his two daughters. He was immersed in designing a new hospital for the city where we lived, and knowing this the nurses used to pop in with design requests: make the doorways wide enough and don't put the pan room in an impossible place.

Sketching the church next door, he gave it to one of the Irish nurses, who was thrilled. She said her mother would be so impressed that she had a picture of a church on the wall!

I used to lie on the hospital bed beside him and they would pop their heads around the door and ask us: "Are ye decent?" It always made us chuckle.

Returning home from this protected environment he needed to organise the final things of his finances and his business.

Having kept so much of it in his head, he now panicked because under such stress he couldn't recall the things he needed to.

This manifested itself in being argumentative and I arrived to find him blaming one daughter for not fixing the bad relationship he had with his other daughter. When I pointed out that it wasn't her responsibility but his, he used the "But I am the one who is dying" card.

I told him it wasn't playable in this game of life. It didn't give any excuse for horrid behaviour.

He was the Dad and he needed to act like it.

He did, and I was proud that he did. Climbing down is always difficult when you are on your high horse, and never more so than in such an emotionally charged situation.

Such a time is certainly one where people close to you cannot but feel the desperation of trying to fill last days and weeks with the important things of life.

But this never excuses anyone from not behaving the way they should.

Step 13 of the Cuban Approach: Keepsakes: We all have a saint in our pocket, for the world is full of saints in waiting.

Adjusting your sails: On my No Plan trip I learnt about saints and beliefs that were different than mine.

It made me think about the need to engage a power other than ours when we feel that we have nothing left with which to fight onwards.

I thought of how precarious is that balance between responsibility for your own actions and handing responsibility to another – especially a non-physical other

.It is one of those scales that I believe to be unique to each of us, for the answer for one may be quite different to the answer for another.

Reading the winds: These days my life is guided quite simply by some guidelines I made for myself when restoring my badly damaged self-confidence after very challenging times.

They hang beside my desk to encourage me.

Make your own to keep your course.

They will remind you to never stop following your dreams.

My guidelines

Walk on the leading edge.

Be the vanguard.

Live passionately.

Find refuge.

Have the courage to be you.

Have faith that the universe will take care of you.

Hold to your course.

Make ideas matter.

The world is your studio.

Be adventurous.

Expect a miracle.

ABOUT THE AUTHOR

Paquita Lamacraft is a traveller and writer who sees the world as her back garden. She travels thoughtfully and with curiosity. This shows in her photos that reveal a fresh side to the places about which she writes. Together with careful research of history, her writings translate into delightful vignettes which others can share as they travel with her through her website www.discover-interesting-places.com.

A native Australian now resident in England, Paquita has lived and worked in many countries over three continents. She says that she finds the challenge of settling into a new area, a new country, or a new place of employment as challenging as anyone – but just has had more practice than most.

Paquita has never lived in one home longer than three years throughout her whole life. This means that she is constantly updating skills to deal with change.

It means refining the ability to let go of the unimportant things and focus on those that have meaning.

It means having the courage to start again.

Despite the many setbacks of her life, she has never stopped believing in her dream.

Perhaps this book
will help you to hold fast to yours.